D0086849

PARTICLES AND IDEAS

Particles and Ideas

Bishop Berkeley's Corpuscularian Philosophy

GABRIEL MOKED

CLARENDON PRESS · OXFORD
1988

Oxford University Press, Walton Street, Oxford OX2 6DP
Oxford New York Toronto
Delhi Bombay Calcutta Madras Karachi
Petaling Jaya Singapore Hong Kong Tokyo
Nairobi Dar es Salaam Cape Town
Melbourne Auckland
and associated companies in
Beirut Berlin Ibadan Nicosia

Oxford is a trade mark of Oxford University Press

Published in the United States
by Oxford University Press, New York

© Gabriel Moked 1988

All rights reserved. No part of this publication may be reproduced,
stored in a retrieval system, or transmitted, in any form or by any means,
electronic, mechanical, photocopying, recording, or otherwise, without
the prior permission of Oxford University Press

British Library Cataloguing in Publication Data
Moked, Gabriel
Particles and Ideas: Bishop Berkeley's
Corpuscularian Philosophy.
1. Berkeley, George
I. Title
192   B1348
ISBN 0-19-824990-X

Library of Congress Cataloging in Publication Data
Data available

Typeset by Cotswold Typesetting, Gloucester
Printed in Great Britain by
Biddles Ltd., Guildford & King's Lynn

B1349
M35
M65
1988

ACKNOWLEDGEMENTS

THE present book is based on my D.Phil. thesis, written in Oxford in 1969–71, under the supervision of G. J. Warnock. My interest in various uses of the concept of particle in Berkeley's philosophy was aroused by some remarks that Warnock made in his well-known book on Berkeley; I have drawn heavily upon his knowledge of the subject, his analytical capacities, and his philosophical insight. As my supervisor, and in some talks after the completion of my D.Phil studies, he has helped me enormously in understanding problems pertinent to Berkeley's thought. He is, however, in no way responsible for all of my views.

I owe a great debt of gratitude to H. R. Harré, Fellow of Linacre College, Oxford, and Oxford Lecturer in Philosophy of Science, who kindly read and remarked on sections of my essay, both during my studies in Oxford and afterwards. Many of Harré's notions are referred to, and, indeed, endorsed, in my discussion of Berkeley's approach to hypotheses and laws of nature. I also owe a special debt to Sir Isaiah Berlin for the encouragement and help he gave me during my stay in Oxford. But for his great kindness, I would never have been able to complete the present book.

My corpuscularian index of *Siris* and some main tenets of whatever is new in my approach to Berkeley's philosophy of science were first published as a discussion-note ('A Note on Berkeley's Corpuscularian Theories in *Siris*') in the Cambridge *Studies in History and Philosophy of Science*, 2/2 (1971), edited by Gerd Buchdahl. Without Dr Buchdahl's great help and patience, as revealed in his critical examination of my views, and also his readiness to suggest many much-needed stylistic corrections, the Cambridge *Note*, which includes the essentials of my entire Berkeleian thesis, would never have been published. Moreover, in my approach to Berkeley's 'corpuscularian philosophy' in *Siris*, I relied to a certain extent on Buchdahl's treatment of Berkeley's *Principles* and *De Motu*, as expounded in his *Metaphysics and the Philosophy of Science*, according to which Berkeley's ideism does not necessitate the rejection of corpuscularian theories, or, indeed, of the very existence of particles. However, as my thesis had been completed in essentials before the publication of Buchdahl's book, I could rely on his analysis of *Principles* and *De Motu* only during

APR 6   1988

some semi-final and final stages of my research. In any case, neither Harré nor Buchdahl are responsible for all of my views. And in the years since the completion of my D.Phil. thesis and the publication of my Cambridge article in 1971, some valuable research has been done on subjects included in or pertinent to my book (notably by Brook and Tipton). I hope that I have succeeded in taking into account whatever is new in their relevant insights, and, of course, reference is made to them in appropriate places. In addition, of course, I relied quite heavily on a number of important books and articles when dealing with various 'non-corpuscularian' issues involved in the Bishop's immaterialism. References to them are to be found in the main body of the present book, and also in the bibliography at its end.

But for the kindness of Sir Lindor Brown, the late Principal of Hertford College, and the Fellows of that College, in offering me a place, I would never have had the opportunity to pursue my research at Oxford. And my thanks are also due to many other persons in Oxford who helped me in my studies, especially Mrs J. L. Austin, and also J. O. Urmson who gave in 1970 a most illuminating seminar on Locke with particular reference to the 'real essence' and to its 'nominal' counterpart.

I would also like to express my gratitude to the Yad Avi Hayishuv Foundation under whose grant a part of my study was done, and to Ben Gurion University of the Negev, under whose sabbatical leave the completion of this book was made possible. I would like to thank too my colleague and friend at the Philosophy Department of Ben Gurion University, Dr H. Marantz, for reading and commenting on an early draft of my Berkeleian thesis. And some of my other friends and colleagues at the Philosophy Department of Ben Gurion University, (e.g. Dr J. Gellman, Professor M. Glouberman, Dr S. Lappin, Dr Y. Louria, Professor A. Paroush, Dr A. Polakov) have also helped and encouraged me during my research.

G.M.

CONTENTS

ABBREVIATIONS   ix

INTRODUCTION   1

1. Corpuscularianism and Inductivism in the *Principles of Human Knowledge* and *Three Dialogues between Hylas and Philonous*   6

2. *Siris* (I): Particles as Theoretical Entities Assumed in Hypotheses   26
   1. Introduction   26
   2. Theoretical usefulness does not prove (or disprove) existence   27
   3. Particles and causality   32
   4. Attraction and corpuscularian 'idiosyncrasies'   34
   5. Analogies and homologies   41
   6. Aether as a theoretical entity; its explanatory role   44
   7. The Bishop's aether and Newton's hypothesis of aether in *Opticks*   61
   8. Aether as light   72
   9. Primary and secondary qualities   84
   10. The anti-Cartesian trend and Berkeley's defence of empty space   95
   11. 'Microcosm' and 'macrocosm'; 'animal spirits'   101

3. *Siris* (II): Particles as Undoubtedly Real   107
   1. References to particles as 'real ideas of sense' on what we would label today an 'atomic (or sub-atomic) level'   107
   2. References to particles as the smallest parts of division of chemical compounds on what we would today label 'a molecular level'   112

4. *Siris* (III): Particles as of Old   120
   1. Active 'souls' and 'spirits of life'   120
   2. Physical seeds of generation   122
   3. 'Forms of all sublunary things', *logoi spermatikoi, homoiomeriae*   124
   4. Particles as the smallest parts of traditional 'elements'   128

APPENDICES   133
   A. Berkeley's Early Atomism as Expounded in his Theory of *Minima*   133
   B. Did Popper Misunderstand Berkeley?   157

C. The Corpuscularian Index of *Siris*   168
D. Index of References to *Minima* in the *Philosophical Commentaries*   170
E. The *Minima*-Theory and the Corpuscularian Theories of *Siris*   175

NOTES   177

BIBLIOGRAPHY   234

INDEX OF SUBJECTS   241

INDEX OF NAMES   244

ABBREVIATIONS

The following abbreviations are used in reference to Berkeley's main works:

Alc.	*Alciphron*
An.	*The Analyst*
M.	*De Motu*
Phil. Com.	*Philosophical Commentaries*
PHK	*A Treatise Concerning the Principles of Human Knowledge*
S.	*Siris, A Chain of Philosophical Reflexions and Inquiries Concerning the Virtues of Tar-Water, and Diverse Other Subjects Connected Together and Arising One from Another*
TD	*Three Dialogues between Hylas and Philonous*
TV	*An Essay Towards a New Theory of Vision*
TVV	*The Theory of Vision . . . Vindicated and Explained*

Pagination of Berkeley's works is given according to the standard edition of *The Works of George Berkeley, Bishop of Cloyne,* ed. A. A. Luce and T. E. Jessop (9 vols., Edinburgh, 1948–57).

Introduction

THE aim of this book is to show that, in sharp contrast to the received view of Bishop Berkeley as a convinced anti-corpuscularian, and, indeed, the arch-Machian, he in fact put forward his own theory of the corpuscularian composition of bodies and light. It is true that Berkeley was very much against Locke's philosophy of 'real essence' and in favour of putting emphasis on 'immediate perception', and his views in the 'heroic age' of his philosophy (1709–13) may accordingly be construed as rejecting not only some metaphysical aspects of corpuscularianism, but also the very existence, and even the usefulness of the concept, of particles. But, in spite of the views of most of Berkeley's commentators (from Dawes Hicks to Popper), there is nothing in the Bishop's phenomenalism, even at the stage of *The Principles of Human Knowledge* (1710) and *De Motu* (1721), that demands the denial of the existence of micro-entities or of the usefulness of hypotheses concerning their role or nature. However, it is certainly true that the author of the *Principles, Three Dialogues*, and *De Motu* did *not* develop his own 'corpuscularian philosophy' in those three books, and used to refer to particles, mostly in deprecatory terms, only within the framework of his rejection of the Lockean 'real essence'.

But (and this is my thesis put in a nutshell) a radical change of mind on this issue occurs in Berkeley's latest philosophical work: *Siris*, of 1744. In *Siris* Berkeley refers to particles in very many of the sections, and develops his own brand of the 'corpuscularian philosophy' within the framework of his phenomenalism, or 'immaterialistic ideism'. It may be maintained that this change of mind had already been adumbrated in a few references to particles in some of Berkeley's works in the 1730s: the *Theory of Vision . . . Vindicated* (1733) and the *Analyst* (1734). However, it is only in *Siris* that Berkeley explicitly asserts the theoretical use of the concept of particles, and also, in some contexts, their reality. It is true that Berkeley's 'corpuscularian philosophy' is developed in his last major work against the background of rather fantastic theories of iatrochemistry and medicine, which, moreover, were interpreted by him as providing grounds for the belief in the healing virtues of tar-water. Furthermore, the corpuscularian bodies are regarded by Berkeley in *Siris* as links in the Neoplatonic 'great chain of beings' in which the 'substance of light' (named also 'invisible fire' or 'aether') fulfils the role of an all-pervading *pneuma*.

Nevertheless, neither Berkeley's reliance on Neoplatonists (and other authorities of Antiquity) nor his devotion to tar-water can conceal the relatively modern aspects of the 'corpuscularian philosophy' in *Siris*, provided one reads it attentively enough. Thus, Neoplatonism and tar-water notwithstanding, the author of *Siris* draws heavily on Newton and other contemporaries. But it should also be noticed that he is by no means an uncritical corpuscularian. On the contrary, he criticizes many corpuscularian tenets (e.g. of Descartes, but also some Newtonian hypotheses), and firmly gears his newly found corpuscularianism to his immaterialistic ideism. He endorses the existence of some brands of particles and the usefulness of some corpuscularian theories, but continues to deny the existence of *matter*, absolute space, and physical powers.

In *Siris* Berkeley ascribes to aether, identified with 'the invisible fire', the then newly computed velocity of light. On his theory, the corpuscularian aether, or the 'substance of light', which moves *in vacuo* 'at the rate of about ten millions of miles in a minute', is slowed down as its path is deflected by attraction and impact of other corpuscularian bodies. He rejects Descartes's cosmological theories (and Newton's tentative references to an aethereal *plenum*-like element). On the other hand, he does accept the hypothesis of 'animal spirits', and considers them as concatenations of aether, although, according to his general treatment of causality, he does not admit that they are efficient causes.

Yet another important aspect of *Siris* is Berkeley's reference to the distinction between hypotheses and 'Laws of Nature'. He asserts that hypotheses are completely different from 'Laws of Nature', which, in his view, only describe well-ordered regularities of 'the ideas of sense'. On the other hand, hypotheses, i.e. explanatory theories, are, in his view, either purely fictitious (or, as he puts it, 'mathematical') or 'existential'. Terms of 'mathematical hypotheses' (e.g. 'parallelogram of forces', 'absolute space') are not capable of any reference to real items in the *rerum natura*. However, those hypotheses which assume the existence of new kinds of items in the *rerum natura* may, according to the Berkeley of *Siris*, sometimes refer to existing entities, i.e. to new series of 'ideas'.

(But, on his premisses, 'new' here means 'new from a finite epistemic point of view', because God perceives all objects whatever, and has no need to have recourse to any index of hypothetical items.) In addition, Berkeley warns the reader of *Siris* not to assume that hypotheses (e.g. those which assume the existence of particles of gases) are true simply because they explain, or enable us to predict, various phenomena.

Concerning causality in the physical realm, Berkeley holds in *Siris* that one may regard particles (and, especially, the corpuscles of aether) as causes of occurrences in the *rerum natura*, to the extent that one only means by 'causes' certain highly important regularities of concomitance. Thus, aether is regarded in *Siris* as the nearly universal 'secondary cause', or the main 'instrument' of the supreme spiritual Agent.

The author of *Siris* also tends to consider colours, and all those 'ideas' which were regarded by Locke as ('ideas' of) 'secondary qualities', as 'effects' of the 'equivocal' activity of particles in general, and of that of the corpuscles of aether in particular. This view is surely quite different from his criticism of the division into primary and secondary qualities, and his rejection of the explanatory role of particles, in the *Principles* and *Three Dialogues*. However, even in *Siris* he does not assert that the corpuscles of aether, or other particles, lack all 'secondary' qualities, nor does he maintain that their weight or number, shapes, configurations, angles, etc., function as the only *explanantia* of all other features of the *rerum natura*. Instead, he prefers to rely heavily on the 'idiosyncrasies' of micro-entities, of which attraction is supposed to be only a species. Moreover, he argues that all those 'idiosyncrasies' (attraction included) may well differ from 'the attraction of gravity', as revealed in the realm of macro- and medium-sized objects.

Berkeley's corpuscularian theory in *Siris* is an attempt to account for many different phenomena, ranging from combustion to the physiology of plants. Although most tenets of the corpuscularian hypotheses of the seventeenth and eighteenth centuries— including Berkeley's corpuscularianism in *Siris*—lost long ago most of their scientific importance, we may note that his views in *Siris* (*a*) contributed something to discussions crucial at the time (e.g. concerning aether), (*b*) reveal that he anticipated some modern approaches to the nature of hypotheses and the role of micro-entities, and (*c*) were, in most respects, geared much more than his early *minima*-theory to the explanatory and predictive function of science. All these issues are dealt with in Chapters 2–4 below.

Now the young Berkeley's *minima*-theory, mentioned in the previous paragraph, which is first and foremost a finitist theory of extension, may also be regarded as a brand of atomism blended with some of his general epistemological and metaphysical tenets. In his view, *minima tangibilia* are the least parts of bodies, and *minima visibilia* function as quanta of 'light and colours', which may 'signify' the tangible *minima*, but are also allowed to constitute their own extension. The *minima*-theory may be regarded as Berkeley's original contribution to the discussion of the ontic and epistemic status of atoms and quanta, in sharp contrast to many (but not all) tenets of his corpuscularianism, which are based on Boyle's, Locke's, and Newton's views and discoveries. Many, if not all, of the newly acquired corpuscularian tenets in *Siris* are, as it were, grafted upon the main body of Berkeley's immaterialism, whereas the *minima*-theory is not only highly original (some medieval and Renaissance *minima*-theories notwithstanding), but is also placed near the very core of his thought, and was always considered by him as one of the main pillars of immaterialism. However, although the *minima*-theory accounts for some haptic–optic correlations, e.g. between kinematics and optics, Berkeley did not succeed in developing it into a hypothetico-deductive theory. Therefore it is not surprising that, although he did not abandon the thesis of finite divisibility, he scarcely referred to the *minima* after the period of *Philosophical Commentaries* and his first Essay on Vision (i.e. after 1709), and did not employ the *minima*-theory when discussing the role that hypotheses play in science. In any case, it should be noticed that there is no contradiction between the young Berkeley's *minima*-theory and his 'corpuscularian philosophy' in *Siris*, as (*a*) particles may, on Berkeley's premises, be considered as concatenations of *minima*, and (*b*) Berkeley never abandoned his 'absolute finitism' (in mathematics, epistemology, and physics alike). His *minima*-theory and finitism are, as it were, a sort of early framework and scaffolding for his much later corpuscularianism. In addition, it seems to me that many aspects of both theories may, and indeed should, be examined on their own merits, quite apart from the Bishop's general metaphysical and ontological, or even some epistemological, tenets.

The above-mentioned considerations make some reference to

Berkeley's finitism and *minima*-theory necessary in this book. Appendix A is, accordingly, devoted to the *minima*-theory. And in Chapter 1 I try to analyse the anti-corpuscularian trend which is conspicuous in the *Principles* and *Three Dialogues*. More specifically, I show that in the period of Berkeley's thought from 1709 to 1713 he identified, at least for all practical and immediate theoretical purposes, 'the corpuscularian philosophy' with the Lockean theory of 'real essence', based in its turn not only on the assumption of the existence of particles, but also on the assumption of (1) infinite divisibility; (2) division into primary and secondary qualities; (3) existence of matter; and (4) causal powers other than spiritual. My conclusion is that in the period of the *Principles* and the *Three Dialogues* Berkeley accepted a sort of 'package deal', suggested by his materialist opponents, according to which the theses 1–4 as above (although every one of them is, in fact, independent of the other three), and also 5 (the corpuscularian hypotheses proper) are blended together in one comprehensive framework, and he rejects the combination of 1–5 lock, stock, and barrel. Accordingly, he does not then refer to particles on their own merits, but only mentions them in the context of his rejection of all the 'corpuscularian philosophy' (i.e. theses 1–5) *as a whole*. Moreover, the rejection of corpuscularianism (1–5) is accompanied in the *Principles* and *Three Dialogues* (and in *De Motu*, too) by a highly inductivist approach to the philosophy of nature. Popper's mistake in attributing this inductivism to *all* Berkeley's works, and in identifying the rejection of thesis 5 with the rejection of 1–4, or with the rejection of 1–5 *as a whole*, is briefly treated in Appendix B. The remaining Appendices (C–E) provide the reader with lists of references to particles and *minima* in Berkeley's writings, and with a concluding comparison between the Berkeleian *minima*-theory and the corpuscularian theories in *Siris*.

I.

Corpuscularianism and Inductivism in the *Principles of Human Knowledge* and *Three Dialogues between Hylas and Philonous*

I

The aim of the present chapter is to describe the young Berkeley's rejection of corpuscularianism, and also to point out its inductivist premisses, as against the background of his later theory of particles in *Siris*.

It would certainly be wrong to say that Berkeley explicitly denied the existence of particles in the *Principles of Human Knowledge* and the *Three Dialogues between Hylas and Philonous*. However, in that 'heroic age' of his epistemology (1710–13), he certainly regarded particles as rather suspect entities which, moreover, fulfilled a very important role in the metaphysics of his materialist opponents (e.g. in 'the corpuscularian philosophy' of Locke and Descartes). It is well known that the 'real essence' of Locke had been conceived on a corpuscularian model;[1] and, in fact, the 'corpuscularian essence' and the 'real essence' may almost be regarded as synonyms in so far as the author of the *Essay* is concerned.[2] Moreover, Berkeley in his early writings accepted, for all theoretical and polemical purposes, Locke's (and Descartes's) ascription of infinite divisibility to particles[3] as a feature of corpuscularian theories in general. Now the thesis of infinite divisibility (e.g. of matter), which was in sharp contrast to Berkeley's own atomism or finitism, invalidated, in his view, the corpuscularian theories of Locke and of the Cartesians alike. It is true that the rejection of the 'infinitist' corpuscularianism may not be identified with the rejection of all corpuscularian theories whatever, especially as corpuscles might have been considered, on Berkeley's view, as concatenations of *minima tangibilia*, whose existence he endorsed. However, the trouble is that he does not mention in either the *Principles* or the *Three Dialogues*, nor, for that matter, in *De Motu*, any alternative model of corpuscularianism (and, in fact, hardly mentions particles in any connection other than the criticism of Locke's corpuscularian 'real essence').

In addition, in many places he also seems to assume[4] that corpuscularian models imply an acceptance of the distinction between primary and secondary qualities (and an unconditional reliance on the causal and physiological story which accompanied it). Thus many of Berkeley's attacks on (1) infinite divisibility, and (2) the division into primary and secondary qualities seem to be launched in the *Principles* and *Three Dialogues* under the banner of a militant anti-corpuscularianism. He certainly accepted in those two crucial works a sort of 'package deal', according to which (1) the thesis of infinite divisibility, (2) the division into primary and secondary qualities, (3) the assumption of matter, (4) the ascription of causal powers to physical entities, and (5) the very assertion of the existence of unperceived minute particles, were identified, or unified, under the name of 'corpuscularian philosophy'. It is, therefore, sometimes quite difficult to evaluate the precise logical force of his attacks on the corpuscularian theory of the 'real essence', as expounded by Locke, or on the Cartesian theory of matter, and to draw clear-cut distinctions between various trends in his apparent anti-corpuscularianism. In most of the relevant passages in the *Principles* and *Three Dialogues*, Berkeley does not say anything in favour of corpuscularian theories of nature; and his attacks on the 'corpuscularian philosophy' of the 'real essence', which is a mixture of theses 1–5, can, accordingly, be easily regarded as the rejection of 5, and not only of 1–4. However, it seems to me that he neither rejected 5 nor needed to do so on his own premises. On the other hand, he certainly did not develop, in that most important period of his philosophy, his own corpuscularian theory (in sharp contrast to *Siris*, his latest work, of 1744), nor did he take pains to refer to 5 alone, nor did he ascribe to particles a theoretical role, like that mentioned, for instance, in the *Theory of Vision . . . Vindicated*.

Section 10 of the *Principles* may be regarded as a *locus classicus* which exemplifies the mixture of 2, 3, and 5:

They who assert that figure, motion, and the rest of the primary or original qualities do exist without the mind, in unthinking substances, do at the same time acknowledge that colours, sounds, heat, cold, and such like secondary qualities, do not, which they tell us are sensations existing in mind alone, that depend on and are occasioned by the different *size, texture and motion of the minute particles of matter* [*my italics*]. This they take for an undoubted truth, which they can demonstrate beyond all exception. Now if it be certain, that those original qualities are inseparably united with the other sensible qualities, and not, even in thought, capable of being abstracted from them, it plainly follows that they exist only in the mind. But I desire any one to reflect and try, whether he can by any abstraction of thought, conceive the extension and motion of a body, without all other sensible qualities. For my own part, I see evidently that it is not in my power to frame an idea of a body extended and moved, but I must withal give it some colour or other sensible quality which is acknowledged to exist only in the mind. In short, extension, figure, and motion, abstracted from all other qualities, are inconceivable. Where therefore the other sensible qualities are, there must these be also, to wit, in the mind and nowhere else.

It seems to me that the blending of theses 3 and 5, and presumably of 1 as well, is also under attack in the young Berkeley's *Philosophical Commentaries* (also labelled *Philosophical Notebooks*; referred to throughout my book as *Phil. Com.*), e.g. in entry 128. That rather cryptic entry runs as follows: 'M Matter tho' allow'd to exist may be no greater than a pin's head.' The same may be said of *Phil. Com.* 234, where he bluntly says: 'My Doctrine affects the Essences of Corpuscularians.' Now this entry, too, may well only refer to the metaphysical aspects of the doctrines of the 'real essence' (or to some Cartesian tenets). But it might also be interpreted as discarding the whole corpuscularian story (especially as the marginal sign *N* which accompanies it refers to the philosophy of nature and the sciences, in contrast to another marginal sign *M*, which refers to purely metaphysical aspects of materialism).[5]

It seems that in *PHK* 10 Berkeley refers to the ideas of secondary qualities as 'secondary qualities',[6] and relies on Locke's famous passage in the *Essay*, II. viii. 15 ('but the ideas produced in us by these secondary qualities have no resemblance of them at all . . . and what is sweet, blue or warm in idea is but the certain bulk, figure and motion of the insensible parts in the bodies themselves . . .'). He rejects here all the story about the division into the primary and secondary qualities, the matterist status of the primary qualities, and the explanation of 'sensations' by a concomitant existence of particles; he certainly rejects the very notion of the existence of 'the minute particles of *matter*' (my italics). This whole section seems to be thoroughly anti-corpuscularian, especially as no immaterialistic corpuscularianism (e.g. of the type developed in *Siris*) is mentioned (nor any possible theoretical use of particles, nor even Berkeley's earlier atomistic *minima*-theory). But, in fact, nothing is said in this section against the very existence of particles. On the other hand, nothing is said in their favour, and they are certainly placed by the author of the *Principles* under suspicion of being connected with the hated creed of his materialist opponents. It seems, therefore, that although Berkeley did not explicitly reject the very possibility of particles' existence, an unwary reader of *PHK* 10 may well regard 'the corpuscularian philosophy' as an inherent part of a metaphysical theory discarded in its entirety, without any attempt to isolate its various strands.

II

In *PHK* 10 Berkeley attacks the corpuscularian theories as embodied in the conjunction of 2, 3, and 5 amongst the five theses mentioned above, but does not mention there theses 1 and 4,[7] which he deals with in other sections of the *Principles*. Thus, for instance, an attack on a mixture of 4 and 5 is launched by him in *PHK* 25:

All our ideas, sensations, or the things which we perceive, by whatsoever names they may be distinguished, are visibly inactive, there is nothing of power or agency included in them. So that one idea or object of thought cannot produce, or make any alteration in another. To be satisfied of the truth of this, there is nothing else requisite but a bare observation of our ideas. For since they and every part of them exist only in the mind, it follows that there is nothing in them but what is perceived. But whoever shall attend to his ideas, whether of sense or reflexion, will not perceive in them any power or activity; there is therefore no such thing contained in them. A little attention will discover to us that the very being of an idea implies passiveness and inertness in it, insomuch that it is impossible for an idea to do any thing, or, strictly speaking, to be the cause of any thing; neither can it be the resemblance or pattern of any active being, as is evident from *Sect.* 8.[8] Whence it plainly follows that extension, figure and motion, cannot be the cause of our sensations. *To say therefore, that these are the effects of powers resulting from the configuration, number, motion, and size of corpuscles* [*my italics*] must certainly be false.

This section may also be regarded as systematically ambiguous in one crucial respect. The contention that 'sensations' are not the 'effects of powers resulting from the configuration, number, motion, and size of corpuscles' may be separately held on two widely different premises: (*a*) that there are no physical powers anyway, or (*b*) that particles do not exist (or, at least, are not known to exist, and the use of the concept 'particle' cannot fulfil any useful role in science). The same result may, of course, be achieved by the conjunction of (*a*) and (*b*). But such a conjunction would in fact be superfluous, since, for instance, (*a*) alone is quite sufficient for the required purpose. However, the trouble is that Berkeley seems to employ in the *Principles* just such an overpowered machinery of conjunction, so that the reader of section 25 may well assume that its author endorses (*a*) and (*b*)—i.e. rejects theses 4 and 5—alike.

A straightforward attack on the thesis of infinite divisibility (1), and its conjunction with 3 (the assumption of matter) and 5 (the assertion of the existence of unperceived minute particles), is the subject-matter of *PHK* 47. Thesis 1 involves, in Berkeley's view, a contradiction, or, at least, generates paradoxes, and allows the sceptics to triumph, even on the materialist premises of the corpuscularians. Accordingly, both Locke's and Descartes's hypotheses are regarded by him as invalidated by the conjunction of 1, 3, and 5. Or, as he himself puts it:

the infinite divisibility of matter is now universally allowed, at least by the most approved and considerable philosophers, who on the received principles demonstrate it beyond all exception. Hence it follows, that there is an infinite number of parts in each particle of matter, which are not perceived by sense. The reason therefore, that any particular body seems to be of a finite magnitude, or exhibits only a finite number of parts to sense, is, not because it contains no more, since in itself it contains an infinite number of parts, but because the sense is not acute enough to discern them. In proportion therefore as the sense is rendered more acute, it perceives a greater number of parts in the object, that is, the object appears greater, and its figure varies, those parts in its extremities which were before unperceivable, appearing now to bound it in very different lines and angles from those perceived by an obtuser sense. And at length, after various changes of size and shape, when the sense becomes infinitely acute, the body shall seem infinite. During all which there is no alteration in the body, but only in the sense. Each body therefore considered in it self, is infinitely extended, and consequently void of all shape or figure. From which it follows, that though we should grant the existence of matter to be ever so certain, yet it is withal as certain, the materialists themselves are by their own principles forced to acknowledge, that neither the particular bodies perceived by sense, nor any thing like them exists without the mind. Matter, I say, and each particle thereof is according to them infinite and shapeless, and it is the mind that frames all that variety of bodies which compose the visible world, any one whereof does not exist longer than it is perceived.[9]

It should be noticed that even on the rather dubious assumption that all this argument is sound, it only proves that the conjunction of 1, 3 and 5 generates paradoxes. In addition, it seems that Berkeley is inclined here to regard thesis 1 alone as responsible for the failure of the conjunction.

Therefore, even if one accepts Berkeley's argument, one has only to reject the conjunction of 1, 3, and 5, or, presumably, 1 alone as well, but neither 3 nor 5. It is true that, according to the *Principles*, 1 and 3 may, or even have to, be regarded as always connected (cf. also *PHK* 130–3). But, even on Berkeley's own premisses as given in the *Principles*, one is not bound to accept this connection. Incidentally, it is interesting that Berkeley himself seems once to have had an afterthought on this issue. In *Phil. Com.* 399 he says: 'The Materialists and Nihilarians need not be of a party.' ('Nihilarians' is his label for the mathematicians who endorsed the thesis of infinite divisibility.) In a similar vein, *Phil. Com.* 61 ('X in every Bodie 2 infinite series of extension the one of tangible the other of visible') may be understood as indicating his early hesitations concerning the connections between finitism and immaterialism. But in all other relevant entries of *Phil. Com.* he accepts the intimate connection between theses 1 and 3 as above, just as in the *Principles*.

III

The status of the 'corpuscular philosophy' as a set of hypotheses which may be used as premises in the sciences (in contrast to its various metaphysical and epistemic aspects and possible implications) is referred to in *PHK* 50. Theses 2, 3, 4, and 5, but not 1, are also evaluated in that section, either directly or by implication. But the main topic of *PHK* 50 is the importance and the possibility of the scientific use of some crucial tenets of the 'corpuscular philosophy', as detached from, or, at least, as not necessarily connected with, more general metaphysical and epistemic frameworks.

Berkeley begins this section by bringing in an argument of his opponents, according to which 5 may not be maintained without 3, nor, by implication, without 2 and 4.

there have been a great many things explained by matter and motion: take away these, and you destroy the whole corpuscular philosophy, and undermine those mechanical principles which have been applied with so much success to account for the phenomena. In short, whatever advances have been made, either by ancient or modern philosophers, in the study of Nature, do all proceed on the supposition, that corporeal substance or matter doth really exist.

Now the crux of the matter is that Berkeley does not simply reply to his opponents by saying that 5 may be maintained quite apart from 3, 2, and 4. On the contrary, what he says is, in fact, that there is no need for explanatory hypotheses in science, which refer to some unobserved new entities, since one can work with reticular hypotheses, which only deal with refined observation-terms.[10]

Berkeley's tendency to rely on reticular theories, and to discard explanatory ones, is very conspicuous in the Preface to the *Three Dialogues* and in the *Third Dialogue* (cf., for instance, vol. ii, pp. 242–3, and, especially, p. 259) where Hylas accepts finally Philonous' tenets, and says that on immaterialistic premisses there would be effected 'a mighty abridgement in knowledge'. And he raises a rhetorical query, or rather exclaims: 'What doubts, what *hypotheses* [*my italics*] . . . what fields of disputation . . . may be avoided by that simple notion of *immaterialism?*' (Cf. also *PHK* 134 and Berkeley's remark in *Phil. Com.* 406 against the 'Hypothetical Gentlemen', who are distinguished by him from 'Experimental Philosophers'.) And G. J. Warnock rightly says, referring to Berkeley's bias against hypotheses as revealed in *PHK* 102: 'Berkeley observes, with misplaced satisfaction, "I need not say, how many hypotheses and speculations are left out, and how much the study of Nature is abridged by this doctrine." Not merely abridged, one might think, but eliminated; and how could this be advantageous?'[11] And Berkeley's own words in the *Principles* concerning this issue (sect. 50) are: 'To this [*i.e. to the argument quoted above*] I answer, that there is not any one phenomenon explained on that supposition, which may not as well be explained without it, *as might easily be made appear by an induction of particulars.*'[12]

The contention that 'an induction of particulars' is a sufficient tool for the establishment of theories in science was abandoned by Berkeley from the *Theory of Vision . . . Vindicated* onwards (and especially in *Siris*). He does, however, endorse it in the section quoted above; and instead of isolating thesis 5 from, say, 3 he rejects 5 as well, in favour of reticular proceedings. He was unable to preserve this Machian trend in his later writings, but it seems to characterize his philosophy of science in the *Principles*.[13] In fact, he seems to widen the scope of interpretation of 'that supposition' (see the two passages quoted above), and to include in it not only thesis 3, according to which 'corporeal substance or matter doth really exist', but also thesis 5 which deals with the 'whole corpuscular philosophy', for example as expounded by those who 'have applied . . . mechanical principles . . . with so much success to account for the phenomena'.

In the *Principles* and the *Three Dialogues* Berkeley not only disapproves of those corpuscularian hypotheses which refer to infinite divisibility, but also condemns some brands of contemporary atomism, which, after all, were close to his finitist premises. But it should be noticed (especially as an unwary reader may well be confused on that issue) that he condemns explanation by 'a fortuitous concourse of atoms', or by a 'confused jumble of atoms' (the *Second Dialogue*, vol. ii, p. 213), on anti-materialist, and not on anti-atomist, grounds. 'Vanini, Hobbes, and Spinoza' are condemned by him not because of their explanatory theories in various sciences, but because of their materialist and atheistic (or allegedly atheistic) tenets. (See also an attack on materialist and fatalist tenets of 'Epicureans, Hobbists, and the like' in *PHK* 93.) In the same vein, he condemns the ancient atomists ('Leucippus, Democritus, and Epicurus') in *Siris* (cf. sects. 259, 273), despite the fact that he expounds there his own highly developed corpuscularian hypotheses which do not contradict, but supplement his finitism.

Moreover, the second half of *PHK* 50 may also be regarded as systematically ambiguous. For instance, Berkeley there says that even on the assumption that matter exists it would be of 'no use' in 'natural philosophy'. Ideas, on the other hand, of the primary and secondary qualities alike 'cannot be the cause of any thing' (ibid.). Again, Berkeley's reader may well assume here that thesis 5—and 'the whole corpuscular philosophy', not only 2, 3, and 4—is (*a*) identified, to all purposes, with 'mechanical principles', and (*b*) completely useless and superfluous from the scientific point of view, just as it is, or should be, discarded both on metaphysical and epistemic grounds. Such a conclusion may seem quite plausible—despite the fact that even in his main works (from the 1709–13 period) Berkeley does not explicitly say anything against the very existence of particles—since the anti-corpuscularian trend is very conspicuous in the *Principles*, and accentuated both by its author's willingness to accept the 'package deal', i.e. the conjunction of 1–5, sanctioned by his materialist opponents, and by his preference of 'an induction of particulars' to explanatory hypotheses.

In *PHK* 101–2 Berkeley refers once more to the connection between 'natural philosophy', which is regarded by him as a 'great province of speculative science', and Locke's theory of the corpuscularian 'real essence'. It seems to me that in those references to 'the corpuscularian philosophy' (which are the last of their kind in the *Principles*) he again unreservedly accepts the notion that thesis 5 is to be evaluated as a part of the 'package deal' mentioned above, and not on its own merits. Again, he does not refer to it alone, but considers it only as a part of the conjunction 1–5 rejected by him in its entirety.

In any event, the feature which distinguishes *PHK* 101–2 from 10, 25, 47, and 50 is the explicit emphasis put on the problems involved in the concept of the 'real essence' (cf. sect. 101), or the 'inward essence' (cf. sect. 102):

101 The two great provinces of speculative science, conversant about ideas received from sense and their relations, are *natural philosophy* and *mathematics*; with regard to each of these I shall make some observations. And first, I shall say somewhat of natural philosophy. On this subject it is, that the *sceptics* triumph: all that stock of arguments they produce to depreciate our faculties, and make mankind appear ignorant and low, are drawn principally from this head, to wit, that we are under an invincible blindness as to the *true* and *real* nature of things. This they exaggerate, and love to enlarge on. We are miserably bantered, say they, by our senses, and amused only with the outside and shew of things. The real essence, the internal qualities, and constitution of every the meanest object, is hid from our view; something there is in every drop of water, every grain of sand, which it is beyond the power of human understanding to fathom or comprehend. But it is evident from what has been shown, that all this complaint is groundless, and that we are influenced by false principles to that degree as to mistrust our senses, and think we know nothing of those things which we perfectly comprehend.

102   One great inducement to our pronouncing ourselves ignorant of the nature of things, is current opinion that every thing includes within it self the cause of its properties; or that there is in each object an inward essence, which is the source whence its discernible qualities flow, and whereon they depend. Some have pretended to account for appearances by occult qualities, but of late they are mostly resolved into mechanical causes, to wit, the figure, motion, weight and such like qualities of insensible particles: whereas in truth there is no other agent or efficient cause than *spirit*, it being evident that motion, as well as other *ideas*, is perfectly inert. See *Sect. 25.* Hence, to endeavour to explain the production of colours or sounds, by figure, motion, magnitude and the like, must needs be labour in vain. And accordingly, we see the attempts of that kind are not at all satisfactory. Which may be said, in general, of those instances, wherein one idea or quality is assigned for the cause of another. I need not say, how many *hypotheses* and speculations are left out, and how much the study of Nature is abridged by this doctrine.

Here Berkeley rejects not only the assumption of the material 'real essence' (3), which, *ex hypothesi*, has to be conceived as never directly (i.e. without a mediation of ideas) perceived by us, but also (2) the division into the truly representative ideas (of the primary qualities) and the non-representative ones (which are said to be only produced in us by some causal powers of the 'real essence').[14]

In addition, he also denies 4 itself, i.e. the causal powers, or activity, of the assumed 'insensible particles' of the 'real essence'. Again he rejects here (at least, by implication) 1 as well, i.e. the thesis of infinite divisibility, according to which—just as according to 2 and 3—'the real essence, the internal qualities, and constitution of every the meanest object, is hid from our view; something there is in every drop of water, every grain of sand, which it is beyond the power of human understanding to fathom or comprehend'. Obviously, if even the smallest parts of extension can yet be infinitely subdivided, and the qualities (or ideas) of 'the outside and shew of things' depend on an 'inward essence' of the minute 'insensible particles', one certainly has no chance thoroughly to 'fathom or comprehend' physical states of affairs. Thus, one seems to be doomed to a sort of 'invincible' epistemic 'blindness' even apart from a general inability to perceive matter without having recourse to ideas, which had then been admitted by nearly all parties. The constitution of physical bodies would, on such premisses, be forever 'hid from our view' in a quite literal sense. The inifinitely small parts may not, *ex hypothesi*, be regarded as wholly perceivable, even on the assumption that we can perceive matter, or ideas which represent truly its real qualities. It seems also, as I have already hinted above, that an 'invincible blindness' referred to by Berkeley in the *Principles* and *Three Dialogues* is specifically epistemic, i.e. cannot be regarded as an outcome of empirical limitations—not even as an epistemically specific handicap which characterizes humans only. It is obvious that 'an invincible blindness', as implied by 1, would not be peculiar to the human species alone, but, on the above premises, should afflict, at least, all species of finite observers. This contention follows from the conjunction of theses 1 and 3, which is, furthermore, combined with 2.

However, the trouble is that Berkeley in fact throws out the corpuscularian explanatory theories along with the theory of the 'real essence'. This last theory is considered by him as a perfect embodiment of muddled metaphysical assertions, and accordingly he rejects *en bloc* all its parts, thesis 5 included. He completely denies the explanatory role of 'insensible particles' (cf. *PHK* 102) not only on a metaphysical level, but also in theories of science (in a modern sense of 'science', e.g. as detached as far as possible from what is considered as philosophy). In brief, he says that it is of no avail to try to explain various 'secondary qualities' (such as colours and sounds) by having recourse to 'primary qualities' of 'insensible particles'. It is true that the very terms 'insensible' and 'explain' may here be regarded, prima facie, as ambiguous. Thus 'insensible' may mean either 'unperceived' or 'unperceivable', e.g. by human observers, and 'hid from our view' may mean either 'hid now' or 'hid forever'. And the verb 'to explain' may be used in widely different senses, especially when referring to physical occurrences. It may indicate some metaphysical assumptions and (supposedly ultimate) interpretations. But it may bear a much more modest meaning, exemplified by various explanatory (or even reticular) hypotheses in science. This second use of 'explanation' was endorsed by Berkeley himself in *Siris*, which deals with many hypotheses, reticular 'laws of Nature' and explanations in the assumedly stronger (i.e. metaphysical) sense alike. One fairly representative example of Berkeley's more modest use of 'to explain' and 'explanation' in *Siris* is to be found in sections 228 and 231, where he distinguishes explanations by means of hypotheses (228) and laws of nature (231) from explanations by final and efficient causes (cf. also sects. 154–5, 198, and especially 227). However, in *PHK* 101–2 he seems to reject any scientific (e.g. corpuscularian) explanation[15] of 'colours or sounds', and, more generally, of all those qualities which may be regarded, according to the principles of his opponents, either as 'secondary' or as 'the outside and shew of things'.

He seems hostile to any explanation by means of an assumed 'inward' constitution of things, even when it is not accompanied by a metaphysical distinction between the real and nominal essence. Thus he says in *PHK* 102 that

to endeavour to explain the production of colours or sounds, by figure, motion, magnitude and the like, must needs be labour in vain. And accordingly, we see the attempts of that kind are not at all satisfactory, which may be said, in general, of those instances, wherein one idea or quality is assigned for the cause of another. I need not say, how many hypotheses and speculations are left out and how much the study of Nature is abridged by this doctrine.

In a similar vein, one has to interpret Berkeley's use of (*a*) 'insensible' and (*b*) 'hid from our view', in the two above-mentioned sections, as (*a*) 'unperceivable, at least from a finite point of view', and, therefore, (*b*) as 'hid forever from *our* [*my italics*] view'.

The 'reticular' trend, already referred to above, does not, in fact, fit well another tendency of Berkeley; namely, his reliance upon observations through microscopes that exemplify the gradual progress into the realm of the *minutiae*. This tendency is very prominent in both his early and later works (from his first *Essay* on Vision—and *Phil. Com.*—to *Siris*; references to the gradual progress into the realm of the *minutiae* are to be found also in the *Principles* and the *Three Dialogues*), despite certain difficulties raised by the notion of 'a fine and exquisite contrivance' of 'the most inconsiderate parts of the universe' within a conceptual framework which stresses the immediate perception of things as they are, and necessitates the rejection of the 'real essence'. The tendency to take into account the gradually unfolding realm of the *minutiae* (e.g. as discovered by microscopes) is amply exemplified in *PHK* where Berkeley tries to refute one of the main objections against immaterialism. According to this objection, eleventh in the order of discussion, immaterialism is not able to explain the role of 'wonderfully fine and subtle' parts of the great 'clockwork of

Nature', since on the immaterialistic premisses they lack causal powers. One of Berkeley's answers to this objection is that the lack of causal powers in the minute parts may function as an argument against immaterialism and materialism alike. He also admits there that 'great part of the clockwork of Nature . . . is so wonderfully fine and subtle, as scarce to be discerned by the best microscope'. He even agrees (ibid. 65) that 'by discerning the figure, texture, and mechanism of the inward parts of bodies, whether natural or artificial, we may attain to know the several uses and properties depending thereon, or the nature of the thing' (see also the first *Letter to Johnson*, sect. 5). Nevertheless, he does not mention corpuscles and corpuscularian theories throughout his answer to the 'eleventh objection', though he does mention them in his criticisms of (1) the infinite divisibility, (2) the division into primary and secondary qualities, (3) the assumption of matter, and (4) the ascription of causal power to physical entities.[16]

According to the anti-hypothetical approach, not only very many metaphysical hypotheses (e.g. of *matter*, of 'seeing all things in God', or even of *absolute space* and *absolute motion*),[17] but also all the explanatory ones are most certainly 'left out', and 'the study of nature' is not only 'much abridged', but, indeed, much impoverished by such ultra-inductivist procedures. Berkeley's bias against explanations by means of hypothetical (or 'supposed') entities is also very conspicuous in the following passage in *PHK* 61: 'Whoever therefore supposes them [*the 'solidity, bulk, figure, motion and the like' of 'machines without the mind'*] to exist (allowing the supposition possible) when they are not perceived, does it manifestly to no purpose; since the only use that is assigned to them, as they exist unperceived, is that they produce those perceivable effects, which in truth cannot be ascribed to any thing but spirit.' In this passage Berkeley apparently denies not only the very existence of (say, minute parts of) 'machines [*and 'intruments'; cf.* ibid.] without the mind', but also the theoretical benefits of reference to various supposed entities (and, since he momentarily argues here from materialist premisses, it would be of no avail to accuse him of confusing 'unperceived by us' with 'unperceived by God'). In addition, it should be noticed that Berkeley maintained in the *Principles* that all parts of (tangible) extension are greater than 'the ten-thousandth part of an inch' (sect. 127). Now this view was utterly nonsensical, and he was not able to maintain it in *Siris*. [In *Siris* he is obviously closer to Newton's references (cf., for instance, *Opticks* ii) to particles 'exceedingly small', which are unperceived because of their minute size, and he might also possibly have agreed with yet another claim of Newton, namely that some minute particles can be regarded as invisible 'by reason of their transparency' (cf. *Opticks* ii. 3, Prop. VII).]

An 'induction of particulars' (cf. *PHK* 50) would thus remain the only scientific method, and the hypothetico-deductive models analysed and endorsed by Berkeley in *Siris* (e.g. in sect. 228; and also mentioned in *Theory of Vision . . . Vindicated* and the *Analyst*) would have to be discarded. Moreover, such an approach would clearly have been inconsistent with the gradual progression into the realm of the *minutiae* to which Berkeley himself referred time and again.[18] After all, Berkeley could not reject the reference to the then already discerned 'figure, texture, and mechanism of the inward parts' of bodies (e.g. of plants or living cells; cf. *PHK* 65), and had to explain such 'artificial and regular combinations' (ibid.) as based on a predominantly linguistic model, i.e. a model of explanation based on a Divine grammar of Nature; and not on efficient causes of mechanism. And he even tries to preserve some remnants of the mechanistic model of 'the inward parts', and incorporates them into his new linguistic theory: 'the reason why ideas are formed into machines [*sic*!], that is, artificial and regular combinations, is the same with that for combining letters into words.'[19]

However, he was certainly not ready in the *Principles* to proceed by analogy from the discerned to the assumed parts. If one even cannot '*assign* [*my italics*] one idea for the cause of another' (ibid., 102) it is no use to invent hypotheses in order to explain various phenomena. On the Berkeleian premises, as expounded in *PHK* 50 and 102, 'laws of Nature' which rely on 'an induction of particulars' would suffice for all practical and theoretical purposes. And, indeed, Berkeley makes a similar anti-hypothetical move at the beginning of the *Second Dialogue between Hylas and Philonous* (vol. ii, pp. 208–10), where he rejects on those highly metaphysical grounds the usefulness of the hypothesis of 'animal spirits', the very hypothesis which is, on scientific grounds, endorsed by him in *Siris*. In brief, although the above-mentioned theses 1–5 do not all *have* to be interwoven within a fabric of one metaphysical-cum-scientific framework, Berkeley accepts their conjunction in a sort of 'package deal', rejects them lock, stock, and barrel, and appears in *PHK* 101–2 as a convinced anti-corpuscularian.

IV

A somewhat more careful attitude in regard to particles is displayed in the *First Dialogue between Hylas and Philonous* (vol. ii, pp. 186–7) in the course of a discussion about the nature of light. Hylas has to concede that 'there is no such thing as colours really inhering in external bodies' ('external' means here 'without the mind', and 'bodies' are 'material substances other than light'). But he tries to defend the contention that colours are 'altogether in the light'. However, light itself is, in his view, a 'contiguous substance, which operating on the eye occasions a perception of colours'. 'Light' stands, therefore, on this view, (*a*) for an 'external' material 'substance' which 'occasions a perception of colours', and (*b*) to the extent that coloured rays of light, rainbows, etc., are concerned, for an epistemic outcome of assumed activities of that hypothetical substance. In addition, the 'substance' of light is conceived by Hylas on the corpuscularian model:

I tell you, Philonous, external light is nothing but a thin fluid substance, *whose minute particles being agitated with a brisk motion* [*my italics*], and in various manners reflected from the different surfaces of outward objects to the eyes, communicate different motions to the optic nerves; which being propagated to the brain, cause therein various impressions: and these are attended with the sensations of red, blue, yellow, etc.

Philonous is very quick indeed to seize upon the source of Hylas' loose usage of the terms 'colours' and 'light', and analyses immediately the lack of fit between the description of the 'external light' and the crucial sentence in which Hylas says that colours are 'altogether in the light'. The relevant passage of the *First Dialogue* runs as follows:

Philonous. It seems then, the light doth no more than shake the optic nerves.
Hylas. Nothing else.
Philonous. And consequent to each particular motion of the nerves the mind
　is affected with a sensation, which is some particular colour.
Hylas. Right.

Philonous. And these sensations have no existence without the mind.
Hylas. They have not.
Philonous. How then do you affirm that colours are in the light, since by *light* you understand a corporeal substance external to the mind?
Hylas. Light and colours, as immediately perceived by us, I grant cannot exist without the mind. But in themselves they are only the motions and configurations of certain insensible particles of matter.
Philonous. Colours then in the vulgar sense, or taken for the immediate objects of sight, cannot agree to any but a perceiving substance.
Hylas. That is what I say.
Philonous. Well, then, since you give up the point as to those sensible qualities, which are alone thought colours by all mankind beside, you may hold what you please with regard to those invisible ones of the philosophers. *It is not my business to dispute about them* [*my italics*]; only I would advise you to bethink your self, whether considering the inquiry we are upon, it be prudent for you to affirm, *the red and blue which we see are not real colours, but certain unknown motions and figures which no man ever did or can see, are truly so*. [*Berkeley's italics*.] Are not these shocking notions, and are not they subject to as many ridiculous inferences, as those you were obliged to renounce before in the case of sounds?

Here, again, one has to draw a distinction between epistemic (and, to a certain extent, metaphysical) aspects of the discussion, and ones which are pertinent to scientific hypotheses only. Thus, from the epistemic, or phenomenological, point of view, Berkeley is certainly right in rejecting the notion that 'the red and blue which we see are not real colours, but certain . . . motions and figures are truly so'.[20]

Obviously, 'the motions and configurations of certain insensible particles', be they 'of matter' or otherwise, may not be identified with the perceived 'light and colours', nor even simply equated with the supposedly unperceived ones. Moreover, even if one is inclined to reject Berkeley's epistemic-cum-metaphysical analysis of all physical constituents of the universe into 'the proper objects' of senses (e.g. of sight and touch), one may yet endorse his more limited epistemic analyses, such as the above-mentioned distinction of the visible light from the assumed, or observed, particles of its 'substance'.

However, Berkeley here again seems quite ready to regard 'the corpuscularian philosophy' as a sort of undifferentiated mixture of theses 1–5. It is true that Philonous' exposition of the relevant subject-matter is, at least in one crucial sentence, more careful than the explicit rejection of all hypotheses in the *Principles* (e.g. 102), or, for that matter, than the attack on the theory of 'animal spirits' at the beginning of the *Second Dialogue*. Philonous, at least, says that it is not his 'business' 'to dispute about' the 'insensible particles'. This dictum may, of course, be explained as expressing Berkeley's opinion that all the corpuscularian subject-matter is not important enough to be discussed, and can be discarded altogether. On the other hand, it may be explained as an attempt to distinguish the epistemic standpoint from the various proceedings in the philosophy of science. But, if so, Philonous did not take pains to maintain that distinction all through the discussion. He is not satisfied to maintain that colours cannot be identified with 'motions and figures' of 'insensible particles' which are supposed to be their causes. He goes farther than that and adds that *'no man ever did or can see'* those 'unknown' corpuscularian entities. The emphasis here has to be put on *'no man . . . can'*, since this turn of phrase clearly indicates epistemic (and presumably also metaphysical) grounds of unperceivability (at least, as far as humans are concerned) in sharp contrast to weaker brands of unperceivability, as due to (1) some generally prevailing empirical limitations (which have nothing to do with basic capacities, or incapacities, of sense-modalities) or (2) logical demands of explanatory theories. Berkeley here relegates the 'insensible particles' to a limbo of total unperceivability, and does not even try to connect them with various data revealed by gradual progress into the realm of the *minutiae* (cf. *PHK* 60–6), nor does he explain that unperceivability by having recourse to limitations imposed by certain conditions of human observation, or by theories, or by the distinction between sight and touch. It is perhaps also noteworthy, in this context, that when Berkeley decided to expound his own corpuscularian theories in *Siris* he took care to qualify the thesis of unperceivability of particles, and clearly indicated that the lack of relevant observations only means that particles have not been 'hitherto' discerned (cf. *S.* 159).

V

In any case Berkeley, in the above-mentioned passage of the *First Dialogue*, closely connects theses 2–4 and 5, and does not consider the 'insensible particles' as parts of an actual epistemic situation, or as useful theoretical devices. He is inclined not to refer to particles, and in most cases brings them under the heading of 'those invisible qualities' (*sic!*) of the metaphysical essence whose mention is not only useless in science, but also meaningless. However, Philonous could not really reject metaphysical excursions outside the realm of the 'proper objects' of sense, since Berkeley did not, of course, reject metaphysics.

In fact, the anti-corpuscularian attitude in the *Principles* and *Three Dialogues* was not the outcome of a completely Machian, or, indeed, Humean, anti-metaphysical approach. What Berkeley always condemned were only certain kinds of metaphysics,[21] and 'the corpuscularian philosophy' had unfortunately been geared by his opponents (and by him as well, at least in the *Principles* and *Three Dialogues*) to those varieties of *philosophia prima* which he completely rejected. And the tendency to connect thesis 5 with 1–4 seems to have been facilitated by his inclination to rely on 'an induction of particulars', although, even in the *Principles*, in his most 'inductivist' period, he never elaborated the inductive procedure into a completely closed theory which would leave no room for hypothetico-deductive models. A loosening of the conjunction of 1–4 and 5, and a new reliance on hypothetico-deductive models as explanatory devices, which may, among other things, guide our progress into the realm of the *minutiae*, are to be found not in the *Principles* and *Three Dialogues*, but in Berkeley's last book, *Siris*.

The first indications of Berkeley's change of mind in regard to 'the corpuscularian philosophy' are to be found in the 1730s in *TVV*43 (see also Appendix A below, and, especially, n. 22 to this chapter), and in a crucial section in *An.* 50, Qu. 56 (see my discussion of Popper's misinterpretation of this Query in Appendix B below). In addition, finite particles are explicitly mentioned in *An.* 4, 11, 41, and 42. It should be noticed that the *Analyst* deals with moments (and fluxions), and, accordingly, refers to finite particles as increments. 'A finite particle' is regarded by Berkeley in the *Analyst* as 'an increment generated in a finite particle of time' (*An.* 11). The 'finite particles' are considered as 'homologous', but, none the less, as of variable magnitudes (*An.* 41–2). Now it is perfectly true that Berkeley refers in the four last-named sections to finite increments of lines or of continuous manifolds, instead of referring to separate particles which may move on in empty space (as mentioned, for instance, in some sections of *Siris*). Particles in the *Analyst* are, as it were, not detached from their 'continuities' (in contrast to *S*. 209 or *TVV* 43[22]). On the other hand, it is obvious that they are not regarded as *minima* (cf. *An.* 41–2).

Perhaps it is also significant that Berkeley referred twice to particles, in the context of the infinitesimal analysis, in the first decade of the eighteenth century (cf. *Of Infinites*).[23] His early finitism enabled him to rely directly on *minima*, the last and least units of 'sensible extensions', instead of having recourse to particles; but in *Of Infinites* he uses, for his own purposes, Locke's distinction between 'the idea of infinity of space' and 'the idea of space infinite'. He approves of Locke's endorsement of the first of these two concepts, and, just like Locke, rejects the second. In addition, he says that one should apply Locke's distinction 'to quantitys infinitely small' (and not only to the infinitely great ones, e.g. not only to macrocosmic space). Accordingly, he appears in *Of Infinites* as a convinced Lockean, and does not criticize (in sharp contrast to his private notebooks, on the one hand, and to his later works, such as the *Principles*, on the other), the entire 'corpuscularian philosophy' of the 'real essence'. Nor does he mention *minima* there, and, in one place, even argues from the 'growing' infinite divisibility against the concept of a 'standing' infinitely small quantity. However, it should be noticed that he tends to confuse in some of his works (although not in *Siris*; cf. sects. 207–9) the concepts of 'indefinite division' and 'infinite division', of which the first is compatible with the assumption of *minima* as theoretical units of division, whereas the second is not.

On the other hand, it is noteworthy that, with but one exception (sect. 132), the *minima* are not mentioned in the *Principles*, in spite of many references to the thesis of finite divisibility. It may well be that Berkeley took notice of the barrenness of the concept of *minima* from any scientific point of view. After all, the *minima*-theory never enabled scientists to predict anything. (See Appendix A below, which deals with Berkeley's theory of *minima*.) Be that as it may, he relied in the *Principles* on a purely inductivist approach, and declined then to refer to either particles or *minima* when dealing with the role of explanations in science. (His sole remark on *minimum sensibile* in *PHK* 132 refers to some aspects of the infinitesimal analysis.)

It seems, therefore, that, in spite of some early indications of atomism in *Phil. Com.* and *TV*, the anti-corpuscularian and extremely 'inductivist' trend, which characterized Berkeley's youthful and vigorous immaterialism in the 'heroic age' of his epistemology (1710–13), was fully revised only thirty years later, in *Siris*.

It is true that *Siris* is, in many respects, a very curious book. Many of its sections deal with the 'salutary virtues' of tar-water, and endlessly quote and eulogize various authorities of Antiquity (in sharp contrast to the young Berkeley's writings). In addition, the topics mentioned in consecutive sections of *Siris* are often very loosely connected with one another. And, on top of all that, he relies heavily on very many obsolete tenets of alchemy, the 'old science'. (It may well be that these rather curious features of *Siris* are the main reason why Berkeley's corpuscularian-cum-hypothetico-deductive change of mind in *Siris* has not been noticed by many commentators.) However, it is clear that, despite all these handicaps, he did elaborate in *Siris* his own brand of 'the corpuscularian philosophy', which perhaps lacks some intransigent features of his epistemology in its heroic age, but takes into account many aspects of philosophy of science without rejecting the basic premisses of immaterialism.

The Berkeley of *Siris* is a convinced corpuscularian; Chapters 2 to 4 below prove this quite clearly.[24] In addition, Berkeley's philosophy of science in *Siris* may be regarded as an attempt to reconcile the inductive and deductive procedures, i.e. the main aspects of the reticular and explanatory theories.[25] Instead of gearing the immaterialistic premisses and the denial of causal powers in the physical realm to the inductivist approach only, he developed in *Siris* his own variety of the 'corpuscularian philosophy', and relied there very heavily on hypothetico-deductive models. But it seems that his rather incautious acceptance of the Lockean (and Cartesian) package deal (i.e. of the conjunction of theses 1–5 mentioned above), if only in order to attack and reject it entirely, and his inductivist approach did not enable him to make such a theoretical move in his earlier and most important writings. In any case, against the background of the 'corpuscularian' evidence in *Siris*, it is extremely difficult, if not impossible, to accept Popper's view that Berkeley was always a Machian or Bellarmino- or Osiander-like instrumentalist, and that instrumentalism and inductivism are a natural outcome of immaterialism. Even the *Principles* does not really supply evidence for Popper's evaluation,[26] and *Siris* surely invalidates it. However, Popper's exposition of Berkeley's philosophy of nature has to be dealt with separately (see Appendix B below).

2.

Siris (I): Particles as Theoretical Entities Assumed in Hypotheses

Even a cursory examination of Berkeley's *Siris* reveals an abundance of remarks, qualitative descriptions, and theoretical considerations concerning the building-stones of the corpuscularian philosophy, 'those minute particles . . . agitated according to certain laws of nature' (*S*. 250). 'The minute corpuscles' which 'are impelled and directed, that is to say, moved to and from each other, according to various rules or laws of motion' (*S*. 235) are mentioned and discussed in *Siris* over and over again in many different contexts, ranging from what at the present day would be called the molecular level to the sub-atomic realm, from the *atomos* of the ancient philosophers to some of the features that belong to the modern atom; fantastical 'seeds', spirits, and *homoiomeriae* exist and flourish in *Siris* side by side with the hypothetical entities of modern theories of science. Berkeley's particles in *Siris*, coming as they do in a confused variety of guises,[1] demand some tentative classification. A list of the occurrences of the term 'particle' (or 'corpuscle') is to be found in Appendix C. In Chapters 2–4 I hope to provide a description and explanation of its uses and functions in its various contexts, and to prove not only that in *Siris* Berkeley abandoned his former anti-corpuscularianism but also that his two main uses of the term 'particle' are to refer (*a*) to particles as hypothetical entities employed in scientific theories (which enable us to deduce various physical—i.e. in Berkeley's view, sensory— phenomena), and (*b*) to particles as real (molecular, atomic, or sub-atomic) existents. The difference between (*a*) and (*b*) is *not* that (*b*) is detached from hypothetico-deductive theories. It is rather that (*a*) does not commit itself to existence-claims.

Particles of light or aether frequently mentioned in *Siris* as a species of the corpuscularian realm are also treated by Berkeley in the manner of either (*a*) or (*b*), although they are mostly related to (*b*); and both (*a*) and (*b*) are connected by him to some relatively modern, but also to some completely antiquated, theories of science.

2. THEORETICAL USEFULNESS DOES NOT PROVE (OR DISPROVE) EXISTENCE

I shall deal with Berkeley's treatment of the corpuscularian aether later. In this section I shall analyse Berkeley's views concerning the theoretical role of particles in general, i.e. not necessarily connected with special reference to parts of aether.

Perhaps Berkeley's clearest statement concerning the theoretical importance of particles within the framework of hypothetico-deductive systems is to be found in *S*. 228:

It is one thing to arrive at general laws of nature from a contemplation of the phenomena, and another to frame an hypothesis, and from thence deduce the phenomena. Those who supposed epicycles, and by them explained the motions and appearances of the planets, may not therefore be thought to have discovered principles true in fact and nature. And, albeit we may from the premises infer a conclusion, it will not follow that we can argue reciprocally, and from the conclusion infer the premises. For instance, supposing an elastic fluid, whose constituent minute particles are equidistant from each other, and of equal densities and diameters, and recede one from another with a centrifugal force which is inversely as the distance of the centres; and admitting that from such supposition it must follow that the density and elastic force of such fluid are in the inverse proportion of the space it occupies when compressed by any force; yet we cannot reciprocally infer that a fluid endued with this property must therefore consist of such supposed equal particles; for it would then follow that the constituent particles of air were of equal densities and diameters; whereas it is certain that air is a heterogeneous mass, containing in its composition an infinite variety of exhalations, from the different bodies which make up this terraqueous globe.

This section of *Siris* may be divided into three parts: part A contains the fundamental exposition of Berkeley's views about the difference between (1) 'general laws of nature', which in this context are broad generalizations of relations between observed sensory data; and (2) 'hypotheses' which enable us to 'deduce the phenomena'. This first part of the section, which includes some fundamental tenets of Berkeley's philosophy of science, ends with the words 'infer the premises'. Part B, from 'For instance' to 'supposed equal particles', exemplifies the difference between hypotheses and general laws of nature by means of the presentation of a corpuscularian theory. (But note that A itself includes yet another example of a hypothesis: an ancient, or at least antiquated, explanation of movements of macrocosmic bodies by means of the 'supposed epicycles'.) Finally, part C includes an attempt to provide an empirical examination of theoretical suggestions mentioned in A and B against the background of problems involved in the composition of the air. Berkeley's general trend of argument in that part of the section seems to be quite sound. But, on the other hand, writing a generation before Priestley, he certainly did not know enough about oxygen, combustion, and the precise composition of the air.

According to Berkeley, 'mechanical principles and universal laws of motions or of nature' are 'proved by experiments, elaborated by reason and rendered universal' (*experimentis comprobatae, ratiocinio etiam excultae sunt et redditae universales, M.* 36). These 'universal theorems of mechanics', which are, of course, subject to the supposition of the Uniformity of Nature, may be applied to 'the movements' of various 'parts of the mundane system' (*M.* 38). Terms like *vis, gravitas, attractio,* etc. which appear in such 'universal laws of motions or of nature', are to be understood here not as *qualitates occultae* (*M.* 6), but as *relations* of ideas in the tangible and/or visible and/or audible, etc., *rerum natura,* describable in mathematical formulae. *Vis, gravitas, attractio,* etc. in this context, stand, therefore, for relation-concepts only, and are not to be viewed as entities which generate motions. Moreover, they are theoretical concepts which, in spite of being 'employed usefully', not only in 'laws of nature' but sometimes in 'hypotheses' as well, cannot appear in any possible state of affairs as real tangible or visible entities, such as even the most hypothetical particles, galaxies, and micro-organisms. By contrast, the latter may be regarded, on the Berkeleian view, as kinds of hypothetical entities that could come to be seen[2] at some future time, perhaps by means of telescopes, or some super-electronic microscope, or in virtue of changes in the human perceptual apparatus.[3] But it would seem impossible to imagine that *vis* itself might surprise us by its naked presence, detached, as it were, from any sensation, impact, or motion.

The importance of *S.* 228 is, first of all, that it establishes a clear-cut distinction between 'hypotheses' and 'general laws of nature', involving a corresponding differentiation of concepts of physics into (1) *relation*-concepts such as *attractio*, and (2) theoretical concepts which appear as terms in *hypotheses* (e.g. *particles* and *epicycles*). An important point to note is that the last-named are in principle capable of changing their epistemic status[4] in passing from the 'hypothetical level' to the 'real' one (or, in Berkeley's language, to the realm of the real ideas of sense). According to *S.* 228, particles and epicycles belong to the hypothetical realms; but laws of motion, together with relation-concepts like *vis*, *gravitas*, and *attractio*, are ascribed to the realm of phenomena, although they may sometimes be applied to hypothetical realms as well. They are merely generalizations, abbreviations, and applications of the perceived data. We 'arrive at general laws of nature from a contemplation of the phenomena', but 'we frame an hypothesis, and from thence deduce the phenomena'. Thus the supposed epicycles, considered by some medieval thinkers either as material spheres or as real paths of motion of the celestial bodies,[5] are, according to Berkeley, premises in an explanatory theory, parts of a hypothesis whose fundamental role was to save the phenomena, and might therefore be regarded prima facie as purely mathematical, that is as a useful device for various complicated computations.[6]

Their theoretical role, has, therefore, to be considered as quite different from the function of 'principles true in fact and nature', as represented by the general laws of motion, and also as different from the function of idealized relation-concepts of the *attractio*-type which appear as links between real events. Astronomers, on Berkeley's view, did not have to ascribe reality to their celestial calculi. Nevertheless, some hypothetical descriptions of the motions of the planets might just come true in spite of the initially mathematical basis of the relevant conjectures, though admittedly epicycles had been less successful than particles in crossing the border between the hypothetical and the real level.

According to my view of Berkeley's intentions in *S.* 228, a double claim is involved here. Firstly, theoretical entities (e.g. various types of particles) may be either real or non-real, which implies that one may, at least in principle, consider them as candidates-for-reality,[7] in sharp contrast to strictly 'mathematical', 'fictitious', and in principle unperceivable terms, like *force* or power-like *attraction*, or 'parallelogram of forces'.[8] Secondly, their existence cannot be inferred from their usefulness and successful function in hypothetical premisses, a contention made explicit in what is the most important part of *S*. 228: 'And albeit we may from the premises infer a conclusion, it will not follow that we can argue reciprocally, and from the conclusion infer the premises.' The exposition of Berkeley's view is here quite clear, remembering that 'premises' in this context means an explanatory set of hypotheses, and 'conclusion' an actually observed state of affairs. In the realm of the 'laws of nature', we can, on Berkeley's view, 'argue reciprocally' from particular data to 'mechanical principles' (by means of experimental methods and inductive generalizations), subject to the uniformity of the *rerum natura*, and then from such general 'principles' to further particular instances by extending the domain of the law and applying it in advance to new sensory data. By contrast, the explanatory hypotheses are not generalizations of relations between 'ideas' in the *rerum natura*, but 'premisses' in deductive procedures, which include useful initial terms ('instrumental devices', 'theoretical entities') for inferring conclusions and 'saving the phenomena'; and the deductive role of such terms does not in itself guarantee reference to existents.

In the domain of laws of nature we may 'argue reciprocally' from some given general law to its particular cases and from the particular cases to the law because the particulars and the law are on the same level, even when we can deduce new cases from the law. That is to say, on Berkeley's view the law has a strictly empirical status, and includes only quantitative relations of regularities among the observed data, always granting a divinely sanctioned principle of uniformity. Hypotheses, on the other hand, lack not only the status of generalizations of empirical data; they also lack the status of inferred and unobserved (or perhaps unobservable) conclusions from given sets of physical observations. In *Siris*, Berkeley quite rightly observes that hypotheses are premisses of, and not conclusions from, the phenomena, and their main explanatory role involves drawing a sharp distinction between them and the laws of nature, even on the assumption that some hypotheses are possible candidates for the status of laws of nature. Hypotheses are non-factual premisses, though matters of fact are inferred from them.

Furthermore, in any possible epistemic order[9] at least some 'ideas of sense' and their 'laws of nature' (or their 'agreements and connections') must precede the formation of hypotheses, for example of those which mention epicycles and particles or, for that matter, micro-organisms and starry giants in the distant parts of the universe, in so far as we are acquainted first with some parts of a real and given *rerum natura*. According to this line of reasoning, we have to be acquainted with some initial data or objects in order to be able to invent hypothetico-deductive systems, although within the framework of hypothetico-deductive systems concepts such as those of epicycles and particles must be taken as preceding 'ideas of sense', because premises have to come before conclusions.

However, this logical priority of premises does not imply in this or any other section of *Siris* that one has to reject the possibility that *some* theoretical terms which function within such premises may actually one day be found as referring to the tangible and/or visible items. On the contrary: Berkeley's view in *Siris* is that in the course of empirical research some of these hypothetical 'premises' may quite possibly come to be transferred to the realm of observed ideas of sense. He only condemns a widespread tendency to assume without further ado that the theoretical terms occurring within hypothetico-deductive systems (e.g. *particles* and *epicycles*) refer to real entities (ideas of sense), let alone metaphysical 'essences' and 'material causes', merely in virtue of their scientific role in explanations. For, as we have seen him say, 'those who supposed' theoretical entities, 'and by them' explained various sets of observed data and inferred entire series of new events, 'may not therefore be thought to have discovered principles true in fact and nature'; their principles are to be understood neither as real complexes and relations of 'ideas of sense' in the *rerum natura*, nor as efficient causes. Some theoretical terms happen to 'work' within the framework of hypothetico-deductive systems; but this kind of success does not immediately enable us to treat such terms as referring to 'ideas of sense'; and, in any event, they are not to be regarded as having reference to entities with causal powers.

Moreover, any given premises, such as the adamantine spheres and the particles of gases,[10] are, of course, not the only possible ground of inference for the actual chains of deductions and conclusions. For every given set of ideas of sense ('the conclusion', according to a Berkeleian *terminus technicus*) a great variety of alternative premises may be assumed. In Berkeley's time, epicycles, for instance, had disappeared from the skyscape of theories in astronomy, and other premises had been introduced in their place, but that part of 'the conclusions' which had been observed in the realm of 'ideas of sense' before the rise of the heliocentric theory had not for that reason suffered any change. *Density* and *elastic force* are perfectly explained by the corpuscularian hypothesis mentioned in *S.* 228. But we are warned by Berkeley not to convert this reasoning and not to move 'backwards' from conclusions to premises, inferring, as it were, some fixed corpuscularian structure from the 'inverse proportion' between the volume of a fluid and its density and elastic force.[11]

3. PARTICLES AND CAUSALITY

Berkeley's reference to the role of particles as hypothetical 'premises' in various hypothetico-deductive theories also includes some remarks on their standing as *causes* of phenomena. Now many sections of *Siris* (e.g. 162, 165, and 227) obviously refer to particles as causes of various appearances on a medium-sized level. But, according to his general immaterialistic premises, and his treatment of causality in particular, he is not prepared to ascribe real causal powers to his newly found *explanantia*, i.e. to various hypothetical micro-entities. Causal powers are ascribed by him to spiritual agents alone, just as in the old days of the *Principles*, *Three Dialogues*, and *De Motu*. Therefore, he ascribes the causal efficiency to particles in only the very qualified Berkeleian (or Humean) sense. However, this caveat has no bearing on the immense explanatory task (or a wide variety of explanatory tasks) assigned to particles in *Siris*. The role of explanation by means of 'the corpuscularian philosophy' as in *Siris* is not encumbered by limitations imposed on the very concept of physical causality, since those limitations have no bearing on the inner structures and *de facto* explanatory powers of various hypothetico-deductive theories, but rather attempt to avoid certain metaphysical misinterpretations of the hypothetico-deductive procedure as a whole.

In any case, Berkeley in *Siris* does wish to employ the concept of causality in his corpuscularian theories, although in a somewhat restricted sense. Therefore, he introduces the concept of 'instrumental' or secondary, cause (see, for instance, *S.* 154 and 160). The hypothetical particles, in conjunction with various fits, attractions, and repulsions within the micro-realm, are regarded in *Siris* as a new universal series of assumed physical phenomena from which one can deduce very many other events. Accordingly, hypothetical micro-entities are regarded by the Berkeley of *Siris* as 'instruments' of deduction, and as possible *significantia* and *explanantia* of 'ideas' perceived on the medium-sized level. They are employed by him as 'equivocal' causes and share, to a certain extent, a special 'instrumental' privilege with the *rector* or *archaeus*, 'pure aether, fire, or the substance of light', regarded as an 'instrumental cause . . . which is applied and determined by an Infinite Mind in the macrocosm or universe, with unlimited power, and according to stated rules' (*S.* 154). Strictly speaking, the 'instrumental' causes, which in *Siris* are a special and privileged set of unobserved and theoretical entities (e.g. aether as 'the spirit of the universe'; and 'the animal spirit in a human body', cf. *S.* 159) although 'applied and determined with unlimited power', neither possess any powers nor are themselves powers as such. They are not even limited and modified powers, because the Aethereal Fire (and light) and its particles—and *a fortiori* all other particles—are assumed in *Siris* to be non-spiritual entities, that is as either purely explanatory or possibly sensory in kind (cf. *S.* 206, 207), and they cannot, therefore, on Berkeleian premisses, be (or have) powers to any degree. The 'unlimited power' is only manifested and presented in the *conjunctions* of these 'secondary' causes, e.g. of particles of aether.[12] The 'stated rules', either the 'laws of motion' in the *rerum natura* or the rules of conjunction of hypothetical terms themselves, depend here on the supposition of the 'unlimited power', present and active in this special (privileged and invisible) medium of aether and its corpuscles, and in the motion of particles which are assumed to exist even without the support of aether.

Berkeley could, of course, employ in his 'instrumental' explanations in *Siris*[13] not only microcosmic entities, but also some parts of the macrocosmic or macroscopic realm of the *rerum natura*: he could isolate various sets of visible and/or tangible data or objects, and ascribe to them the role of 'secondary causes'. For instance, this could be done on the non-corpuscularian level of celestial mechanics and in biology, chemistry, and botany. However, he preferred to ascribe his 'secondary' causality mainly to the purely theoretical realms of particles and aether,[14] perhaps because he did not find any sufficiently universal 'concause' in the macroscopic and macrocosmic *rerum natura*.

Berkeley's warning that explanation by means of hypothetical hidden micro-entities is not to be understood as validating causal powers in the physical realm is even more conspicuous in those sections of *Siris* in which he unconditionally assumes the reality of particles. For instance, compare the following sentences from *S*. 250 with *S*. 228:

Sir Isaac Newton asks, Have not the minute particles of bodies certain forces or powers by which they act on one another, as well as on the particles of light, for producing most of the phenomena in nature? But *in reality* [*my italics*] those minute particles are only agitated according to certain laws of nature, by some other agent, wherein the force exists and not in them, which have only the motion; which motion in the body moved the Peripatetics rightly judge to be a mere passion, but in the mover to be ἐνέργεια or act.

Here the causal powers of the 'minute particles' are treated as fictitious, but the 'minute particles' themselves seem to be considered as real parts of the *rerum natura*, a new microcosmic series of 'ideas' of sense. In a similar way, Berkeley incorporated into the framework of his immaterialistic ideism the new visual data revealed by the microscope, as shown, for instance, in the discussion of the 'eleventh objection' in *PHK* 60–6. 'Force' alone remains as a fictitious concept.[15] Particles, or at least some series of particles, are incorporated into the *rerum natura* as real ideas of sense. But, being new series of sensory phenomena, they share here the sheer passivity of all ideas of sense, and are described therefore as 'only agitated according to certain laws of nature, by some agent,[16] wherein the force exists and not in them, which have only the motion'.

Particles as theoretical entities are terms in hypotheses which explain the phenomena (see, especially, Berkeley's theory of the corpuscularian aether, referred to in Sections 6 and 7 below). But particles as real ideas of sense behave according to their new status and cannot explain their own motions which are described and brought under the rubric of 'laws of nature'.

4. ATTRACTION AND CORPUSCULARIAN 'IDIOSYNCRASIES'

Berkeley bestows upon his hypothetical particles a wide variety of qualities; and he assumes, among other things, that one may ascribe to the 'hitherto unperceived' (*S*. 159) particles various regularities of motion, best brought under the common denominators of (*a*) 'attraction of gravity', and (*b*) certain 'idiosyncrasies' of attraction (different from 'attraction of gravity'), repulsion, etc. One of the *loci classici* for all this is *S*. 227, in which the author prefers, among other things, Newton's original view of an independent role of attraction to its Cartesian or semi-Cartesian explanations by means of (*a*) aether, and (*b*) cohesion of 'hamate atoms'. (See also *S*. 131–3, where he rejects Homberg's explanation of cohesion by certain fits between angular configurations of particles,[17] and maintains that Newton's account of the relevant phenomena, which does not deduce attraction from configuration of particles, is 'better than others'.)

Berkeley does not reject in *Siris* the notion that particles are characterized by, at least, certain 'primary qualities', such as shape (see the relevant *locus classicus*, *S*. 162, to which I refer later). However, he does not think that the actual shape of particles, be they of various observed compounds or of aether, may be the explanation of attraction. This is one of the most persistent tenets in his corpuscularian theories, and it appears time and again in very many sections of *Siris*. In his view, neither 'attraction of gravity' on micro- or macro-level, nor 'idiosyncrasies' of attraction on a corpuscularian level, may be explained by reference to various shapes of particles of aether and of other bodies. Thus, for instance, he explicitly says in *S*. 227 that attraction can be explained neither by 'hamate atoms'[18] (e.g. of 'oil and water, mercury and iron'), nor by aether. He adds that the *density* and *elasticity* of aether cannot 'account for the rapid flight of a ray of light from the sun' (ibid.).[19] The main argument of *S*. 227 runs as follows:

Or how can it [i.e. '*the density and elasticity of aether*'] account for the various motions and attractions of different bodies? Why oil and water, mercury and iron, repel, or why other bodies attract each other? Or why a particle of light should repel on one side and attract on the other, as in the case of the Icelandic crystal? To explain cohesion by hamate atoms is accounted *ignotum per ignotius*. And is it not as much so to account for the gravity of bodies by the elasticity of aether?

I have already referred above to *S*. 228, which is crucial in the context of Berkeley's approach to various theories concerned with both aethereal and non-aethereal particles. The next relevant sections of *Siris* (232, 236, 238, 239, 244, and 277) mainly deal with (*a*) the rejection of the mechanistic concepts of the Cartesian *plenum* in general, and of their application to the corpuscularian realm in particular; and (*b*) the explication of Berkeley's own thesis, according to which gravity is only one of the various basic 'attractions and repulsions' or 'idiosyncrasies' of bodies and particles in the *rerum natura*. Thus, in *S*. 232, Berkeley tends to assume that 'the mineral, vegetable, and animal parts of the creation' are composed of particles. But he rejects the contentions of '*some* corpuscularian philosophers of the last age' who 'have . . . attempted to explain the formation of this world and its phenomena by a *few* simple laws of mechanism' (my italics). The case instanced by him in this section is the Cartesian hypothesis of a circular motion; he says that 'nothing could be more vain and imaginary than to suppose with Descartes that merely from a circular motion's being impressed by the supreme Agent on the particles of extended substance, the whole world, with all its several parts, appurtenances, and phenomena, might be produced by a necessary consequence from the laws of motion'.

I hope to show by analysis of sections like *S*. 232 that the general trend in *Siris* is to accept certain qualified principles of Newton's physics and optics (provided that they are not interpreted from the materialist point of view), and to reject the approach of the Cartesians. Newton is mentioned (and eulogized in most cases) in tens of sections in *Siris*, whereas Descartes seems to be regarded as the ultra-mechanistic villain of the piece (cf. also *S*. 243 and 246). In addition to the Newtonian physics, chemistry, too, looms large in *Siris*, but Boyle appears as a rather minor, though not unimportant, figure in comparison to Newton, and references to him are fewer than those to Berkeley's contemporaries Homberg and Boerhaave.

Berkeley's thesis that all the natural phenomena and movements of bodies may be explained by *various* mostly 'insensible' 'attractions and repulsions', but not by a few 'principles merely mechanical' (*S*. 232), is also very prominent in *S*. 238. In that section he seems to assume, first, the corpuscularian composition of all bodies in the universe; secondly, that 'attractions and repulsions' obtain among various particles, and, thirdly, that *attraction* may be endorsed as the universal explanatory term under the following conditions only: (1) that it is not regarded as detached from various particles and bodies; and (2) that it is conceived as a convenient umbrella-term which covers different correlations of the corpuscularian motions. The attraction which is precisely computed on the macrocosmic and 'medium-sized' level (and equated with gravity), is, on this view, *only one* of the basic correlations between the natural phenomena. First, the 'cohesion, dissolution, coagulation, animal secretion, fermentation and all chemical operations' can be deduced neither from the macroscopic attraction, or gravity, nor from 'a circular motion' (but 'a circular motion' suggested by Descartes is, on Berkeley's view, of no avail whatever, whereas the Newtonian rules of attraction in the macrocosm are regarded by him as generalizations of real motions). Secondly, even on the macrocosmic, or macroscopic, level, 'the laws of gravity, magnetism, and electricity are diverse' (ibid., 235). 'We behold iron move towards the loadstone, straws towards amber, heavy bodies towards the earth. The laws of these motions are various.' (Ibid., 236.) Thirdly, no law of nature, be it of gravity, or of a hypothetical 'circular motion', may be known as absolutely universal. 'And it is not known which other different rules or laws of motions might be established by the Author of nature. Some bodies approach together, others fly asunder, and perhaps some others do neither.' (Ibid., 235; see also *PHK* 106 where he urges that gravity might well not be universal.)

In brief, Berkeley rejects the assumption that all occurrences in the *rerum natura* may be explained either by one major mechanistic principle, or by one unified mechanistic theory which does not take into account 'magnetism and electricity', on the one hand, and various 'idiosyncrasies' of particles, on the other. It is especially noteworthy that, according to *Siris*, the actual properties and interactions of particles of the hypothetical aether, and also of particles of all bodies whatsoever, are extremely *diversified*, and even their 'attractions and repulsions' *may not be deduced from, or modelled on, the macrocosmic 'general laws of motion'*. The two relevant sections of *Siris* (238 and 239) are very important, and I will quote them in their entirety:

238. It is an old opinion, adopted by the moderns, that the elements and other natural bodies are changed each into other (Sect. 148). Now, as the particles of different bodies are agitated by different forces, attracting and repelling, or to speak more accurately, are moved by different laws, how can these forces or laws be changed, and this change accounted for by an elastic aether? Such a medium—distinct from light or fire—seemeth not to be made out by any proof, nor to be of any use in explaining the phenomena. But if there be any medium employed as a subordinate cause or instrument in attraction, it would rather seem to be light (Sects. 152, 156); since, by an

experiment of Mr. Boyle's, amber, that shewed no sign of attraction in the shade, being placed where the sunbeams shone upon it, immediately attracted light bodies. Besides, it hath been discovered by Sir Isaac Newton, and an admirable discovery it was, that light is a heterogeneous medium (Sects. 40, 181), consisting of particles endued with original distinct properties. And upon these, if I may venture to give my conjectures, it seemeth probable the specific properties of bodies, and the force of specific medicines, may depend. Different sides of the same ray shall one approach and the other recede from the Icelandic crystal: can this be accounted for by the elasticity of a fine medium, or by the general laws of motion, or by any mechanical principles whatever? And if not, what should hinder but there may be specific medicines, whose operation depends not upon mechanical principles, how much soever that notion hath been exploded of late years?

239. Why may we not suppose certain idiosyncrasies, sympathies, oppositions, in the solids, or fluids, or animal spirit of a human body, with regard to the fine insensible parts of minerals or vegetables, impregnated by rays of light of different properties, not depending on the different size, figure, number, solidity, or weight of those particles, nor on the general laws of motion, nor on the density or elasticity of a medium, but merely and altogether on the good pleasure of the Creator, in the original formation of things? From whence divers unaccountable and unforeseen motions may arise in the animal economy; from whence also various peculiar and specific virtues may be conceived to arise, residing in certain medicines, and not to be explained by mechanical principles. For although the general known laws of motion are to be deemed mechanical, yet peculiar motions of the insensible parts, and peculiar properties depending thereon, are occult and specific.

All the obsolete trappings of Berkeley's approach to physiology (e.g. of plants) and chemistry should not conceal the fact that he appears in these two sections as a convinced opponent of the extreme mechanistic approach. It is also noteworthy that he actually uses some assumptions of the 'corpuscularians' in order to argue from the 'idiosyncrasies' of 'heterogeneous' particles against any unified mechanistic explanation of nature, and also against an unqualified reliance on macroscopic gravity. In addition, it should also be noticed that, besides putting an emphasis on the 'idiosyncrasies' of particles (and, more generally, of bodies 'with regard to' particles), Berkeley here draws a distinction between (1) various 'attractions and repulsions' in the corpuscularian realm, and (2) other properties ('the different size, figure, number, solidity, or weight') of the minute corpuscles. Another important point here is that he speaks of particles of aether (or 'light or fire'), and of particles of 'minerals', 'vegetables', and 'animal spirit' alike. He obviously assumes a wide variety of theoretical entities (or, as he puts it in *S*. 238, of 'particles of different bodies . . . agitated by different forces, attracting and repelling, or to speak more accurately . . . moved by different laws'). Finally, yet another crucial point here is that he rejects anew (cf. also *S*. 232 and 237) an explanation of (*a*) gravity, and (*b*) the corpuscularian 'idiosyncrasies' by the 'elasticity and density of aether' (I shall return to that last issue somewhat later in Section 6 below within the context of Berkeley's theory of the corpuscularian aether.)

In any event, even a cursory examination of *S*. 238 and 239 reveals that, on Berkeley's view, particles of light do not move in an aetherial *plenum* of the Cartesian type. On the contrary, they are assumed to be identical with the corpuscles of (supposedly discontinuous) aether, and their motions *in vacuo* are not regarded by him as derivable from rules of dynamics of any *plenum*, be it their own or of other media.

It might also perhaps be interesting to notice how he draws boundaries (in *S*. 238) between observations and *conjectures* (to use his own term). The explanatory forces of particles are, on his view, purely conjectural (even when applied in the restricted sense of concomitance). An instance of the relevant observations, referred to in that section, is Newton's 'admirable discovery . . . that light is a heterogeneous medium'. The assumption that the 'heterogeneous' light consists of heterogeneous particles is used by Berkeley as a 'bridge-statement' which connects conjectures (e.g. the various explanatory roles ascribed to particles) with actual observations. However, in contrast to the admirable rules of usage of theoretical terms set forth in *S*. 228 (quoted at the beginning of this chapter), Berkeley himself now slips in one place into an inaccurate usage of those terms, and the sentence which refers to Sir Isaac's 'admirable discovery' seems to imply that particles themselves had been observed (see the text of *S*. 238 above).

In *S*. 244 and 277, Berkeley again emphasizes that 'the great masses are held together in their orderly courses, as well as the minutest particles governed in their natural motions, according to the *several* [*my italics*] laws of attraction, gravity, electricity, magnetism, and the rest' (*S*. 277), and says that many interactions of bodies 'seem to be effected' 'by peculiar compositions and attractions' of the corpuscularian realm (*S.* 244). In both these sections he puts stress on the diversity of laws of nature. In fact, when referring to particles, he speaks in many cases not of 'attraction', but of 'attractions' (and 'repulsions') in the plural; e.g. in *S.* 240 (or of the 'laws'—again in the plural—'of attraction and repulsion', e.g. in *S.* 245). In many other cases one has to read 'attractions' for 'attraction' in order to understand Berkeley's view. Thus, at the beginning of *S.* 244, he says: 'The size and shape of particles and general laws of motion can never explain the secretions, without the help of attraction, obscure perhaps as to its cause, but clear as a law.' Now *the* attraction (or what Berkeley calls 'the attraction of gravity'; cf. *S.* 245) is certainly incorporated within the universal framework of the Newtonian 'general laws of motion', which according to him *cannot* explain 'the secretions' etc., without the help of . . . attraction. Accordingly, prima facie, it is not easy to understand here what is the logical force of the above-mentioned distinction between the two terms 'general laws of motion' and 'attraction'. I may, of course, be wrong, but on my view, and in consonance with the line of reasoning developed for instance in *S.* 244 and 277, 'attraction' is here a portmanteau-term which stands for various 'idiosyncratic' motions of particles that are, or may be, different from instances of the 'general laws of motion' in the macroscopic realm. It seems to me that this trend, a tendency to draw a line of distinction between (1) corpuscularian 'idiosyncrasies' and (2) macroscopic, or macrocosmic, laws of motion, in addition to the emphasis put on differences between gravity, electricity, and magnetism, is very prominent in *Siris*.

S. 244 may also be regarded as a representative instance of Berkeley's account of correlations between two kinds of particles, those of the hypothetical aether and those of other bodies. Particles of both kinds are assumed to attract (or repel) each other. The rejection of the Cartesian *plenum* is followed in this section by the rejection of the notion that small particles have to fit precisely 'the pores' between 'gross' particles (or between aggregates of 'gross' particles) of 'substances' in which they are 'detained or imprisoned'. Berkeley's explanation of cohesion between small and 'gross' particles is quite different from the Cartesian one, or from the explanation by the 'hamate atoms'. The magnitude of particles of aether (i.e. of 'pure fire' or 'the substance of light') is regarded by him as smaller (and not equal to, or greater) than that of 'the pores' between particles of grosser bodies. They may nevertheless be conceived as 'detained', *in vacuo*, or in the air, etc., by the non-aethereal particles due to the 'peculiar attractions' in the microcosmic realm. He also assumes that, at least, some 'peculiar attractions' between various micro-entities *depend* on the presence of aether, that 'instrumental cause' concomitant in the entire *rerum natura* (see, for instance, *S.* 161). But the gist of his argument in *S.* 244 is that reference to 'peculiar attractions' of particles, be they of aether or of 'grosser' bodies, is the best explanation of various medium-sized phenomena, quite apart from 'the size and shape' of particles themselves and the 'general laws of motion' (ibid.).

Berkeley's views in *Siris* concerning 'peculiar attractions' and 'idiosyncrasies' of all corpuscles whatever, be they parts of aether or of 'grosser' bodies, are also summarized by one crucial sentence in *S.* 267. Berkeley says there, eulogizing the 'ancient philosophers', that 'they supposed a concord and discord, union and disunion, in particles, some attracting, others repelling each other: and that those attractions and repulsions so various, regular, and useful, could not be accounted for but by an intelligence presiding and directing all particular motions'. This corpuscularian thesis, ascribed by him to the 'Platonists', and incorporated in *Siris* within the immaterialistic framework, is applicable, on his view, to all bodies whatever, be they actually observed and well known or purely hypothetical. In any case, it is obvious that Berkeley's treatment of the corpuscularian realm reveals a pluralistic tendency not only with regard to particles' sizes and qualities, but also when he deals with various interactions on the micro-level. A more detailed examination of this pluralistic tendency as applied to the hypothesis of aether is to be found in Section 7 below.

5. ANALOGIES AND HOMOLOGIES

Berkeley tries in many sections of *Siris* to strengthen his corpuscularian theory by means of various *arguments from analogy and homology*,[20] supposed to function as 'bridge-statements' between assertions concerning a completely hypothetical level of the smallest corpuscles (e.g. of 'animal spirits' and aether) and the perceived data. The 'grosser' particles of acids and 'earth' mediate here, as it were, between the actual observations and the 'smallest particles of light'.

Thus, for instance, particles referred to in *S*. 228 and at the beginning of *S*. 238 are not considered as parts of the assumed aether. Theoretical assumptions concerning various non-aethereal particles, be they on a molecular or sub-molecular level, are also to be found in *S*. 134, 147, 150, and 151. In *S*. 134, Berkeley does not refer at all to aether, and only suggests that a certain corpuscularian hypothesis (in regard to magnitude and attraction of 'the parts of acid . . . and water') may be more useful than another one. In *S*. 147, 150, and 151, on the other hand, he expounds various hypothetical assumptions concerning the interspersion of 'grosser particles' amongst the corpuscles of aether. In a rather similar vein, he tries in *S*. 194 to rely on experiments of Homberg in order to explain the composition of gold, that is, he assumes that bits of gold consist of very small particles of mercury, and yet smaller particles of aether, or 'the substance of light', which are 'introduced into the pores' of mercury. Those aethereal and non-aethereal particles are regarded by him as 'attracting and fixing' each other.

The same hypothesis, according to which there are certain fixed proportions between the particles of various bodies and the much smaller particles of aether ('or light or fire'), is adumbrated in *S*. 222. Berkeley now accepts in essentials Newton's explanation of the reflection of light, and refers again to 'the great porosity of all known bodies' which 'affords room' for many 'particles of light or fire to be absorbed and latent in grosser bodies'. It is noteworthy that, in this section, Berkeley refers to different levels of explanation, ranging from an almost empirical to a completely theoretical one. The non-aethereal particles—e.g. of 'acids' and 'earth' mentioned above—function as a mediatory realm between (1) the actual observations and experiments concerning the porosity of bodies, and (2) the 'deeper' hypothetical level of the assumed corpuscularian aether:

it is certain the great porosity of all known bodies affords room for much of this light or fire to be lodged therein. Gold itself, the most solid of all metals, seems to have far more pores than solid parts, from water being pressed through it in the Florentine experiment, from magnetic effluvia passing, and from mercury entering, its pores so freely. And it is admitted that water, though impossible to be compressed, hath at least forty times more pores than solid parts. And as acid particles, joined with those of each in certain proportions, are so closely united with them as to be quite hid and lost to all appearance, as in *mercurius dulcis* and common sulphur, so also may we conceive the particles of light or fire to be absorbed and latent in grosser bodies.

Particles of 'acids' (be they 'pure'—and cf. *S*. 159—or 'common') and of compounds of mercury mentioned above may be here regarded as hypothetical entities, being 'hid and lost to all appearance', i.e. not discerned in the actually observed compounds or elements.[21] However, they might also be regarded by Berkeley as verging, as it were, on the observed realm, because chemists had actually isolated in a pure or mixed form 'substances' and 'minute parts' supposed to consist of them. Particles of aether, on the other hand, have to be regarded not as theoretical parts of observed parts or elements, but as theoretical parts of a theoretical medium, since aether itself is only assumed *ex hypothesi*.

Our lack of capacity to perceive the assumed aether is explained in *S*. 222 by means of an analogy endowed with certain homological features.[22] The basic differentiation in the section above is between the smallness of the corpuscles of aether and the relative 'grossness' of other particles. What is analogical here is the capacity of both 'acid particles' and the corpuscles of aether to penetrate the 'grosser' bodies, and be instrumental in the relevant chemical reactions. This would be a similarity of function. The analogy is also supported here by a comparison with empirical investigations showing that many solid bodies which seem, on the face of it, to lack any pores become literally soaked with water. (But note also that, besides referring to parts of water (and mercury), Berkeley also speaks of 'magnetic effluvia' which themselves are connected with the porosity-model in a rather theoretical fashion.) This too is primarily a comparison based on processes and functions. On the other hand, the analogy itself is explained on the grounds that both particles of aether and of acids (such as were supposed to inhere in grosser compounds, as in the case of *mercurius dulcis* and common sulphur) are smaller than particles of other bodies, and can, therefore, be 'pressed' through them. This would be an instance of homology, at least in a less detailed, or weaker, sense, i.e. of dependence on similarity of structure. (But the homology may here perhaps be interpreted in the strong sense as well—see n. 20 below—provided that all the very minute particles assumed by Berkeley in *Siris*, e.g. of acids and 'the substance of light', are regarded as members of one family, in contrast to all others.) The analogy is supported here by an argument from observed data (water and other components) to hypothetical candidates-for-reality. But Berkeley proceeds here in the identical way concerning the homological aspect as well. He relies on the structure of water, and argues from it to that of other compounds and elements. It is true that, when speaking of water, he does not refer to *particles*, but merely to pores and parts. But he refers to particles of water in many other places; see for example an interesting reference to them in *M*. 62, and also *S*. 134. Still, a structure is a structure; and the reference to pores and parts provides him with an argument from observed data interpretable in favour of the homology. Another theoretical point in *S*. 222 is that, in fact, even the exact proportion between 'pores of water' and the solid parts as assumed by Berkeley had to be regarded as partly hypothetical because of the prevailing observational limitations. In fact, he himself says rather cautiously: 'And it is *admitted* that water . . . hath *at least* forty times more pores than solid parts' (my italics). In any event, the structure of scientific explanation, as conceived by the author of *Siris* in his reference to the corpuscularian aether in the section above, seems to take into account both homological and analogical aspects.

6. AETHER AS A THEORETICAL ENTITY; ITS EXPLANATORY ROLE

Berkeley explains in many sections of *Siris* that in using the concept of aether he is referring to a purely hypothetical entity. He sometimes tries very carefully to avoid any misunderstanding in regard to the actual status of aether, and frequently indicates that this subtle and universal 'instrumental cause' has never been separately observed in the *rerum natura*. Thus, he entirely approves of Homberg's opinion 'that this principle of sulphur, fire, or the substance of light, *is in itself imperceptible* [*my italics*], and only becomes sensible as it is *joined* [*my italics*] with some other principle, which serves as a vehicle for it' (*S*. 189). In fact, he tries to identify Homberg's 'principle of sulphur' with aether *qua* pure fire. We perceive, as it were, only various 'vehicles' of such a hypothetical 'true chemic principle' (ibid.) which 'itself' is 'imperceptible'. I interpret 'becomes sensible' here as indicating that certain events (e.g. chemical reactions), supposedly explained by 'the substance of light', take place, because Berkeley explicitly stipulates that the hypothetical 'principle' referred to is regarded as 'always lost . . . in the analysis of bodies . . . escaping the skill of the artist, and passing through the closest vessels' (ibid.). And in *S.* 190 he says that, according to 'moderns' and ancients alike, 'the pure fire is to be *discerned by its effects alone*[23] [*my italics*], such as heat, dilatation of all solid bodies, and rarefaction of fluids . . .'. The fire 'which smokes and flames' (ibid.) is also an effect only of that pure and invisible one, whose particles move according to various laws of 'attractions' and of geometrical optics (e.g. like rays along straight lines; cf. *S.* 208 and 226), and are 'collected in the focus of a mirror or burning glass'.

It is also noteworthy that Berkeley employs tentative verbs, such as 'seem' and 'suppose', when describing the influence of the hypothetical aether. The invisible fire '*seems* the source of all the operations in nature' (*S.* 190); it 'is *supposed* to be everywhere, and always present' (ibid.; my italics). The supposed aether is, however, not to be regarded as unperceivable *ex principio* (or because of our intrusion in the very process of observation). Its invisibility (which seems also to signify in *Siris* all other kinds of imperceptibility) may be regarded as due to its sheer 'subtlety and elasticity': 'This aether or pure invisible fire, *the most subtle and elastic of all bodies* [*my italics*] . . . seems to pervade and expand itself throughout the whole universe' (*S.* 152). The aether, just as various non-aethereal particles mentioned above in Section 2, is a 'candidate-for-reality'. Berkeley himself evaluates (in *S.* 159) the precise logical force of the hypothetical elements in the concept of aether:

No eye could ever hitherto discern, and no sense perceive, the animal spirit in a human body, otherwise than from its effects. The same may be said of pure fire, or the spirit of the universe, which is perceived only by means of some other bodies, on which it operates, or with which it is joined. What the chemists say of pure acids being never found alone might as well be said of pure fire.

Aether is assumed here as a 'candidate-for-reality', a hypothetical entity which has never been observed in the *rerum natura*. Thus, in nearly one hundred sections of *Siris*, Berkeley tends to speak of a hypothetical entity, i.e. of the corpuscularian aether, as the main pillar of his theory of nature. In fact, the theory of the corpuscular-

ian aether (just like the theory of the corpuscularian structure of all
bodies) is endorsed by him much more strongly than many
particular references to non-aethereal particles, important as they
may be within the framework of, say, eighteenth-century science.
We should remember that in some sections (e.g. 228) dealing with
non-aethereal particles, he warns the reader not to 'argue reciprocally' from empirical 'conclusions' (e.g. computations of density
and volume of gases) to theoretical 'premises' (e.g. the molecular
structure of gases) just because of the remarkable success of the
diametrically opposite 'inference'. But he refers to the corpuscularian aether in many tens of sections without issuing a single similar
warning. In fact, he seems to have more doubts concerning the
reality and features of molecules of gases(!), and of some other non-
aethereal particles (cf., *inter alia*, *S*. 131–4), than in regard to the
reality and characteristics of the corpuscles of aether. The
corpuscles of aether are 'candidates-for-reality' just like many non-
aethereal particles mentioned in *Siris*; but their option for reality
seems, on his view, to have more chance of coming true than the
option of some of their non-aethereal analogues. Their status in
Siris is, therefore, closer to that of the unobserved 'animal spirits'
(cf. *S*. 153), the existence of which had been accepted in the second
half of the seventeenth and the first half of the eighteenth century by
almost all sides, than to the rather mathematical role ascribed to
particles in *TVV* 43, the dubious footing of molecules of gases
(cf. *S*. 228), and the theoretical function of a 'subtle element'
assumed by the Cartesians (cf. *S*. 246). The 'corpuscles of aether'
in what the author of *Siris* labels the 'macrocosm' (i.e. the non-
organic part of the entire *rerum natura*), and the 'animal spirits' in
what he calls 'microcosm' (i.e. the realm of occurrences characteristic of animate bodies in general, and of the human body in
particular), are apparently regarded by him as having more chance
to be real physical entities than some particles assumed as premises
in deductive models which do not take aether into account. In a
similar vein, he seems to think that aether has more chances than
epicycles of keeping its useful theoretical status. It should perhaps
be mentioned here that the Cartesian influence on the one hand, and
a curious return to the vitalistic and Neoplatonic philosophy of the
Renaissance on the other, are very prominent in the use of the term
'animal spirits'. The Renaissance influence is, of course, also
exemplified by the reference to 'microcosm' and 'macrocosm'.

Be that as it may, even Berkeley's more cautious references to aether (e.g. in *S*. 159 above) express his view that it is presumably a real, though as yet unobserved, entity. 'Unobserved' here means 'unobserved by us, but presumably observed by other 'finite spirits' or by God'. It is also noteworthy that on this view, aether and the 'animal spirits' could not 'hitherto' be discerned not only by sight, but by any sense whatever. (In addition, 'perceive' and 'discern' as in *S*. 159 seem to be synonyms.) And, at least, some particles of the heterogeneous aether may, according to him, be 'indefinitely small' (*S*. 208–9). In any case, 'hitherto' seems to be the most important word in *S*. 159, since it indicates a vacillation between two approaches to the assumed aether, the first of which would only be that aether is unperceived, whereas the second would have to take into account its unperceivability from, at least, the human point of view. 'Pure fire' above might, of course, be interpreted as a refined, i.e. 'idealized', version of the 'culinary' or 'grosser' fire (cf. also *S*. 190), just as the concept of 'pure acids' mentioned in many sections of *Siris* (e.g. 129–35) might only be an idealized version of references to *observed* 'acid solvents' (*S*. 131), and 'acid spirits', or 'salts', 'discernible also in many parts of the earth, particularly in . . . sulphur, vitriol, and alum' (*S*. 135). However, the very assumption of the corpuscularian structure, and also of differences between the corpuscularian structures of observed and unobserved entities, does not enable us to treat explanatory terms of aether-type as standing for refined (i.e. idealized) references to well-known bodies. An instance of the crucial difference between the refinement of terms which stand for observed bodies, relations, etc., and the invention of new explanatory terms would be a comparison of the concept of 'idealized' motion with that of the corpuscles of aether. The ordinary motions of (at least, all earthly) bodies are involved in various kinds of friction. But the refined concept of motion does not refer to any friction whatever. The concept of particles, on the other hand, is not just a refined concept of subdivided extension, which merely declines to take into account some of the observed concomitant occurrences.

S. 197 is yet another instance of reference to the hypothetical status of the invisible aether. In that section, Berkeley does not refer at all to the observability of aether, but only evaluates the logical situation implied by his theory. According to that section, the aethereal 'fire' 'is a subtle invisible thing, whose operation is not to be discerned but by means of some grosser body'. The 'grosser bodies' 'serve not for a pabulum to nourish the fire, but for a vehicle to arrest and bring it into view' (by its 'effects'). Now I take the sentences above (and, especially, the verb 'is') as indicating that aether may well be described as 'a subtle thing' (i.e., on Berkeley's view, a spirit or a real 'collection of ideas').

'Thing' is in the Berkeleian dictionary of technical terms either 'idea' or 'spirit' (see *PHK* 39). Aether, referred to above as 'a subtle invisible thing', may, accordingly, be regarded (on the assumption that it is real) as either corporeal or incorporeal. Those would be, according to Berkeley's general metaphysical assumptions, the only two options of existence for the real aether. And, in fact, he examines those two possibilities, and rejects the very concept of the incorporeal aether, in *S.* 206–9. There, aether is regarded as an extremely subtle *corporeal* entity, whose particles are 'exceedingly small' in relation to 'the empty spaces', or to other particles. But the invisibility of the corpuscles does not indicate in that group of sections, nor, indeed, in any other section of *Siris*, a total inaccessibility to vision. It seems to mean rather 'not visible by any known means', or, at most, 'epistemically inaccessible to human vision' (see also Section 8 below). Besides, even a total inaccessibility to all 'visive faculties' whatever does not, of course, mean, on Berkeley's view, that the invisible items have no right to belong to the *rerum natura*, because, after all, the real particles might be tangible only.

In any case, Berkeley certainly has to admit that in our present epistemic situation we cannot 'discern' single particles, or groups of particles, of aether, and they come 'into our view' by means of some 'grosser bodies' only. In other words, we only 'discern' the *'effects'* of the assumed corpuscles (*S.* 159). The aethereal microbodies have to be regarded as observed neither single nor *en masse* when 'lodged' in various other bodies. In addition, they have to be conceived as never singly observed even in their own 'common ocean' (*S.* 165). However, they may perhaps be regarded as observed *en masse* as the visible light *in vacuo* to the extent that a visual observation of objects which are not revealed by touch (e.g. glows) is an indication, or, to use Berkeley's term, a signification, of things moving in (kin-aesthetic) space. In this last sense, particles of ('the substance of') light may be regarded (i.e. on the assumption that they are real) as observed, seen, etc., only when being *en masse*, in the same manner that one sees trees whenever one sees, say, a forest without being able to see its trees separately. But, in fact, Berkeley is rather wary of equating even the visible light with the 'substance of light' seen *en masse*, and speaks of the '*invisible* [*my italics*] elementary mass' of aether (*S.* 198).

In any event, the aethereal 'pure fire' is supposed in *Siris* to exist not only in conjunction with other bodies, but also, as it were, on its own, in its separate 'invisible elementary mass' (*S.* 198). It is assumed to be 'ingenerable and incorruptible by the course of nature', i.e. to exist independently of, and to be prior to, all other natural processes and bodies. (It seems that, according to the cosmology of *Siris*, light which appeared on the first day of the Creation was identical with, or, at least a concomitant of, the corpuscularian aether.) Now, according to sections like 159, particles of aether are never observed, be it singly or *en masse*, in conjunction with other bodies (such as metals and air). However, according to other sections (e.g. 165), they are also never singly observed *in vacuo*. Even varying colours of stars, or of rays of light parted by prisms, only indicate, on this view, *groupings* of the corpuscles of ('the substance of') light according to their kinds, i.e. aggregates which are an outcome of reflection and refraction. Thus, the homogeneous light is diversified when refracted by separating devices; but its 'substance' is regarded as diversified into groups of similar particles, and not into single ones. There is nothing infelicitous within the logical framework of Berkeley's theory of aether in the notion of singly observed corpuscles; but it was rather difficult to refer to such observations in absence of any empirical data. The visible rays of light could be geared to groups of particles of aether, but what could a single particle of aether be geared to? Therefore, within the framework of his scientific theory, Berkeley emphasizes in *Siris* the perceivability of single corpuscles much less than he had previously emphasized the perceivability of single *minima* in *Philosophical Commentaries* and his first work on vision, even though *minima* have to be regarded as smaller units than corpuscles. (The visible particles of light may, on Berkeley's premises, be regarded either as bigger, or, at most, as equal to, but obviously not as smaller, than the *minima visibilia*.) The corpuscles of aether are 'lost to sense', be it singly or *en masse*, 'when fixed and imprisoned in a compound' (cf. also *S.* 198), i.e. when being relatively static; are not singly observed *in vacuo* (cf. *S.* 209); and are not unconditionally regarded as seen *en masse* when one sees light in the air, or even *in vacuo* (cf. *S*. 198). In the same vein, the transition of the corpuscles of aether from various compounds to their 'invisible elementary mass' is discerned, according to *Siris*, by its effects only, as we do not observe these 'incorruptible'[24] particles in either of the above-mentioned states of affairs.

I would like also to point out that, according to Berkeley's theory of the corpuscularian structure of all bodies, the particles of aether are, of course, not the only items seen *en masse* when one sees various objects, say a stone, or the sun (in contrast to instances of seeing rays of light in the intervening space), and they may also not be seen at all when seeing certain parts (e.g. superficies) of bodies, since they are not the elementary stuff of which bodies are supposed to consist. It would possibly make sense to say that one sees atoms *en masse* when observing stones or stars, if stones or stars are supposed to consist of atoms. But the corpuscles of aether, assumed by Berkeley's theory, constitute, *ex hypothesi*, only a very minor part of opaque bodies in whose 'pores' they are 'lost to all appearance'. It would seem, therefore, that (*a*) to see, or, for that matter, to touch, any compound[25] whatever has, on these premises, to be a very different occurrence from seeing, or touching, anything which consists of the corpuscles of aether only; (*b*) to the extent that even the 'pores' of opaque bodies are opaque, the observed segments of such bodies may be regarded as not including any corpuscles of aether. (In a similar vein, it might make sense to say that one touches particles whenever one touches a (surface of a) stone; but it certainly would not make sense to say that one touches all the particles of a stone when touching a stone.) In addition, 'aether or the substance of light' is regarded by Berkeley as a 'secondary *cause*' *of all vision*, but *not as* always *seen* when seeing bodies. And it should also be remembered that, on Berkeley's view, one has to draw a distinction between the physical (tangible) particles of light and their visual counterparts, which might 'signify' quite different sets of physical units. On top of it, visual space is regarded by him as 'blended' with kinaesthetic data, i.e. as a fusion of visual bi-dimensional manifolds with kinaesthetic clues.

'The general ocean of aether', i.e. the assumed 'invisible elementary mass', is mentioned too in *S*. 192. In that section Berkeley also draws a distinction between visible flames and the assumed 'invisible fire'. But he certainly wavers on the issue of the invisibility of aether, or 'the substance of light', *en masse*. *S.* 192 and 198 imply that 'the general ocean of aether' is invisible (at least, from our point of view) just like its single particles. On the other hand, in some other sections of *Siris* the author is inclined to speak of the 'common mass' of aether, or 'the substance of light', as 'seemingly homogeneous' from our point of view, i.e. as 'seemingly' *white*, rather than as invisible (cf. *S.* 191). The 'seemingly homogeneous . . . common mass' of aether is assumed to include various *kinds* of particles 'lost and blended together' (ibid.). It seems to me that there is a difference between this last view, and the one expounded in *S.* 192 and 198. Thus, in *S.* 198 the emphasis is put on the invisibility of the common mass of aether, whereas in *S.* 165 and 191 Berkeley merely stresses the theoretical tenet that the colour of that 'common mass' is different from the colours of its components, and, in addition, he does not say that the components (i.e. various basic kinds of the corpuscles of aether) cannot be seen separately. In fact, he assumes (*S.* 165) that the separation of the 'common mass' of aether into its heterogeneous kinds is analogous to the observed separation of white light by a prism into the various colours (and connects in *S.* 191 observations and theory by rather dubious 'bridge-statements' which deal with 'several distinct kinds of sulphur').

Incidentally, it seems to be a good policy always to put in doubt Berkeley's 'bridge-statements' in *Siris*. He refers in most cases to sound observations (e.g. of Newton and Boyle), and his theories are, in many cases, very interesting even from the modern point of view (and certainly were not obsolete against the background of the eighteenth century). But sometimes he relies on misinterpreted experiments (see, for example, his reference to the transmutation of mercury and light into gold in *S.* 194), and his 'bridge-statements' are often most spurious, and reflect the influence of the 'old science'. T. E. Jessop says in his introduction to *Siris* (cf. Luce-Jessop edition, vol. V, pp. 8–12) that Berkeley says many things 'which the most mediocre student of today knows to be wrong'. Now I would say that this statement may be primarily applied to 'bridge-statements' which figure in *Siris*, rather than to some logical features of Berkeley's corpuscularian hypotheses, on the one hand, or to his reference to Newton's observations or to the discovery of the velocity of light, etc., on the other. The case in point would be an analysis of the bridge-statement in *S.* 193 where the corpuscularian theory of aether and perfectly sound observations are incorrectly connected. The relevant observations are that 'lead, tin, or regulus of antimony, being exposed to the fire of a burning-glass, though they lose much in smoke and steam, are nevertheless found to be considerably increased in weight'. But those observations are connected with the theory of the corpuscularian aether by the assumption that the increase of weight is an outcome of 'the introduction' of aether (or 'light or fire') 'into the pores' of these bodies.

Now I turn again to the corporeal status of the invisible 'substance of light' as expounded in *Siris*. We have already seen that, on Berkeley's premisses, the explanatory and universal 'concause' is too subtle to be caught 'in the analysis of bodies' (*S*. 189). We 'always lose' it in every analysis, because it 'escapes' 'the skill of the artist . . . passing through the closest vessels' (ibid.). In brief, it 'is in itself imperceptible' (ibid.). But the very use of 'hitherto' in a crucial section (159) quoted above implies that the lack of observations in the past (e.g. concerning particles of aether) does not necessarily mean unobservability in the future. Moreover, we have seen that Berkeley insists that the hypothetical entities assumed by him are not incorporeal. Thus, in *S*. 154, aether is called a 'corporeal' cause (cause in 'a subordinate sense'), and it is also referred to as 'physical' (*S*. 160). It is true that he sometimes refers to aether as 'spirit', but this must be understood in a purely metaphorical sense. (But the very use of such a metaphor seems to draw on the ambiguity of meaning of 'spirit', and of some other nouns which may indicate things corporeal and incorporeal alike, or, at least, had been used so in the first half of the eighteenth century.[26]) Two *loci classici* in which Berkeley warns the reader of *Siris* that, strictly speaking, 'the vital spirit of the universe', i.e. aether or 'the substance of light', is corporeal are to be found in *S*. 206–7 and 220. In *S*. 206–7 he draws a distinction between his own theory of 'the substance of light' and the extreme Neoplatonic one (expounded by Ficinus), according to which light is *incorporeal*, being 'the act of a pure intelligence'. (The discussion with Ficinus is dealt with in Section 8 below, which relates in detail to various problems involved in Berkeley's identification of aether with light.) And in *S*. 220 he says: 'Force or power, strictly speaking, is in the Agent alone who imparts an *equivocal* [*my italics*] force to the invisible elementary fire, or animal spirit of the world.' He also says there that an infinite Agent is the first 'link' in the great 'chain' of beings, and aether is only the first amongst the 'intermediate' and 'corporeal' links[27] of that 'chain', 'capable of motion, rarefaction, gravity, and other qualities of bodies' (ibid.). In brief, aether is regarded by him neither as an 'incorporeal' *force*, nor as an observed entity, but as an explanatory term and a 'candidate-for-reality', which, on his view, has to be either non-existent or *corporeal*.

I have referred above to Berkeley's treatment of the assumed reality, invisibility, and corporeality of the particles of aether. But in *Siris* he is mostly inclined to speak not only of the general characteristics of aether, but also of the peculiar features of particles of which this 'vital flame' is supposedly composed. At times he speaks only of particles, without any reference to aether. Sometimes he mentions aether without any reference whatever to particles (as in many sections quoted at the beginning of this chapter). But in most sections of *Siris* in which reference is made to particles or aether he connects those two theoretical tenets and interweaves them within the framework of one explanatory hypothesis. Thus, for instance, he refers in *S*. 202 to the 'peculiar parts' of aether; and in *S*. 226 he says that the parts of aether, or 'the substance of light', may be regarded as the smallest and most 'moveable' of all corpuscles. In *S*. 162 he suggests that 'the pure aether or invisible fire contains parts of different kinds, that are impressed with different forces, or subjected to different laws of motion, attraction, repulsion, and expansion, and endued with divers distinct habitudes towards other bodies'. The corpuscles, or the 'original particles', of aether are regarded by him as 'subtler', smaller and quicker than all other particles. Their 'extreme minuteness' is emphasized time and again in *Siris* (cf. for instance, *S*. 165), and seems to follow logically from the assumption of aether as the subtlest medium (cf. *S*. 161). Obviously, if the 'latent and unobserved' aether is the subtlest medium ('the most subtle and elastic of bodies') which is able to 'pervade' the entire *rerum natura* (cf. *S*. 152 and 157), and consists of corpuscles, it would follow, or at least be very probable, that its corpuscles are 'subtler', or smaller, than parts of all 'grosser' bodies.

Berkeley assumes (e.g. in *S*. 162 mentioned above) that even 'the original particles' of aether are not homogeneous. But he certainly ascribes to all those 'original particles' certain decisive common 'instrumental' properties, such as the capacity to be 'diversely separated and attracted by the various subjects of the animal, vegetable and mineral kingdoms' (*S*. 162), and also to penetrate all those 'grosser' bodies, and 'be detained' in their 'pores' (*S*. 244), in spite of being very small (e.g. smaller than the 'pores' between other particles; ibid.) and moving with the velocity of light (*S*. 226). Berkeley also emphasizes (e.g. in *S*. 227) that 'the particles of aether' (or 'the substance of light') 'fly asunder with the greatest force', apparently because he assumes that *vis impressa* and velocity *in vacuo* may be equated.

The 'equivocal' greatest force (e.g. as manifest in capacity to 'pervade' other bodies), greatest velocity, and 'extreme minuteness' are regarded by him as the three fundamental quantitative features of the heterogeneous corpuscles of aether, which set them quite apart from corpuscles of all other compounds or elements. He also assumes that the greatest velocity of particles of aether has to indicate that 'according to the Newtonian doctrine' 'they . . . attract each other with the greatest force'. All those assumed quantitative features of the corpuscles of aether and their motions (and their other basic 'idiosyncrasies' in regard to the non-aethereal particles) are, on his view, applicable to all of them in spite of their heterogeneity. However, various kinds of the corpuscles of aether reveal, according to him, various degrees of 'attraction and repulsion' in conjunction with different kinds of non-aethereal particles (see, *inter alia*, *S*. 162).

We may, therefore, conclude that the corpuscles of aether are regarded by Berkeley as having the smallest size (but they are not to be identified with *minima tangibilia*, nor, of course, with *minima visibilia*, referred to in *Phil. Com.* and the *Theory of Vision*), and the greatest velocity and 'force' of attraction in the entire *rerum natura*. However, being regarded as almost always mixed with (and 'detained by' aggregates of) other and 'grosser' corpuscles, and as imparting to them, as it were, their own motion, they tend, in Berkeley's view, to lose their original velocity and 'subtlety'. 'But action and reaction being equal, the spring of this aethereal spirit is diminished by being imparted. Its velocity and subtlety are also less from its being mixed with grosser particles' (*S*. 147). Thus also the particles of the 'heterogeneous' air are described by Berkeley as 'cohering with particles of aether'. Particles of aether are 'attracted and clogged' by particles of air, and, accordingly, become 'less active' (*S*. 150–1). This 'diminution' in the velocity and 'force' of particles of aether, owing to their involvement in various mixtures with 'grosser' bodies, is described as follows in *S*. 163:

As the soul acts immediately on pure fire, so pure fire operates immediately on air; that is, the abrasions of all terrestrial things being rendered volatile and elastic by fire (Sects. 149, 150, 152) and at the same time lessening the volatility and expansive force of the fire, whose particles they attract and adhere to (Sect. 147) there is produced a new fluid, more volatile than water or earth, and more fixed than fire. Therefore, the virtues and operations imputed to air must be ultimately attributed to fire, as that which imparts activity to air itself. [*The reference to various sections of* Siris *is Berkeley's own.*]

The 'extreme minuteness and volatility' of 'peculiar particles of light or fire' is also mentioned in *S*. 165, which has already been referred to above. This 'extreme minuteness' and 'subtlety' of the corpuscularian structure of aether, or, ('the substance of') light, is maintained by the author of *Siris* not only for purely theoretical reasons, i.e. as the best general explanatory hypothesis which connects all finite 'links' of the 'great chain of beings' (and cf. *S*. 274). He endorses his particular theory of aether also on what seem to him more immediate and practical grounds. Thus, first, he tries to subtantiate his claim concerning the 'minuteness' of the aethereal particles by means of some curious alchemical reports and experiments, as for example in *S*. 194 where he refers to a venerable tradition according to which 'mercury' is 'the mother' and 'sulphur' 'the father' of metals. The 'element' sulphur is identified by him with aether *qua* 'the substance of light', and he also accepts the supposed results of Homberg's experiment according to which gold is a compound of mercury and light. Accordingly, he interprets Homberg's assertions in his own corpuscularian vein, and says that 'from the foregoing experiment it appears that gold is only a mass of mercury penetrated and cemented by the substance of light, the particles of those bodies attracting and fixing each other'. In this section, both the alchemic and relatively modern tendencies and sources of such an explanation are quite conspicuous. An even more uncritical, or, one may say, 'unscientific', approach is conspicuous in many sections of *Siris* which refer to the 'Hermetic' and oriental alchemy; e.g. *S*. 178. But Berkeley's argument in favour of the 'minuteness' of particles of aether does not really depend on mere alchemical notions. The very mixture of alchemical notions and relatively modern experiments described in *S.* 194, misconceived as it may be, is a hint that he tried, even when referring to the 'old science', to explain by means of the corpuscularian aether many empirical data and assumptions accumulated and expounded by the 'spagyrists',[28] and by scientists at the second half of the seventeenth and the first half of the eighteenth century.

However, Berkeley's rather uncritical acceptance of some assertions of the spagyrists (and of some scientists of his time)[29] does not mean, of course, that he endorsed only theories which were doomed to failure. On the contrary, it may be said that, on the whole, his theory of aether, light, and combustion was much more modern than those of many of his contemporaries. Thus he clearly preferred the hypothesis of the corpuscularian aether to de Stahl's *phlogiston* as an explanation of combustion. (Another case in point would be his rejection of the Cartesian *plenum.*) He declined to accept, even within a hypothetical framework blended with a few fantastic alchemical assumptions, the notion that a mysterious substance, the 'matter of fire', is disengaged during combustion of bodies; he preferred to assume that the 'spirit of fire' is *added* to the burning bodies (see also many of the sections of *Siris* quoted above). He tended to think that the various burning bodies receive 'the substance of light', i.e. the conflagration and the subsequent additional weight are to be explained by 'mixture' of 'the substance of light' and particles of other compounds and elements (see, for instance, *S.* 195). In fact, in his view, particles of aether may be conceived as 'imprisoned' (cf. *S.* 203) in *all* 'grosser' bodies; and the transition from the 'pure fire' to the 'visible flame' is explained by him as an outcome of special correlations prevailing between the 'invisible fire' and particles of certain compounds (e.g. an *increase* in quantity of the aethereal corpuscles). 'Nothing flames but oil, and sulphur with water, salt, and earth compose oil, which sulphur is fire; therefore fire enclosed attracts fire, and causeth the bodies whose composition it enters to burn and blaze.' (*S.* 195.)

The additional weight acquired by bodies after combustion, or calcination, is, therefore, easily explained in *Siris*. The relevant bodies do not lose any substance, but, on the contrary, acquire, as it were, 'the substance of light', or the 'invisible fire', which is 'attracted' by the 'oil', or the 'enclosed fire', and 'in order to become sensible, must have some subject to act upon' (*S.* 198). See also

S. 196: 'When common lead is put into the fire in order to make red lead, a greater weight of this comes out than was put in of common lead. Therefore the red lead should seem impregnated with fire. Mr. Hales[30] thinks it is with air. The vast expansion of compound *aqua fortis*, Mr. Nieuwentyt[31] will have to proceed from fire alone. Mr. Hales contends that air must necessarily co-operate.' Berkeley's own solution in *Siris* is a fairly reasonable compromise between Hales and Nieuwentijdt. According to him, the 'visible flame', and, indeed, many other phenomena, e.g. heat, 'caused' by the 'invisible fire', may be regarded as being ordinarily effected by means of air. But, in his opinion, air itself is 'nothing more than particles of wet and dry bodies volatilized and rendered elastic by fire' (*S.* 197). On this view, air always includes particles of aether (just like other bodies. However, the proportion between the aethereal and non-aethereal particles is not regarded by him as equal in various compounds). In addition, air, 'being less gross than other bodies', is, according to him, 'of a middle nature and therefore more fit to receive the impressions of a fine aethereal fire, and impart them to other things' (*S.* 199). The 'pure aether' is, in most cases, too subtle to act 'immediately and of itself' on 'grosser bodies' (*S.* 200), and air, whose particles are, on the whole, regarded by him as smaller than those of other non-aethereal bodies, is supposed normally to function as a 'vehicle' of aether (*S.* 199).

However, despite the suggestion that 'they who hold the opposite sides in this question [*of dependence of* all *conflagrations on air*] may be reconciled' (*S.* 197), because 'what is done by air must be ascribed to fire' (ibid.), he seems, in fact, to be closer to Nieuwentijdt's view than to Hales's. The reason for this is, in my view, that he does not really say that the existence, or even influence, of 'pure fire', i.e. of aether or 'the substance of light', always depends on the existence of air. He only says that aether always permeates air; but, following the *Elementa Chemiae* of the celebrated Boerhaave, he rejects the view that the 'elemental fire' needs 'a pabulum' (say, of air) 'to nourish' it. On his theory, particles of grosser bodies do not 'nourish', but only 'arrest', the particles of aether, and, indirectly, 'bring them into view', i.e. indicate their presence (*S.* 197–8). The particles of the 'elemental fire' are extremely 'volatile' and 'invisible'; and their 'operation is not to be discerned but by means of some grosser body' (ibid.). Berkeley maintains that what depends on air is, strictly speaking, only a 'visible flame', and some other 'sensible effects' of the assumed presence of aether (such as certain fluctuations of 'volatility' and 'elasticity'). But (*a*) the very presence, and (*b*) some 'sensible effects', of the 'invisible fire', or aether, do not seem to depend, in his view, on air. Thus with regard to (*b*) he apparently assumes that many 'sensible effects' of the activity of aether may be discerned even *in vacuo*. At least, 'heat' and 'melting' (mentioned in *S.* 198) do not demand the presence of air. Berkeley says that 'fire, in order to become sensible, must have some subject to act upon'. But such a 'subject' may be air, a piece of rock, 'the focus of a glass *in vacuo*' (cf. *S.* 196), and, indeed, one's own body. In regard to (*a*) he explicitly says that aether, in spite of being a corporeal part of the created[32] *rerum natura*, may be regarded, 'for aught that appears', as 'ingenerable and incorruptible by the *course* of nature' (my italics), since its particles are never dissolved in various compounds,[33] and may even exist independently of all other objects (in a separate 'invisible elementary mass' *in vacuo*; cf. also *S.* 201 and 207–9).

In any case, it should be noticed that the corpuscularian structure of aether, whether it is mentioned in the context of air or as related to occurrences *in vacuo*, is actually regarded by Berkeley as an explanation of many particular problems in physics, chemistry, botany, physiology, optics, and other sciences. He not only regards the corpuscularian aether as the theoretical universal 'concause', but also actually tries to explain by means of it widely diversified states of affairs[34] (e.g. 'heating, flaming, melting', the movement of light, problems related to the physiology of plants), in accordance with his basic assumption that the 'invisible fire' is 'active' (i.e. active in the rather peculiar Berkeleian sense of 'secondary' causation) in different ways in various physical contexts. Now I have already mentioned above that those detailed explanations of physical events by aether range from references to sound experiments (and quite modern theories) to an acceptance of fantastic contentions propagated by various pseudo-sciences and old authorities. (The rather shadowy realm of the spagyrists' chemistry, to which he also refers, verges on both alchemy and new science, and may, accordingly, be regarded as belonging to both the old and the modern sources of influence on *Siris*.)

I would like to cite two final examples in order to emphasize that the theory of the corpuscularian aether is employed by Berkeley both in fantastic and in quite modern contexts. *S.* 110 is an instance of application of the theory of aether in a completely fantastic way: 'It must be owned that light attracted, secreted, and detained in tar (Sects. 8, 29, 40), and afterwards drawn off in its finest balsamic particles . . . is a safe and mild alterative, which penetrates the whole system, opens, heals, and strengthens, the remote vessels, alters and propels their contents, and enters the minutest capillaries', etc. Another rather fantastic, although, prima facie, not implausible, conjecture concerning aether is also to be found in *S.* 213 where he says that 'it is . . . known that certain persons have fits of seeing in the dark', and suggests that such phenomena may be explained by assuming that those people, and some animals as well, need smaller amounts of aether in order to discern whatever can be seen. And he exemplifies this rather bold conjecture by referring to Tiberius who 'was said to have had this faculty or distemper'.[35]

But in other instances his references to aether seem to be very good examples of an analytical approach to theories of modern science. A case in point would be *S.* 225 which refers primarily to the corpuscles of aether, but has a bearing on other corpuscularian theories as well. Thus, for instance, he says there that

to explain the vibrations of light by those of a more subtle medium seems an uncouth explication. And gravity seems not an effect of the density and elasticity of aether, but rather to be produced by some other cause: which Sir Isaac himself insinuates to have been the opinion even of those ancients who took vacuum, atoms, and the gravity of atoms, for the principles of their philosophy, tacitly attributing (as he well observes) gravity to some other cause distinct from matter, from atoms, and consequently from that homogeneous aether or elastic fluid. The elasticity of which fluid is supposed to depend upon, to be defined and measured by, its density; and this by the quantity of matter in one particle, multiplied by the number of particles contained in a given space; and the quantity of matter in any one particle or body of a given size to be determined by its gravity. Should not therefore gravity seem the original property and first supposed?

The difference between sections like this and references such as are found in *S.* 110 and 213 is amazing. It seems, therefore, that any attempt to classify various kinds of particles mentioned in *Siris* would need to take into account many different levels of conceptual use, ranging from completely obsolete traditions to most interesting (and quite modern) theoretical suggestions.

I shall conclude this Section with some remarks concerning the 'secondary causality' of aether (the 'secondary causality' of particles in general was dealt with in Section 3 above). We have seen that Berkeley correlates the velocity of particles in general, and of the corpuscles of aether in particular, with their *vis impressa*, i.e. with 'forces' inherent in them ('force' being an abbreviated term for, among other correlations, a capacity of a body to penetrate other bodies; and cf. *S.* 226–7). The velocity of the corpuscles of aether is the greatest (*S.* 226); and they are also assumed to 'fly asunder with the greatest force' (*S.* 227). Their 'idiosyncrasies' are regarded as the most important in the entire *rerum natura* (cf. for instance, *S.* 162, 191, and 239). However, the author of *Siris* is very careful not to ascribe to them any real powers. I have already referred to the concept of 'secondary causality' and the 'instrumental' but not unreservedly instrumentalist (in the modern sense of 'instrumentalism') approach of Berkeley in Section 3 above. Here I would like only to mention briefly that the 'instrumental' role fulfilled by aether at large (i.e. the assumed function of a universal explanatory medium which 'activates', according to God's design, the entire *rerum natura*) has, *ex hypothesi*, to characterize also the aethereal *corpuscles*, which are in this respect regarded as very different from the non-aethereal ones.

Berkeley's *definition* of 'instrumental causality' (referred to, *inter alia*, in *S.* 154) is also applied by him to the role of particles of aether (cf., for instance, *S.* 161–2). And he even bases the 'instrumental' causality of aether (which is also regarded by him as 'mechanical' (ibid.) to the extent that it refers to impact) on corpuscularian mechanisms and 'idiosyncrasies'. According to *S.* 162, the 'heterogeneous' particles of the all-pervasive aethereal medium may explain the 'secondary qualities', or 'the specific properties' (cf. *S.* 238) of all bodies. The very presence of various particles of aether is supposed to be a main 'instrumental cause' of various (at least, secondary) macroscopic qualities (*S.* 162): 'The pure aether or visible fire contains parts of different kinds . . . These seem to constitute the many various qualities, virtues, flavours, odours, and colours which distinguish natural productions.'

However, Berkeley emphasizes time and again that all this 'medium', i.e. aether and its particles, is only employed as a 'subordinate cause' and instrument. The causality of aether and its particles, as mentioned in *Siris*, refers, strictly speaking, to a conjecture concerning certain widespread, or indeed universal, concomitances, based partly on analogies with observed occurrences in the regular course of nature. It is, therefore, completely different from what has to be, on his assumptions, the only model of real causality, i.e. 'acts of will' which are regarded by him as the only sources of motion.[36] The 'idiosyncrasies' of the particles of aether are not to be explained by their own causal powers, but by spiritual 'vis or force' (*S.* 248), or 'by some other agent, wherein the force exists and not in them, which have only the motion' (*S.* 250). Particles are neither efficient nor final 'causes of appearances' (*S.* 251). They may rather be terms in hypothetical 'grammars of nature', analogical to the 'grammar' of the perceived *rerum natura*, and subject once more to the thesis of the uniformity of phenomena (*S.* 252–4).[37] References to them, or terms which purport to 'signify' them, may, accordingly, function as premisses of prediction (or, as Berkeley puts it, of 'natural vaticination'). In the same vein, he maintains in *S.* 277 that 'the minutest particles' referred to above as 'instrumental causes' are themselves 'governed in their natural motions' by laws which are not explainable by them. In this section, just as in *S.* 250, it is also very clear that although, to a certain extent, all hypothetical particles whatever may be regarded as 'secondary causes', the author ascribes the main and almost universal explanatory role to particles of aether which are supposed to 'activate' other observed and unobserved bodies (and see, for instance, *S.* 192 and 201, among many other sections). In addition, there are some other few terms in *Siris* which designate 'secondary causes', such as 'animal spirits' mentioned, *inter alia*, in *S.* 161 (see also Section 11 below).

7. THE BISHOP'S AETHER AND NEWTON'S HYPOTHESIS OF AETHER IN *OPTICKS*

Particles of aether fulfil the most important explanatory role within the framework of Berkeley's theories in *Siris*. However, he does not regard them as all-explaining causes, not even in the 'secondary' and 'subordinate' senses of causality. References to particles in general, and to the corpuscles of aether in particular, are, for instance, incorporated by him within the respective theoretical frameworks of physics and chemistry, optics, physiology, and botany. But he does not consider them as explanatory concauses of

all those 'laws of nature' according to which they are assumed to
account for the phenomena. In particular, he does not ascribe to 'the
minute parts' of aether an ability to generate gravitational fields. On
his view, it is impossible to 'deduce' gravity from the structure of
the corpuscularian aether.[38] The corpuscles of aether which are, as
it were, extremely agile 'instrumental agents' of an infinite Spirit,
and gravity, both function as essential explanatory terms in
Berkeley's theories of science (at least, as expounded in the *Siris*-
period). Gravity cannot be defined by means of, or deduced from,
the size or shape of the hypothetical particles of aether (*S.* 162 and
225). On the other hand, gravity, being in Berkeley's view only a
term standing for well-ordered descriptions of motions of bodies,
may not be identified with real forces 'considered as prescinded
from gravity and matter, and as existing only in points or centres'.
Real force, in contrast to gravity, is 'incorporeal', or 'spiritual'
(*S.* 225).

When dealing with laws of nature in the perceived universe, and
sometimes also with hypothetical entities like aether and particles,
Berkeley relies heavily on Newton. He is very keen throughout *Siris*
to draw a distinction between the main scientific contributions of
Newton, whose opinion, in many cases, he actually endorses, and
those utterances and tenets of the Newtonians, and of the great man
himself, which may be regarded as metaphysical assumptions.[39] He
refers in many sections (e.g. in 225, 227, 236, 238, 240, 241, 245, and
246) to 'Sir Isaac' (or 'Sir Isaac Newton', the author of 'the
Newtonian doctrine', etc.) as the main authority on 'laws of
Nature'. But he does reject at least one fundamental tenet of
Newton; namely, 'the doctrine of real, absolute, external space'
(*S.* 270).[40] This rejection of absolute space (and absolute motion),
prominent in the *Principles* and *De Motu*, is reiterated in *S.* 271
where he says: 'Concerning absolute space, that phantom of the
mechanic and geometrical philosophers, it may suffice to observe
that it is neither perceived by any sense, nor proved by any reason
. . .'. Besides, he had criticized some suppositions of Newton's
theory of fluxions in the *Analyst*[41] (1734) and *A Defence of
Free-thinking in Mathematics* (1735). He also certainly rejected the
thesis of infinite divisibility of space which looms large in Newton's
thought (see, for instance, *Opticks* iii, Qu. 31; Dover edn., pp. 403–
4). However, it might seem that he *fully* endorses in *Siris* the
Newtonian hypothesis of the corpuscularian aether, which had

mainly been expounded in *Opticks*. But on closer inspection it gradually becomes clear that he introduces into it some modifications, and accepts only its main outlines. I shall refer here only to some of the major and most obvious of those modifications, which deal with the concepts of matter, gravity, forces, and laws of nature.

First, particles are accepted by Berkeley either as theoretical entities in hypothetico-deductive systems, or as new series of 'ideas of sense' in the *rerum natura* (see also Section 2 above). But they are never regarded, after the period of the *Theory of Vision*, as material, i.e. as particles of *matter*. They are obviously regarded by him as bigger than the *minima* (see also Appendix A below); and, to the extent that they are real, may be located on the map of 'ideas of sense' somewhere between the *minima* and the *minutiae* dealt with in *PHK* 60–6 (in the discussion of the 'eleventh objection'). In any case, the use of the concept of 'particle' is regarded by the Berkeley of *Siris* as fitting the general *immaterialistic* framework of his metaphysics, and as fitting also what seemed to him the correct linguistic analysis of the term 'existence'. He seems to have applied to particles a sort of bifurcating logical approach, or what may possibly be called *Berkeley's fork*. The use of such a label is, to my mind, much more justified than Popper's reference to *Berkeley's razor*. According to Popper, Berkeley eliminates in an instrumentalist way any possibility of existence in so far as theoretical entities are concerned (be they forces, micro-entities, or absolute space and motion; cf. Appendix B below, in which Popper's treatment of Berkeley's philosophy of science is analysed in detail). Berkeley's razor is supposed by Popper to be a rather undiscriminating tool; whereas Berkeley's fork indicates a dual approach, according to which 'particles', and, indeed, any other not purely mathematical terms in hypotheses, may signify real 'ideas of sense'. The same may be said of the application of Berkeley's view in *Siris* to 'the corpuscles of aether'. This term, too, may but does not have to refer to real particles. In fact what Berkeley did in *Siris* was, among other things, to incorporate the Newtonian brand of 'the corpuscularian philosophy' in general, and the tentative hypothesis of aether in particular, within the framework of his immaterialistic metaphysics and of his qualified positivism (and of his admirably modern approach to hypothetico-deductive systems). The adaptation of the Newtonian approach to immaterialistic, and partly instrumentalist, purposes is accompanied in *Siris* by a violent attack on the Cartesian *plenum* which has already been mentioned above, and to which I shall devote Section 10 below and some lines in the present section. But this attack on the Cartesians, launched under the Newtonian banner (see, for instance, *S*. 243 where he says: 'Nature seems better known and explained ... by Sir Isaac Newton, than Descartes') should not conceal his criticism of Newton in cases where it seems to him that the great man 'may be thought to forget himself in his manner of speaking' (*S*. 246). The point at issue is that, on Berkeley's view, the very reference of Newton to various corpuscles as parts of *matter* moving in *absolute* space may be interpreted as a departure from both the observed data and the logic of the theoretical situation. Berkeley's reiteration of the principles of immaterialism is to be found, *inter alia*, in *S*. 251; Newton refers to particles as material bodies in *Opticks* iii, which is mentioned several times in *Siris*—see, for instance, *Opticks* iii, Qu. 31, (Dover edn., p. 400).

I took up above Berkeley's rejection of the entire materialist framework of the 'mechanical philosophy' from which follows his first criticism of Newton's concept of particles in general, and of the corpuscles of aether in particular. This criticism is ordinarily implicit in *Siris*; it does not come to the fore in most cases. However, in *S*. 251 (mentioned above), and also *S*. 292, 294, 304, and 311, the author's rejection of matter is prominent. Berkeley's second, and much more explicit, criticism of the Newtonian concept of particles deals with the great man's references (in, at least, some passages of his works) to *forces* inherent in the material particles. He accuses the author of *Opticks* (Berkeley refers in *Siris* mostly to *Opticks*, and not to Newton's other works) of a misuse of terms, according to which it might seem that there are 'physical agents', and that 'real forces ... exist in bodies, in which, to speak truly, attraction and repulsion should be considered only as tendencies or motions, that is, as mere effects, and their laws as laws of motion' (*S*. 246; cf. also the reference to *S*. 250 in Section 2 above).

Berkeley's attempts to clarify and delimit the conceptual scope of terms like 'force', 'attraction', etc., are very conspicuous in his discussion of gravity and its relations to the corpuscularian realm. He accepts Newton's distinction (cf., *inter alia*, *Opticks* iii, Qu. 31; Dover edn., pp. 375–6) between the phenomena of gravity on the one hand, and the corpuscularian hypotheses on the other. But he certainly stresses much more (and—presumably—in a more consistent manner) than Newton the logical background of such a distinction. On his view, the distinction is necessitated not only on purely empirical grounds (i.e. because the corpuscularian realm includes unobserved entities). The more important reason for detaching, as it were, gravity from particles, is, on his view, that particles, be they observed or assumed *ex hypothesi*, may not be endowed with forces. This view is the leitmotif of *S*. 250 (quoted above), and is quite conspicuous in many other sections. And even if *gravity* is considered as a uniform description of motions, it is not, in Berkeley's view, to be applied without further qualifications to the corpuscularian realm. The particles of aether are supposed to be characterized by 'different modes of cohesion, attraction, repulsion and motion' (*S*. 162), or 'certain idiosyncrasies' (*S*. 239). Those '*different* modes of motion' (my italics) cannot be brought under one common denominator. Newton, too, refers to 'the Attractions of Gravity, Magnetism and Electricity' in Qu. 31 of *Opticks*, and also to attractions between particles which may be explained by electricity 'without . . . Friction'. But Berkeley certainly emphasizes more than Newton the 'diversity' of those 'attractions'.

The reference to 'insensible attractions' (in the plural) 'of most minute particles' is to be found also in *S*. 236. Moreover, in that section Berkeley explicitly says that 'laws of motion' have to be regarded as 'various' in both macrocosmic and microcosmic realms. 'The laws of gravity, magnetism, and electricity' are regarded by him as 'diverse' (*S*. 235), and the same is maintained by him in regard to 'fermentation' and 'all chemical operations' actually discerned in medium-sized bodies and explained by means of 'divers distinct habitudes' of particles in general, and, especially, by those of the corpuscles of aether. However, on his view, even if all 'attractions and repulsions' in the macrocosmic and microcosmic realm alike could be brought under a common denominator, one should still have to make a distinction between (1) the observed, or assumed, entities and (2) the relations binding them according to various laws of motion. On his view, we may not assume that it is possible to deduce mathematically laws of motion, or the law of motion, from the quantity and density of particles in the universe. For instance, Berkeley maintains in *S*. 237 that gravity should not be regarded as 'an effect of the density of aether'. Accordingly, even the universal scope of a unique law of motion would not mean that it depended on quantitative characterizations of particles. I here mean by 'quantitative characterizations' measurements which do not refer to the above-mentioned law(s) of motion (see also Section 4 above, which does not specifically deal with aether).

But in fact, says the author of *Siris*, it is not the case that the same law(s) of action, or motion (under which all physical changes whatever would be able to be subsumed) has or have been discerned in the macrocosmic and microsmic realms alike, nor that, at least, each of those respective realms is, or has to be, characterized by its own unique and all-embracing law of motion.

Berkeley maintains that (*a*) there are many kinds of corpuscles (even the invisible aether is regarded by him as consisting of heterogeneous parts; cf., for instance, *S.* 162); and (*b*) there are heterogeneous laws of nature which differ from the macrocosmic to the microcosmic realm, and, for that matter, in each of those realms as well. The 'idiosyncrasies' of all particles (and of the corpuscles of aether in particular) with regard to each other, which may be assumed and applied by analogy to different states of affairs, do not depend, in his view, on other measurable qualities of particles, nor on 'the general laws of motion', such as the rules of gravity, nor, again, on the general characteristics of the assumed aether (not necessarily conceived of as corpuscularian), e.g. on its density or elasticity. The *locus classicus* in which he expounds this theory is *S.* 239, already quoted above. The crucial passage in that section is: 'Why may we not suppose certain idiosyncrasies [in the corpuscularian realm] . . . not depending on the different size, figure, number, solidity, or weight of those particles, nor on the general laws of motion, nor on the density or elasticity of a medium . . .'

The corpuscles of aether cannot, on this view, explain gravity; and gravity cannot explain various qualities of the corpuscles of aether (*S.* 225, 232, 239). At most, one may translate 'the quantity of matter in any one particle'[42] (but not other corpuscularian qualities) into terms of gravity. But before examining briefly Berkeley's reference to the definition of 'the quantity of matter' by gravity, it should be noticed that his rejection of the 'comprehensive view' according to which all the corpuscularian 'idiosyncrasies' have to be brought under a unique law, or a few laws, of motion, is at times couched in terms of an attack on mechanism. He condemns the tendency 'to explain the formation of this world and its phenomena by a few simple laws of mechanism' (*S.* 232). And he says that 'if we consider the various productions of nature, in the mineral, vegetable and animal parts of the creation, I believe we shall see cause to affirm that not any one of them has hitherto been, or can be, accounted for on principles merely mechanical' (ibid.). This quotation shows, among other things, that Berkeley was most careful in his use of 'hitherto'. Here he qualified it by adding 'or can be'. But in *S.* 159, which refers to aether, he did not qualify 'hitherto' by any amendment, because, in my view, he did not want to imply the complete imperceptibility, or unperceivability, of aether (even from the human point of view).

The precise logical force of this opposition to mechanism in *Siris* must be carefully evaluated, especially against the background of Berkeley's endorsement of basic tenets of 'the corpuscularian philosophy' in the 1740s. It is certain that he rejected mechanism as a metaphysical theory. But it is difficult, if not impossible, to accept T. E. Jessop's evaluation (cf. vol. v, p. 116, n. 4) that *S.* 232 refers only to Berkeley's *metaphysical* (or, indeed, anti-metaphysical) opposition to explanation by mechanism. Berkeley rejected the deistic view of God as the temporally First Cause (i.e. as the beginning of the series of events whose subsequent links are effects of mechanically interacting bodies) on most general grounds, whereas *S.* 232 deals with a much more detailed problem, namely the impossibility of deriving the observed phenomena from 'a few simple laws', and, *a fortiori*, from one law of motion (e.g. from 'a circular motion' in a continuous *plenum*; ibid.). The arguments of *S.* 232 may, of course, be used in order to invalidate the metaphysics of mechanistic design; but they are also (or primarily) employed against certain well-defined interpretations of the corpuscularian theories (e.g. against the Cartesian hypothesis of 'a circular motion' mentioned in the second half of *S.* 232, and referred to above). In fact, what Berkeley does in *S.* 232 is not (or not only) to attack the metaphysics of mechanism, but rather to reject certain primarily Cartesian, but to some extent also Newtonian tendencies of the 'corpuscularians' to base all natural changes or motions (e.g. the 'idiosyncrasies' of particles) on one and only one principle (such as 'the vibrations of aether'; cf. *Opticks* iii Qu. 18–19). On his view, the indubitable success of bringing many diverse phenomena of motion in the macrocosm under certain general 'rules' does not mean that pushing this process of explanation further and further can always be effected, or indeed, usefully attempted.[43]

But, on the other hand, when he says that not all phenomena can be explained by 'principles merely mechanical', does this mean that he assumes occult qualities, rejected by him (and condemned as scholastic) in *De Motu*? It seems to me that such an interpretation would run against all the explanatory trends in *Siris*. Particles are introduced by Berkeley in *Siris* as premises in hypothetico-deductive proceedings, or as new series of data which may be discovered by modern science; and even their 'idiosyncrasies' refer to their actual or assumed behaviour, and not to scholastic pseudo-explanations of the *vis dormitiva* type, according to which each entity, or kind of entities, on the phenomenal level, has to be considered as endowed with its special form, species, or *vis* (e.g. sedatives are considered as substances which just happen to have the special power of soothing the nerves, producing calm, etc.), without having recourse to hypotheses, or to laws of Nature. A more correct interpretation of Berkeley's anti-mechanistic utterances seems to be, first, that in *Siris* he is extremely wary of explanation 'by a *few simple* laws of mechanism' (*S.* 232; my italics). But he is not against mechanical explanations as such, especially in the macrocosm. Secondly, he is not inclined to accept the view that *all* events in the *rerum natura* can be explained by 'principles merely mechanical', be they few or many. Now 'principles merely mechanical' does *not* mean here, on my view, 'laws of interaction between bodies in the macrocosm and microcosm'. It only means (*a*) the rules of mechanics fitting the Cartesian *plenum* (cf. the second half of *S.* 232, where Descartes and the assumed 'circular motion' are referred to); and (*b*) the prevailing laws of motion in the macrocosm (and cf. again *S.* 239). The various 'idiosyncrasies' of particles are not explainable, according to Berkeley's view, by the Cartesian hypothesis, nor by the general laws of motion discovered in the macrocosm. Those two tenets certainly enable him to uphold the anti-mechanistic statements which loom large in *S.* 232 and 239 in consonance with his general approach to metaphysics and science. But it should be noticed that, in spite of his anti-mechanistic arguments, he accepts in *Siris* the main factual tenets of 'the corpuscularian philosophy' which were neither endorsed by him in the *Principles* and the *Three Dialogues*, nor mentioned in *De Motu*.

It seems, therefore, that if by 'mechanistic tenets' one means the 'corpuscularian philosophy' at large, or various assumptions concerning quantitative aspects of particles' features and motions, or, again, mathematical deductions of various phenomena from the corpuscularian structure, it would follow that the author of *Siris* did *not* reject explanation by mechanism. If, on the other hand, explanation by mechanism means that one assumes (*a*) that the same laws of motion prevail in the macrocosm and in the realm of particles, or that motions of all particles have to be explained by one law, or (*b*) that interactions between particles, and, indeed, between all bodies whatever, occur in a continuous *plenum* (according to the Cartesian hypothesis), and necessitate, as it were, a permanent impact, then Berkeley *did* most certainly reject it. In fact, his emphasis on the independent role of gravity which, in his view, cannot be 'deduced' from various features of the corpuscularian aether, fits very well his rejection of (*a*) and (*b*).

Now it seems that at least one feature of particles in general, and of the corpuscles of aether in particular, is allowed by Berkeley in *Siris* to be deduced from, if not to explain,[44] gravity. I refer to a hypothetical '*quantity of "matter"* [*my italics*] in any particle' mentioned, for instance, in *S*. 225. Berkeley is not inimical to an attempt to 'determine' such an assumed 'quantity of matter in any one particle' by its gravity (ibid.). On this view, even the density, and, ultimately, the elasticity, of the corpuscularian aether would be partly[45] translatable into terms of gravity in any given spatial field. Thus, gravity and the corpuscles of aether are correlated within the framework of one explanatory hypothesis, according to which most features of particles (e.g. their mutual 'idiosyncrasies') are not derivable from gravity, whereas the quantity of 'matter' 'in any one particle' may be translated into its terms. However, such a translation is, on Berkeley's view, possible only because gravity and 'quantity of matter' are synonyms. And to the extent that *gravity* obtains in the corpuscularian realm it would, according to him, designate an actual behaviour of particles, just as it designates an actual behaviour of observed bodies. Thus, he also says in *S*. 319 that the conceptual moves from 'quantity of matter' to gravity and vice versa, are in 'a . . . circle'.[46] And, of course, *matter* has to be interpreted by him as *tangible extension*.

Berkeley's contention that gravity, and, more generally, various kinds of 'attraction and repulsion', may be regarded neither as force(s) nor as derivable from an assumed structure of the

corpuscularian aether is also stressed in *S.* 245–6 where he
eulogizes Newton as the greatest and most successful of all
corpuscularians, but criticizes him in regard to issues raised above:

Sir Isaac Newton, by his singular penetration, profound knowledge in
geometry and mechanics, and great exactness in experiments, hath cast a
new light on natural science. The laws of attraction and repulsion were in
many instances discovered, and first discovered, by him. He shewed their
general extent, and therewith, as with a key, opened several deep secrets of
nature, in the knowledge whereof he seems to have made a greater progress
than all the sects of corpuscularians together had done before him.
Nevertheless, the principle of attraction itself is not to be explained by
physical or corporeal causes . . . The Cartesians attempted to explain it by
the nisus of a subtle element, receding from the centre of its motion, and
impelling grosser bodies towards it. Sir Isaac Newton in his later thoughts
seems (as was before observed) to have adopted somewhat not altogether
foreign from this notion, ascribing that to his elastic medium (Sects. 237,
238) which Descartes did to his second element. But the great men of
antiquity resolved gravity into the immediate action of an intelligent
incorporeal being. To which also Sir Isaac Newton himself attests and
subscribes; although he may perhaps sometimes be thought to forget
himself in his manner of speaking . . .

It is also noteworthy that in *Siris* he puts an emphasis not only on
attraction, but on repulsion as well. His old fascination with the
'algebra of Nature', a science of computation of those things which
are 'signified' by *natural* signs,[47] inspires him anew in *S.* 236 where
he compares the 'idiosyncrasies' of attraction and repulsion with
positive and negative quantities in algebra (mentioned also in
Newton's *Opticks* iii, Qu. 31). In the same section he also accepts
the analogical 'inference' from the 'attraction and repulsion' of
observed bodies[48] to the behaviour of the hypothetical particles,
again drawing heavily on Qu. 31. And the same tendency is very
conspicuous in *S.* 235.

In any case, concerning co-ordinations between gravity and
attractions-cum-repulsions, and the non-mechanistic evaluation of
those corpuscularian 'idiosyncrasies', it is certainly true that gravity
of particles is regarded by Berkeley in *Siris* as covering much less
ground than all their various other 'idiosyncrasies'. However, he
connects both those categories of 'rules of motion' (i.e. gravity, and
various attractions and repulsions) by assuming that an equivalent
of the Newtonian law of motion and reaction may be applied to
both: 'The most repellent are, upon contact, the most attracting

particles' (*S.* 240). (But this general contention of *S.* 240 is exemplified in a very obsolete manner in *S.* 241; and both these sections rely heavily on Newton's Qu. 31 in *Opticks* iii.) I have already mentioned above that the assumption of the variety of corpuscularian 'attractions and repulsions' is regarded by Berkeley as a rejection of the prevailing mechanistic interpretations of nature. Size, number, figure, weight, or even solidity, are on the Bishop's view, less important than various micro-idiosyncrasies: I would only add that if the variety of these corpuscularian 'idiosyncrasies' refers to changes of motions of particles which depend on which particles meet each other, then even such 'attractions and repulsions' may yet be regarded as measurable, and perhaps also as being in a consonance with, at least, certain variegated rules of mechanics (in the broadest, but admittedly rather loose, sense of mechanics). In this last case, the 'idiosyncrasies' of changes of motions of particles would only have to be regarded as 'non-mechanical' in compliance with a stricter sense of the term 'mechanics', according to which that science deals exclusively with a few uniform laws of impact in an assumed *plenum* which do not even cover gravity *in vacuo*. Now, according to such a strict definition of mechanics, both Berkeley's insistence on 'idiosyncrasies' of particles and his preference of Newton's approach to gravity (which does not necessarily imply an aethereal *plenum*) to the Cartesian one, reveal certainly a 'non-mechanical' tendency. But if mechanics is referred to in a broader sense, then even variegated changes of motions of particles may yet be 'deemed mechanical' (cf. *S.* 239), despite Berkeley's opposition to that term. However, to the extent that 'idiosyncrasies' of particles refer also to qualitative changes, be they on the micro- or macro-level, they certainly have to be considered, on any interpretation whatever, as utterly different from occurrences ascribable to the realm of mechanics.

I referred above to some major modifications introduced in *Siris* into the Newtonian hypothesis of aether: the detachment of the concepts of aether from (*a*) the concepts of matter and absolute space, (*b*) the concepts of hypostatized force and mechanism, and (*c*) gravity. Other modifications of the Newtonian aether as in *Siris* will be dealt with in Sections 8 and 10 below, which refer respectively to light and to some basic aspects of the *plenum*-hypothesis.

8. AETHER AS LIGHT

Berkeley states quite explicitly in *S.* 221 that the 'pure aethereal spirit' 'ignites bodies', but is itself neither the visible fire nor 'an ignited body'. It is clear from sections like this (see also *S.* 214 and 220) that the *invisible* corpuscularian aether, 'the vital spirit of the universe', and 'instrument' and all-pervading 'medium' of 'the incorporeal Agent', is identified by the author of *Siris* with what he calls 'the pure elementary fire', which is distinguished from its perceived 'culinary' counterpart. The third synonym for 'aether', or 'invisible fire', is in *Siris* 'light', or rather 'the substance of light'. (See, for instance, the last sentence of *S.* 191, and the first sentence of *S.* 195, in which 'light' and 'fire' are used as synonyms.) The 'pure invisible fire', aether, or light, which 'mixeth with all bodies' (*S.* 195), is also, in Berkeley's view, rightly called 'occult', or 'celestial' (cf. *S.* 211–13), in distinction from the visible light, although it is not allowed to be incorporeal (cf. *S.* 207). Berkeley certainly draws heavily in *Siris* on mystic and semi-mystic (e.g. Neoplatonic) sources, and maintains that the macrocosm and microcosm alike are literally soaked with the unperceived 'substance of light', of which the visible light is but a manifestation.

However, in spite of a certain Neoplatonic bias, Berkeley's differentiation of the visible from invisible light is, in fact, largely maintained on empirical and theoretical rather than semi-mystic grounds. The visible light is, on his view, the 'proper object of vision' (according to his old basic contention from *Phil. Com.* and the *Theory of Vision* onwards); but 'the substance of light' ('substance' in a metaphorical sense only) indicates a certain arrangement of particles of aether. In fact, there are, on his premisses, visible and invisible fire, and also visible light and its invisible counterpart. The visible fire and the visible light differ from one another; Berkeley does not think that every colour, or 'mode of light', is an instance of a visually or non-visually perceived combustion. But he identifies the invisible light and the invisible fire with one another, and with aether.

On Berkeley's theory, whatever is seen is 'light, and its several modes or colours' (*TVV* 41). But the crux of the matter is that the particles of aether might have been regarded (on the assumption that one will have been able to rely on new relevant observations) as correlated with quite different 'modes' of light than those previously revealed. Berkeley does not maintain that it is logically, or epistemically, impossible to see the particles of aether, either singly or *en masse* under other forms than the 'hitherto' perceived glows, flames, coloured rays of light, an undifferentiated brightness, or various other visible configurations which 'signify', on his view, the known physical objects, nor that their invisibility is required by the very structure of his corpuscularian theory. (See also Section 6 above, and 9 below, where some connections of this problem with, respectively, the explanatory role of aether and the division into primary and secondary qualities are discussed in detail.) In *Siris* he makes a distinction between (1) the visibility of the assumed corpuscularian aether via the actually visible light (or the 'visible flame', etc.; see also *S.* 226 in which he refers to 'determinations' and 'effects' of 'the substance of light'), and (2) the invisibility of its corpuscles or, for that matter, of its mass, under guises different from that of the visible rays of light, of an undifferentiated brightness, and of the various formerly perceived configurations of colours. But this distinction is made by him on at least partly empirical grounds, i.e. he takes into account that 'no eye could ever hitherto discern' the 'pure fire' which has never been 'found alone'.

One should perhaps also note that the Berkeleian hypothesis of the corpuscularian aether had been much more successful as an explanatory theory of light than as a parallel theory of ignition. The concept of 'the particles of light' was usefully incorporated within the framework of geometrical optics, the velocity of the assumed particles was quite reasonably equated with the then newly computed velocity of the visible light ('about ten millions of miles in a minute', as Berkeley puts it in *S.* 226), and they were identified (at least by Berkeley, if not by the Cartesians and Newton) with the corpuscularian aether, which exists and moves in empty spaces, that is, according to *Siris*, with those 'most minute particles' which in most cases move and 'remain *in vacuo*' (cf. *S.* 223), even in the absence of all other bodies, but are not contiguous, being interspersed with 'empty spaces' (cf. *S.* 209). It may, therefore, be maintained that at least some aspects of Berkeley's theory of light are not completely obsolete. His pre-oxygen theory of ignition, on the other hand, conceived by him as a branch of the unified theory of aether, was already sadly outdated at the end of the eighteenth century, although it was certainly closer to the description and explanation of the relevant occurrences than the *phlogiston*-theory.

I have already mentioned above that the particles of 'the substance of light' and the visible light were assumed in *Siris* to move with the same great velocity, despite its author's distinction between *visibilia* and *tangibilia*. And the visible light may be regarded on Berkeleian premisses as moving in a sort of 'blended' space, i.e. in a visible extension 'mediated' by kinaesthetic clues, and constituted as an analogue of real (i.e. kinaesthetic) space (see also Appendix A below). In fact, the velocity of aether under both its visible and invisible aspects seems to be regarded in *Siris* as the swiftest in the entire *rerum natura*.[49] One of the theoretical justifications of such an assumption[50] is, in Berkeley's view, the extreme 'minuteness-cum-volatility' of the relevant particles. The double identification of (1) the velocity of visible light with that of its hypothetical 'substance', and (2) of aether with the selfsame 'substance', is very clearly expounded in *S.* 226:

It doth not seem necessary, from the phenomena, to suppose any medium more active and subtle than light or fire. Light being allowed to move at the rate of about ten millions of miles in a minute, what occasion is there to conceive another medium of still smaller and more moveable parts? Light or fire seems the same with aether. So the ancients understood, and so the Greek word implies. It pervades all things, is everywhere present. And this subtle medium, according to its various quantities, motions, and determinations, sheweth itself in different effects or appearances, and is aether, light, or fire.

This identification of aether with the corpuscles of light is not only anti-Cartesian (as it eliminates the theory of *two* subtle celestial elements), but is also a modification of Newton's theory in *Opticks* iii.[51] Newton's tentative hypothesis of aether which is supposed to explain the movements of particles (and rays) of light, and partly also their reflection and refraction, is summarized in *S.* 223–4:

It is the opinion of Sir Isaac Newton that somewhat unknown remains *in vacuo*, when the air is exhausted. This unknown medium he calls aether. He supposeth it to be more subtle in its nature, and more swift in its motion, than light, freely to pervade all bodies, and by its immense elasticity to be expanded throughout all the heavens. Its density is supposed greater in free and open spaces than within the pores of compact bodies. And in passing from the celestial bodies to great distances, it is supposed to grow denser and denser continually, and thereby cause those great bodies to gravitate towards one another, and their respective parts towards their centres, every body endeavouring to pass from the denser parts of the medium towards the rarer.

The extreme minuteness of the parts of this medium, and the velocity of their motion, together with its gravity, density, and elastic force, are thought to qualify it for being the cause of all the natural motions in the universe. To this cause are ascribed the gravity and cohesion of bodies. The refraction of light is also thought to proceed from the different density and elastic force of this aethereal medium in different places. The vibrations of this medium, alternately concurring with or obstructing the motions of the rays of light, are supposed to produce the fits of easy reflection and transmission. Light by the vibrations of this medium is thought to communicate heat to bodies. Animal motion and sensation are also accounted for by the vibrating motions of this aethereal medium, propagated through the solid capillaments of the nerves. In a word, all the phenomena and properties of bodies that were before attributed to attraction, upon later thoughts seem ascribed to this aether, together with the various attractions themselves.

In these two very crucial sections, Berkeley refers to the function of the Newtonian hypothesis of aether in regard to (1) gravity, and 'various attractions' in general; and (2) the movement and velocity of light. As I have already dealt with (1) in Section 7 above, I shall refer here only to some aspects of (2) which have not yet been clarified. First, it should be noticed that Berkeley had always drawn a sharp distinction between the visible light and the hypothetical corpuscularian structure supposed to be its concomitant or 'cause'; see, for instance, the first *Dialogue between Hylas and Philonous* (vol. ii, pp. 186–7). We have seen that Berkeley did not endorse there, in sharp contrast to *Siris*, the corpuscularian theory of light (Philonous says that 'it is not' his 'business to dispute about' the 'invisible' structure of light (ibid.)); but he expounds very clearly the logical distinction between the visible light and the invisible corpuscularian 'real essence' supposed by his opponents. There-fore, to the extent that he admits the possibility of existence of the corpuscles of light (as a new series of ideas of sense, and not as parts of unperceivable substratum), he already has to take into account two factors: the empirical one (visible light), and its theoretical counterpart (the corpuscles—of 'the substance'—of light) which explains, in his view, the relevant phenomena. Accordingly, and following some of his other tenets, he sees no reason for assuming yet another theoretical entity, i.e. aether as distinguished from 'the substance of light'. And he says that 'to explain the vibrations of light by those of a more subtle medium seems an uncouth explication' (*S.* 225). He also says (in *S.* 227): 'We are not therefore obliged to admit a new medium distinct from light, and of a finer and more exquisite substance, for the explication of phenomena which appear to be as well explained without it.' Moreover, he suggests (in *S.* 225) that most of Newton's own theories might be maintained without the distinction of 'the substance of light' from aether ('in the philosophy of Sir Isaac Newton, the fits, as they are called, of easy transmission and reflection seem as well accounted for by vibrations excited in bodies by the rays of light, and the refraction of light by the attraction of bodies').

It is noteworthy that in *S.* 225, and also in *S.* 227 where Berkeley seems to assume that the path of motion of the rays of light is modified by the gravitational field of the sun, or that they are slowed down by it, 'various attractions' (of which gravity is, on Berkeley's view, but an instance) are supposed to exert their influence on the corpuscularian 'substance of light' *in vacuo* without any need to have recourse to the vibrations of a *continuous* aethereal medium modelled on the Cartesian *plenum*.

In contrast to the Newtonian hypothesis paraphrased in *S.* 223 and 224, particles and gravity (or other 'attractions') are, in Berkeley's view all that is needed in order to explain the relevant phenomena; and he does not leave room for aether as distinct from the corpuscularian 'substance of light'.[52] In brief, the aethereal *plenum* is discarded by him in favour of the particles of the aethereal 'substance of light', assumed to exist and move *in vacuo*. This point—against (1) the continuous aether, and against (2) aether as distinct from light, and also against the conjunction of (1) and (2)— is made by him again in *S.* 238: 'Such a medium—distinct from light or fire—seemeth not to be made out by any proof, nor to be of any use in explaining the phenomena. But if there be any medium employed as a subordinate cause or instrument in attraction, it would rather seem to be light.' In this last section he also tries to explain that the hypothesis of an aethereal *plenum* is followed[53] by the assumption of only one set of 'general laws of motion', whereas his theory which identifies the corpuscularian 'substance of light' with aether (and cf. also *S.* 151 and 164) takes into account a more plausible hypothesis, namely that 'particles of different bodies are agitated [at least on micro-level] by different forces . . . or, to speak more accurately . . . moved by different laws.'[54]

This seems to be a valuable theoretical contribution to the general debate on aether which raged from the seventeenth to the end of the nineteenth and even the beginning of the twentieth century. But, of course, not all of Berkeley's remarks on 'the substance of light' show such a theoretical turn of mind: in *S*. 43 and 110, he speaks of light as a 'medicine' and 'principle of life', 'detained', for instance, in tar (*S*. 110).

A more valuable theoretical suggestion (at least in comparison with those made in *S*. 43 and 110) is to be found in *S*. 165. There Berkeley correlates various colours of the 'parted rays' of light with various types of particles. On this theory, even the particles of 'the substance of light' or aether, are 'heterogeneous'. The intimate connection, assumed in *Siris*, between (1) the heterogeneity of particles of aether, (2) 'parted rays' of light, and (3) various colours may be summed up as follows. All particles of 'the substance of light' are regarded by him as smaller, faster, and more 'active' than other corpuscles; but they are not conceived as identical with each other. In addition, the heterogeneous kinds of particles of 'the substance of light' are regarded by him as 'blended', in many cases, in 'one common ocean' (see, *inter alia*, *S*. 165 quoted below). In this 'blended' state they 'conceal', on his view, their 'distinct forms', i.e. according to his interpretation they do not then reveal, or 'cause', those 'specific properties' (the separate *colours* included) which they are supposed to manifest in conjunction with particles of other bodies:

Blue, red, yellow, and other colours have been discovered by Sir Isaac Newton to depend on the parted rays or particles of light. And, in like manner, a particular odour or flavour seemeth to depend on peculiar particles of light or fire . . . These particles, blended in one common ocean, should seem to conceal the distinct forms, but, parted and attracted by proper subject, disclose or produce them; as the particles of light, which, when separated, form distinct colours, being blended are lost in one uniform appearance. (*S*. 165.)

It seems that Berkeley is here expounding the view that each colour is characterized by a certain concomitant corpuscularian structure of the substance of light which usually, i.e. when being 'blended', is, under certain conditions, a concomitant of whiteness only. He refers to the corpuscularian structures of various bodies which separate 'rays or particles of light',[55] but puts an emphasis on the heterogeneity of particles of light proper. His acceptance of the division of all qualities into primary (e.g. some corpuscularian features) and secondary (e.g. colours) is dealt with in Section 9 below.

Some crucial problems involved in the reference to the corporeality and magnitude of the corpuscles of 'the substance of light' are raised in *Siris* in sections 206–10. That group of sections deals mainly with the criticism of the Neoplatonic concept of the incorporeality of light as expressed in the writings of Ficinus.[56] Berkeley is inclined throughout *Siris* to rely quite heavily on ancient authorities, and, especially, on the Neoplatonic ones. But even in cases where he is very glad to prove that the hypothetical aether looms large not only in the expositions of Newton's theories, but also in the writings of antiquity, he is extremely wary of any spiritualization of theoretical entities. The real forces are, on his view, spiritual (i.e. express the wills of real conscious spirits). And, according to him, aether and other theoretical entities, geared as they are, to the physical realm of *rerum natura*, may not be regarded as spiritual in the non-metaphorical sense. Aether is only assumed to be very 'subtle' and unperceived (by us). He does not assume that aether (to the extent that it is real), is, or has to be, unconditionally unperceivable by human observers, and still less does he ascribe to it incorporeality, i.e. non-sensory attributes.

He certainly is one of those who, in contrast to many Neoplatonists, *are* 'content to suppose light the most pure and refined of all *corporeal* beings' (my italics); but he is not ready to 'go farther', and to 'bestow upon it some attributes of a yet higher nature' (cf. his exposition of the problem in *S.* 206). Moreover, he denies the spiritual nature of light not once, but twice: (1) when considering visible light, and (2) when considering the corpuscularian structure of 'the substance of light' (the selfsame corpuscularian structure which he had not been inclined to consider in the *Three Dialogues*).

(1) The 'modes', or 'determinations', of visible light continue to be, on his premises, the 'proper objects of sight'. Proper objects of sight, i.e. arrangements of the 'blended' (white) light and other colours (see for instance, *S.* 165), are indeed, on his view, incorporeal—*but only in a rather restricted sense of 'incorporeality'*— since they are *indiscernible by touch*. But they most certainly were not regarded by him as being outside the realm of *passive* and nonspiritual *ideas*. Therefore he declined to accept the Neoplatonic tradition, according to which 'a pellucid and shining nature, pure,

impassive, and diffused throughout the universe' is 'incorporeal', being 'the *act* of a pure intelligence' (my italics). He is, indeed, quite ready to assume that the 'pellucid and shining nature' is 'pure' (i.e. does not include anything which is not pertinent to its proper nature, and its concomitants are the 'subtlest' particles, be it after or before the 'parting of its rays'). In the same vein, if 'purity' would refer to 'the substance of light' only, it would, accordingly, mean 'an absence of grosser particles'. But he rejects the very notion of the 'impassivity' of ideas, or 'appearances',[57] to the extent that it is understood as the opposite of 'passivity'; and, especially, denies the characterization of the visible light as 'spiritual', because, on his view, only spirits are incorporeal or non-sensory. In the same vein, he cannot accept the opinion that light is 'the *act* of a pure intelligence', because, in his view, it is a visible sign 'compounded' of 'passive *ideas*' only, and like other ideas, lacks spiritual activity and perfection.[58]

(2) Moreover, Berkeley of course denies not only the spirituality of the visible light, but also that of its hypothetical structure. In particular, he rejects the incorporeality of the particles of ('the substance' of) light. This second point is referred to in *S.* 207–9, where the very reference to 'solid particles' clarifies the terminological distinction between the visible light and its invisible structure, or, more precisely, between it and its invisible concomitants, regarded by Berkeley in *Siris* as 'instruments' of an active Creator. The boundary between the conceptual locations of references to (*a*) the visible light and (*b*) the 'solid particles of light' must always be taken into account whenever one reads the relevant sections in *Siris*. But even the 'particles of light', and not only various rays of visible light, may, in Berkeley's view, be a real—and new—series of 'ideas of sense'; and the terms which stand for them may, accordingly, be something more than mathematical devices or designations of useful conjectures. In addition, he mentions in his hypothesis the 'solidity' of 'particles of light' (for 'solid particles' see, especially, *S.* 209; in Berkeley's view, the 'solid particles' also have weight; cf., for instance, *S.* 169, 193, and 207). He is inclined to ascribe to the particles of light not only the status of ideas of sense in general (such as of scents and sounds), but also geometrical properties, and corporeality in the strong sense of Lockean 'solidity', which is a non-geometrical feature. The 'solid particles of light' may be 'exceeding small relatively to the empty spaces' (*S.* 209); but to the

extent that they exist they must, on Berkeley's view, be tangible parts of the *rerum natura* in spite of that extreme smallness.

Berkeley's ascription of corporeality to the hypothetical 'substance' of light is defended by him (within the framework of discussion of Ficinus's views) throughout *S*. 206–9. (References to 'solid particles' mentioned above are instances of his summarizing argument only.) He remarks, first, that 'Ficinus . . . undertakes to prove that light is incorporeal by several arguments'. Those arguments are paraphrased in *S*. 206, and may be summed up as follows:

(1) 'Light cannot be defiled by filth of any kind.'

(2) It 'is not fixed in any subject'.[59] It cannot be condensed or rarefied.

(3) It meets no opposition in space, not because space is empty, but 'because several lights meet without resisting each other'.

(4) It moves instantaneously. It 'expands itself. . . without delay (or 'collision'; and see argument 3 above) throughout the vastest space'; and 'fills a great space in an instant'.

Argument 1 is not rejected by Berkeley. He simply ascribes the suggested 'purity' to the *corporeal* light ('the most pure and refined of all corporeal beings'; cf. the beginning of *S*. 206). Argument 2 is rejected by him (in *S*. 207), because, according to his contention, bodies are literally soaked with light; or, at any rate, with particles of light. His contention is that ('the substance of') light 'is capable of condensation' and 'rarefaction'; and also that it can be mixed with other bodies, enter their composition, and increase their weight (*S*. 169, 192, 193).[60] Argument 4 is rejected by him quite easily. He refers to the then recent discovery of the velocity of light by Roemer, and discards quite happily the argument of his Neoplatonist opponent by saying: 'But it is now well known that light moves; that its motion is not instantaneous' (*S*. 207). Finally, he rejects argument 3 with regard both to visible light and to its corpuscularian 'substance'.

However, Berkeley's treatment of argument 3 is much more complicated and interesting than that of its two predecessors, and of 4, and has to be examined with special care. He answers Ficinus in detail, and his solution is ingenious. But one has also to notice that he only chooses one possible answer out of three, or four; and, in addition, relies heavily, though in an indirect way, on some assumptions of his *minima*-theory, which is not mentioned in other sections of *Siris*.

Ficinus argues that light 'meets no opposition' and does not collide with other entities, nor is it subject to resistance when meeting other parts of its own 'nature'. But all 'corporeal' entities collide with, and are hampered by, each other. Ergo, concludes Ficinus, light is incorporeal. Now Berkeley might easily answer (*a*) that light, too, is hindered in its motion at least by opaque, if not by all, bodies; and (*b*) that some moving bodies (e.g. stones falling down) seem not to be hampered by other ones (e.g. water or air), but a more careful examination reveals that they are, in fact, slowed down. He might maintain that the same contention must, or can, be applicable to light as well, though to a lesser or indeed negligible extent. In addition, he might simply agree that (*c*) light does not encounter any resistance *in vacuo*, but stipulate that in this particular respect it is most certainly not different from moving bodies. However, he did not use in *S*. 207–9 either the second or the third out of those three basic arguments, nor did he simply rely on the first of them, and, having perhaps regarded them as infelicitous, or not elaborate enough, preferred instead to employ with great ingenuity yet another set of explanations. Thus, for instance, he relies on the small size of the particles of 'the substance of light', i.e. he accepts the contention that light, to the extent that it arrives directly at its destination, moves without opposition, i.e. is hindered neither by its own various particles, or rays, nor by other bodies whose velocity is, on empirical grounds and *ex hypothesi* alike, regarded as slower than its own—see, for instance, *S*. 226–7; and he explains all this by means of his corpuscularian theory.

Berkeley rejects (e.g. in *S*. 225–7) any assumption that it is necessary to postulate a theoretical medium 'of still smaller and more moveable parts' than light. The particles of light, being, *ex hypothesi*, the smallest and most 'active' amongst all entities in the *rerum natura*, are also, in his view, the fastest-moving. However, he admits (in *S*. 207) that his hypothesis concerning the movement and velocity of the particles of light *in vacuo* seems to be involved, 'at first sight', in certain difficulties. He says that 'there appears indeed some difficulty at first sight about the non-resistance of rays or particles of light occurring one to another, in all possible directions or from all points. Particularly, if we suppose the hollow surface of a large sphere studded with eyes looking inwards one at another, it may perhaps seem hard to conceive how distinct rays from every eye should arrive at every other eye without jostling, repelling, and confounding each other.' But his answer (in *S.* 208) is that

these difficulties may be got over by considering, in the first place, that visible points are not mathematical points, and consequently that we are not to suppose every point of space a radiating point. Secondly, by granting that many rays do resist and intercept each other, notwithstanding which the act of vision may be performed. Since as every point of the object is not seen, so it is not necessary that rays from every such point arrive at the eye. We often see an object, though more dimly, when many rays are intercepted by a gross medium.

And he adds in *S.* 209:

Besides, we may suppose the particles of light to be indefinitely small, that is, as small as we please, and their aggregate to bear as small a proportion to the void as we please, there being nothing in this that contradicts the phenomena. And there needs nothing more in order to conceive the possibility of rays passing from and to all visible points, although they be not incorporeal. Suppose a hundred ports placed round a circular sea, and ships sailing from each port to every other; the larger the sea, and the smaller the vessels are supposed, the less danger will there be of their striking against each other. But as there is by hypothesis no limited proportion between the sea and the ships, the void and solid particles of light, so there is no difficulty that can oblige us to conclude the sun's light incorporeal from its free passage; especially when there are so many clear proofs of the contrary. As for the difficulty, therefore, attending the supposition of a sphere studded with eyes looking at each other, this is removed only by supposing the particles of light exceeding small relatively to the empty spaces.

'The hollow surface of a large sphere studded with eyes looking inwards one at another', mentioned in *S.* 207 and 209, stands for the inner envelope of any given spherical volume of space 'studded' with sources of light. Berkeley's first argument here is that only some 'points of space' have to be regarded as actually 'radiating'; some parts of 'the hollow surface' would be dark. This argument is in accordance with Berkeley's theory of heterogeneous *minima* (see Appendix A below), although 'points' may also mean here 'the smallest seen particles', or 'concatenations of *minima*'. Thus, on this theory, the *minima visibilia* (1) do not have to 'signify' all parts of the kinaesthetic space; (2) nor do they have to 'signify' all *minima tangibilia* as distinguished from the 'empty space' relative to bodies assumed to consist of such 'sensible atoms'; (3) they do not even have to stand for all points of the purely visual space,[61] because such a space might be conceived of as relative to the visible 'bright' quanta, and not as composed of their continuous series.[62] In any event, if only some 'points of space' are actually radiating, there is no necessity to regard the rays, or particles, of light as intercepting each other.[63] Moreover, on Berkeley's finitist premises, no given extension consists of infinity of points, and the assumption that the amount of points in general, and of the 'radiating' ones in particular, is finite facilitates the assumption of 'non-interception'.

Berkeley's second argument in this group of sections (207–9) is that even if some rays, or particles, of 'corporeal' light *are* intercepted by each other, or by a grosser medium,[64] we can still see the relevant objects, 'though more dimly', provided that a fairly high percentage of rays, or particles, 'arrive at the eye'. It is noteworthy that here too he uses an analogy between observed and hypothetical states of affairs, namely between the partial interception of the visible light by various media, and the interception of some of its particles, i.e. of particles of its 'substance', either by various media, or by each other. And it might also be assumed that many particles of 'the substance of light' do not initially meet resistance, but, on the contrary, penetrate the 'pores' of opaque bodies, and are lost there 'to all appearance'. Now, first, it should be noticed that this argument in favour of the corporeality of 'the substance of light' is propounded by Berkeley, as it were, on top of the former argument from the finite divisibility of extension. It seems that he did not consider the empirical argument from interception by 'gross media' as sufficient for his purposes, presumably because it has direct bearing on visible light only. Secondly, it is obvious that in section 208 he emphasizes again, just as in *Phil. Com.* and the *Theory of Vision* (see also Appendix A below), that, in his view, one may well see the object without seeing all its 'points', or *minima*. And it seems that he now applies this contention to the particles of light as well.

Berkeley's third argument in favour of the corporeality of 'the substance of light' is that the possibility of interception may be minimized, for all practical purposes, or even completely eliminated, by supposing 'the particles of light to be indefinitely small' in comparison with 'the empty spaces'. This last argument exempli-

fies Berkeley's distinction between the assumption of the corpuscularian aether, or 'the substance of light', on the one hand, and
conjectures concerning the sizes of its particles on the other. But
'indefinitely small' does not mean 'infinitely small'. The author of
Siris only says that according to (*a*) the observed phenomena, and
(*b*) the given hypothesis, we may assume that the particles of light
are 'as small as we please', in other words one may ascribe to them
any size required by various empirical and theoretical considerations.

Berkeley's criticism of Ficinus' hypothesis of 'incorporeal' light
clarifies some tenets of his own approach to theoretical entities in
general, and to aether, or 'the substance of light', in particular.
Therefore, any student of the Berkeleian view of hypotheses and
laws of nature should regard sections 206–10 of *Siris* as crucial.
Moreover, they should also be recommended to anyone interested
in the fascinating and dangerous area that lies on the border
between epistemology and the philosophy of science.

9. PRIMARY AND SECONDARY QUALITIES

The concept of particles of aether is used in *Siris* not only in order to
explain a wide variety of physical phenomena, but also as an all-
important principle of co-ordination between epistemology and
philosophy of science. The corpuscularian hypotheses are supposed
in *Siris* first and foremost to explain various regular and perceived
occurrences referred to in the realm of physics, geometrical optics,
etc. (such as behaviour of gases, or of rays of light) and to enable the
scientist to deduce accurately chains of useful computations.
However, they are also meant to fulfil a yet wider role, namely to
account for differences between what may be respectively regarded
as the *primary* and *secondary qualities*. The very assumption of a
differentiation between the primary and secondary qualities may
certainly be considered as a quite radical change of Berkeley's view,
and as a major modification within the framework of his immaterialism; he certainly would not have admitted such a differentiation in
the *Principles*.

T. E. Jessop is right in saying (in the Editor's Introduction to
Siris, p. 14) that while Berkeley now 'mentions with some approval
the distinction of primary and secondary qualities', he still holds

'that epistemologically a primary quality is not the "truth" or "reality" of its connected secondary quality, and that ontologically the former is not an agent, does not produce the latter as a subjective effect within a finite mind'. The primary qualities, as considered, for instance, in *S.* 162, are certainly regarded as characterizations of 'instrumental causes' (e.g. of the corpuscles of aether), and not as being, or belonging to, efficient causes. Jessop is also right in pointing out that Berkeley's distinction in *Siris* between the primary and secondary qualities 'falls wholly within the province of physics; it stands there so far as a regular concomitance can be empirically established between the two sets of qualities' (ibid.). It is also true that, in the view of the author of *Siris*, both the primary and secondary qualities are real (because equally perceived by an infinite Observer, and equally perceivable by all finite observers) and mind-dependent.[65]

Nevertheless, the distinction introduced in *Siris* between the primary and secondary qualities, the second of which are explained by the first, is quite new in comparison with the *Principles* and the *Three Dialogues*; and it is worth while inspecting it closely. This distinction, according to which some qualities of the corpuscles of aether, which may be called 'primary', provide an explanation for the occurrences of 'flavours, odours, and colours', and other 'various qualities' of 'natural productions' within the realm of medium-sized and macrocosmic objects, is to be found mainly in *S.* 162, 165, 181, 240, and 266.

The most important of those, in the context of reference to the primary and secondary qualities, is *S.* 162, which in its entirety runs as follows:

The pure aether or invisible fire contains parts of different kinds, that are impressed with different forces, or subjected to different laws of motion, attraction, repulsion, and expansion, and endued with divers distinct habitudes towards other bodies. These seem to constitute the many various qualities (Sects. 37, 40, 44), virtues, flavours, odours and colours which distinguish natural productions. The different modes of cohesion, attraction, repulsion, and motion appear to be the source from whence the specific properties are derived, rather than different shapes or figures. This, as hath been already observed [cf. *S.* 132 ff.], seems confirmed by the experiment of fixed salts operating one way, notwithstanding the difference of their angles. The original particles productive of odours, flavours, and other properties, as well as of colours, are, one may suspect, all contained and blended together in that universal and original seminary of pure elementary fire; from which they are diversely separated and attracted by the various subjects of the animal, vegetable, and mineral kingdoms, which thereby become classed into kinds, and endued with those distinct properties which continue till their several forms, or specific proportions of fire, return into the common mass.

In this section, Berkeley develops two main arguments:

(1) The corpuscles of aether 'are impressed with different forces, or subjected to different laws of motion, attraction, repulsion, and expansion' (cf. also the remarks above—mainly in Section 7—on gravity and attraction).

(2) The corpuscularian aether 'constitutes', i.e. is the 'secondary cause' of, 'the many various qualities' on the macrocosmic and medium-sized levels. Qualities explained by the assumption of the corpuscularian aether are represented here by colours, odours, etc. On the view of the author of *Siris* the particles of aether cause (in the restricted sense of 'cause', i.e. they function as concomitants, or, in other words, are 'productive' of) the various secondary qualities, mainly owing to their various 'idiosyncrasies', and not to their 'different shapes and figures'.[66]

Within the conceptual framework provided by *S*. 162, one may also note some further interesting points:

(*a*) The 'specific properties' of, say, medium-sized bodies, 'derived' from 'different habitudes' of the particles of aether, are exemplified by the 'secondary qualities' only. 'Flavours, odours, and colours', mentioned in this section of *Siris*, are all 'secondary qualities', according to the distinction made by men of science and philosophers in the seventeenth and eighteenth centuries. It seems, therefore, that the Berkeleian particles of aether fulfil at least part of the role ascribed by Locke to particles of the corpuscularian 'real essence'. In a similar vein, it is certainly not misleading to say that Locke (drawing heavily on Boyle) maintains, in fact, that the hidden 'real essence' may consist of any particles whatever, whereas Berkeley assumes that the main part of the role he ascribes to particles is exerted by the particles of aether (although he rejects the assumption of an aethereal plenum 'subtler than light'). The particles of aether are assumed by him to be nearly universal 'concomitants' of chemical, optical, and physiological events.

(*b*) It should also be noticed that, even on Locke's premises, microscopic and macroscopic primary qualities cannot be regarded as identical. Particles of the 'real essence' are supposed by Locke to be characterized by solidity and extension, shape, position, and weight, rest and motion, and also to be countable. But, of course, the solidity of tables, or the size of stars, are not to be confounded, even on Locke's premises, with the solidities or sizes of (the conjunctions of) particles of the relevant 'real essence'.[67] The obvious reason for this impossibility of equating a macro-size with the relevant addition of micro-sizes is the assumption of empty spaces between macro- and micro-entities alike. Only the assumption of a Cartesian-like *plenum* enables one to identify any given macro-size with the relevant sum of micro-sizes.

(*c*) But, even after taking into account the limitations imposed by the assumption of empty space, the author of *Siris* might yet, no doubt, consider particles as 'secondary causes' not merely of secondary but also of some primary qualities of macro- and medium-sized objects. The 'tangible extension', for instance, is in fact referred to in *Siris*, without any inconsistency with the Berkeleian premises, as imbued with particles of aether, and those particles might in turn be considered as *explanantia* of most of the basic qualities of bodies, primary and secondary alike. However, almost all the qualities and 'virtues' explicitly mentioned in *S.* 162, and explained by reference to the corpuscularian aether (flavours, odours, etc.), are to be found in Locke's list of the *secondary* qualities. The 'received' primary qualities of macro-objects depend, in Berkeley's view, on the corpuscularian aether only in regard to 'volatility', 'plasticity', and various 'attractions and repulsions' (cf., *inter alia*, *S.* 162–3). Thus, aether is assumed to operate on air, and 'renders' it more 'volatile and elastic' (*S.* 163). On the other hand, the very shape, weight, size, and motion of air at large, and of its 'heterogeneous' particles as well, cannot, on his view, be explained by the corpuscles of aether only, since these last entities can neither account for the specific weight of particles of various compounds and elements, nor wholly explain their actual distribution in space.

We may therefore sum up section (*c*) as follows: (1) Locke explains the 'secondary qualities' by referring to the corpuscularian 'real essence' which is supposed to differ from species to species (or, presumably, even from one physical object to another). (2) In *Siris*

Berkeley explains the 'secondary qualities', such as 'flavours, odours, and colours', and also the 'volatility' and 'elasticity' of observed objects, by means of one unique medium, namely the corpuscularian aether, conceived as a universal concomitant involved in various mixtures, or textures, of non-aethereal particles. (For the assumed role of textures of observed bodies in producing 'various specific qualities', see *inter alia*, *S.* 37.) In addition, Locke nearly identified (at least, it seems so in many chapters of the *Essay*[68]) the 'primary qualities' of micro- and macro-bodies, in spite of the assumption of empty spaces, whereas, on Berkeley's view, such a move would necessitate taking into account at least (*i*) the corpuscles of aether, (*ii*) all other heterogeneous particles, (*iii*) various 'idiosyncrasies' of 'attractions and repulsions' prevailing within the corpuscularian realm, and also (*iv*) the resulting amount of empty spaces in each body. In any event, it is quite obvious that, according to the tenets expounded in *Siris*, no assumption in regard to shapes, figures, motions, numbers, and specific weights of the corpuscles of aether may be completely translated into terms of their observed counterparts. The corpuscles of aether, assumed in *Siris*, are regarded as explanations of the 'secondary qualities', and of some other 'specific properties' of bodies (e.g. 'elasticity'), but the actual bulk, or weight, of any given body cannot be explained by simply computing the gravitational values, angles, or radii, etc., of those 'aethereal' particles, since such a measurement would demand in any given state of affairs taking into account, at least (*i*), (*ii*), and (*iv*) among the factors mentioned above. In addition, according to *Siris* (e.g. sect. 162), the 'pure aether' also consists, *ex hypothesi*, of 'corpuscles of different kinds' whose separate primary qualities cannot be uniformly computed by division of a mass of that invisible medium into an assumed number of its parts.

(*d*) One may certainly agree with Jessop that Berkeley, even in *Siris*, does not regard the primary qualities as 'more real' than the secondary ones, and that both are considered by him as mind-dependent (see also my Introduction, and Section 1 of this chapter). However, Jessop's brief notes and Introduction (vol. v) do not deal in detail with the problems discussed in (*a*), (*b*), and (*c*) above, nor with some other problems of 'the corpuscularian philosophy' as in *Siris*. And he most certainly does not emphasize Berkeley's conversion from an inductivist anti-corpuscularianism to a hypothetico-deductive corpuscularianism. In any event, the mind-dependence and the equal ontological and even causal and epistemological status of both secondary and primary qualities (despite the distinction made between them in *Siris*) seem to be logically connected in Berkeley's last book with the following tenets:

(*i*) The universal concomitance of the corpuscles of aether provides physical, but not metaphysical, explanation of some (i.e. at least of so-called *secondary*) qualities of macroscopic bodies (which are, however, not to be considered as merely subjective effects sensed by certain finite (e.g. human) minds; see (*ii*) below). In addition, the instrumental role of particles is not to be identified with real powers, which, in Berkeley's view, have to be spiritual only, and cannot characterize corpuscularian 'substance'.

(*ii*) The whole system of the *rerum natura*, 'immense, beautiful, glorious beyond expression and thought'[69] is not to be 'deprived of all reality', and reduced to the mechanical[70] primary qualities only (such as impact and sizes, and even 'attractions and repulsions', or spheres of interaction, of macroscopic and microscopic bodies). Whatever we perceive is a real part of the *rerum natura*, perceived by God and us alike,[71] and not a subjective modification of our minds. Berkeley crosses swords on this issue with Malebranche. He rejects Malebranche's theory of *modifications*, and also Locke's classification of (ideas of) qualities into objective and more subjective ones.

(*iii*) There are no unperceived objects, and whatever is perceived by one observer may, in principle, be perceived by others.[72]

Therefore Berkeley, on his premises, has certainly to reject the very possibility that God perceives only the primary qualities (or, according to his identification of (1) the contents of the divine perception with (2) the ontic status of objects, he has to reject the assumption that only the primary qualities exist 'outside' our minds). He could not admit, on premises (*i*), (*ii*), and (*iii*) above (the first of which is characteristic of *Siris*, and the other two of his immaterialism at large), that only the primary qualities are objective, be they of macro- and medium-sized bodies, or of all particles whatever, or of the corpuscles of aether which have a privileged position within his explanatory theories in *Siris*, and, in any case, may well emerge as a new (from an epistemic point of view) and real series of 'ideas of sense'. The theological considerations concerning the undeceiving communication between finite spirits and their infinite Creator, who is also the Creator *ex nihilo*[73] of the entire *rerum natura*, and the epistemological contention that whatever is perceived is real on all ontological levels, are here clearly interwoven. An outcome of those epistemological and theological evaluations of the perceivability of various properties of objects is, in fact, that the author of *Siris* is not ready to ascribe to the 'secondary' qualities the rather dubious ontic status of pain which, in spite of certain crucial arguments (which equate its standing with that of heat, etc.) in the *First Dialogue between Hylas and Philonous*, is, according to him, only '*known*', and not 'felt' or 'perceived by sense', by God (cf. the *Third Dialogue*, vol. ii, pp. 240–1).[74] Berkeley's intransigent doctrine of an equal reality of both primary and secondary qualities is certainly not abandoned by him in *Siris*, in spite of his references to the corpuscles of aether, as 'sources' 'from whence the specific properties are derived' (*S.* 162). Moreover, even the archetypal (and not only chronological) priority granted in *Siris* to the divine ideas[75] (which endangers the reality of all 'ideas of sense') does not make the primary qualities more real than the secondary ones, because on Neoplatonic premises our ideas of solidity would have the same ontological status as our ideas of various colours; both kinds of ideas would be but reflections, or shadows, of their divine Archetypes.

(e) According to the Berkeleian hypothesis in *Siris*, the heterogeneous corpuscles of aether may be assumed under two forms: (1) 'all contained and blended together' in their own medium, i.e. in the 'universal and original seminary of pure elementary fire' (*S.* 162). In this pure and unmixed state they are 'blended' only with themselves ('blended', because, *ex hypothesi*, there are different sorts of those elementary parts of aether); and (2), 'separated and attracted by the various subjects of the animal, vegetable, and mineral kingdoms'. Various 'idiosyncrasies' of 'attractions and repulsions' prevail between the corpuscularian stuff of aether and particles of other bodies; and the secondary qualities (e.g. 'flavours, odours, and colours') are regarded as an outcome of those 'diverse distinct habitudes'. Here, too, the non-aethereal particles seem to play an independent, though limited, role, since one has, presumably, to take into account not only the 'idiosyncrasies' of aether, but also, to a lesser extent, those of other bodies. The aether is conceived of as diversified by an interplay of 'attractions and repulsions' with other bodies, and its heterogeneous particles and the particles of 'grosser bodies' are supposed to explain the constitution of species (or, indeed, any 'generation'), and corruption. However, in Berkeley's view in *Siris*, the non-aethereal particles are not sufficiently quick, minute, and 'active', cannot exert a decisive influence on each other, and are only a natural background for an activity of the main explanatory 'cause', i.e. aether. The constitution of species is explained by diversification, and the corruption of bodies by restlessness, of the corpuscles of aether. The corpuscles of aether, i.e. of the 'invisible fire', are not supposed to rest in the sensory bodies. According to Berkeley's corpuscularian hypothesis, they tend to 'move to and fro', and, after an indefinite sojourn in the 'grosser bodies', return into their own pure 'common mass', disrupting an uneasy balance of 'specific proportions of fire' in various 'natural bodies', and *eo ipso*, corrupting their 'distinct properties'.

In *S.* 165, 181, 240, and 266, Berkeley accentuates various aspects of dependence of the 'secondary qualities' on the corpuscularian structure of aether. In *S.* 165 he relies on Newton, and connects his corpuscularian theory with tenets of the new optics; he also tries to subtantiate his claim that not only colours, but various other secondary qualities as well, depend (in his sense of 'dependence') on 'the substance of light' as identified with aether. He says that 'blue, red, yellow and other colours have been discovered by Sir Isaac Newton to depend on the parted rays or particles of light. And, in like manner, a *particular odour or flavour seemeth to depend on peculiar particles of light or fire.*' (My emphasis.)[76]

In the last part of *S.* 165 he argues again that the corpuscles of aether have to be considered in two different context: (*a*) 'blended in one common ocean'; and (*b*) 'parted and attracted' by various bodies. In *S.* 162 he mainly stresses the process of diversification assumed to occur in various corpuscularian compounds whenever the corpuscles of aether join and 'specify their parts'. In *S.* 165 he puts a stress on diversification of 'the substance of light', or aether, whose various kinds are described as 'blended' in 'one common ocean', and 'parted' by 'attractions' which prevail between them and other bodies.[77] Thus the various kinds of particles (and rays) of

light are regarded as 'blended in one uniform appearance' and
colour (presumably white). They reveal their different colours, due
to their diversification, just like 'the rays of light' 'parted' by a
prism. 'These particles, blended in one common ocean, should
seem to conceal the distinct forms, but, parted and attracted by
proper subjects, *disclose or produce* them' (my italics). As I have
already mentioned above, it seems to me that Berkeley wavers
between (1) the ascription of various relevant colours to heterogeneous particles 'blended' in one common white mass, and the
assumption that we can 'disclose' such colours; and (2) a rather
different assumption that such colours (i.e. other than white) are
'produced' only *after* the separation of particles from their
'common mass' by 'attractions', prisms, etc.

It is also noteworthy that in *Siris* he relies heavily on Newton's
own shift of argument from rays to particles of light.[78] He accepts
Newton's rather cautious incorporations of corpuscularian
assumptions within the framework of (reticular) laws of optics, and
modifies the theoretical part of that framework by identifying
aether with 'the substance of light', whose fixed velocity *in vacuo* is
considered by him as greater than in any *medium*—since, in his
view, particles of other 'substances' and their 'attractions' hinder
the movement of the corpuscles of 'the substance of light'.

The similarity between the corpuscularian explanations of (1)
different colours, and (2) other 'specific (secondary) properties', is
also pointed out in *S.* 181:

The heaven is supposed pregnant with virtues and forms, which constitute
and discriminate the various species of things. And we have more than once
observed that, as the light, fire, or celestial aether, being parted by
refracting or reflecting bodies, produceth variety of colours, even so, that
same apparently uniform substance, being parted and secreted by the
attracting and repelling powers of the diverse secretory ducts of plants and
animals, that is, by natural chemistry, produceth or imparteth the various
specific properties of natural bodies. Whence the tastes, and odours, and
medicinal virtues so various in vegetables.

Various qualities of 'natural productions' are here regarded as
specified by heterogeneous 'forms', or parts, of aether. Berkeley in
Siris certainly wanted to suggest a comprehensive explanatory
principle in, at least, optics and 'natural chemistry', and to account
in the same encompassing manner for 'attractions and repulsions'

instrumental in 'production' of colours, tastes, odours, and 'medicinal virtues'. (The same explanation—by means of the corpuscularian aether—is applied by him to sounds;[79] cf. *S.* 147.) It may also be noteworthy that most qualities mentioned in *S.* 181 are again 'secondary', according to Locke's use of the term (see, for instance, *Essay* II. viii. 10 and 23). But 'medicinal virtues' may be regarded as Locke's 'tertiary qualities' (cf. ibid.).

In any event, it is quite obvious that the references in the above-mentioned sections are made to optics and 'natural chemistry' only, and not, for instance, to motion, sizes, and shapes of bodies as described in physics and geometry, and they may accordingly be interpreted as *restricting* the explanatory powers of the theory of the corpuscularian aether (and the assumed scope of activity of the corpuscles of that 'invisible fire') to the realm of the secondary (and tertiary) qualities.[80] According to such an interpretation, the corpuscles of aether cannot really explain changes of shape and weight of other particles and bodies, and even solidity would presumably not be included in the list of 'the various specific properties' 'produced', or 'generated', by the minute 'instrumental causes'. At least, some changes of shape, size, weight, etc. might be considered, even on the premises of *S.* 162, 165, and 181, as concomitant with movements of non-aethereal particles, and not with those of the main explanatory medium. Even changes of solidity (which *qua* elasticity seem mainly to depend, on Berkeley's premisses—and see also *S.* 163—on the corpuscles of aether) would yet be explainable without reference to the direct presence—in contrast to the total sum of attractions, or gravitational influences—of those extremely minute parts of the *rerum natura*. And even in computations of the sum total of 'attractions and repulsions', the 'grosser' (non-aethereal) particles have yet to be taken into account. However, changes of the secondary (and tertiary) qualities, and, presumably, even most[81] of the secondary (and tertiary) qualities themselves, depend, according to the doctrine expounded in the three sections mentioned above, on the direct presence of the corpuscles of aether.

It seems that one may similarly interpret the following sentence in *S.* 240: 'And in that sense it may be said that peculiar attractions or repulsions in the parts are attended with specific properties in the wholes.' The 'specific properties' may here quite safely be assumed to refer, first, to the secondary (and tertiary[82]) qualities. Secondly,

they may also provide a *part* of an explanation of the primary
qualities of macro- and medium-sized objects. Thus, according to
S. 200, aether is assumed to contribute to the 'expansion' and
'contraction', and, according to *S.* 147, to the 'volatility' and
'elasticity' of bodies. It 'actuates and enlivens the whole visible
mass' (*S.* 152; but 'enlivens' may well refer here to changes of
colours). Still, the solidity, shape, weight, etc. of particles of various
bodies, and of various entire bodies as well, are, on Berkeley's
hypothesis, not exclusively explainable by aether.

The distinction between primary and secondary qualities is
regarded in *Siris* not only as a valuable tenet of the new
'corpuscularians' and their 'new way of ideas', but also as a
praiseworthy contribution of some 'ancient philosophers'. It is
ascribed by the author to 'the Pythagoreans and Platonists' who
'had a notion of the true system of the world' (*S.* 266). Those
'Pythagoreans and Platonists' are eulogized by him because 'they
allowed of mechanical principles, but actuated by soul or mind . . .
distinguished the primary qualities in bodies from the secondary,
making the former to be physical causes . . . understood physical
causes in a right sense . . .', 'knew there was no such thing as real
absolute space . . .', and maintained that 'there was a subtle aether
pervading the whole mass of corporeal beings . . . itself actually
moved and directed by a mind'. In *S.* 267 he says that 'the
Pythagoreans and Platonists' 'supposed a concord and discord,
union and disunion, in particles, some attracting, others repelling
each other; and that those attractions and repulsions so various,
regular, and useful, could not be accounted for but by an
intelligence presiding and directing all particular motions, for the
conservation and benefit of the whole'. In those two sections
(266–7) Berkeley ascribes to the 'ancient philosophers' three major
tenets of his own theory, according to which the corpuscularian
aether is the explanatory concomitant medium. First, they are said
to have assumed the existence of aether. Secondly, they (i.e. 'the
Pythagoreans and Platonists', and not only the Epicureans) are
regarded as convinced corpuscularians. Moreover, they are even
assumed to have put stress on 'attractions and repulsions' of
particles. Thirdly, according to *Siris*, they endorsed the distinction
of the primary and secondary qualities, and understood (*a*) that only
the first are 'physical causes', or 'instruments'; and (*b*) that those
'physical causes' are (*qua* particles) explanations of the secondary

qualities. Now even if those two sections do not provide us with a very good explanation of the Pythagorean-cum-Platonist point of view, they certainly put in a nutshell some important tenets of Berkeley's late philosophy of nature. And it should be noticed again that it is not too difficult for the Berkeley of *Siris* to rely here on Platonic premises, according to which *all* qualities are based, as it were, on their ideal Forms. Thus, on such premises, not only Ideas of geometrical qualities but also those of, say, solidity and whiteness are the ideal Forms of their inferior counterparts in the changing, physical universe (although mathematics, of course, enjoys a special status in Plato's system). Therefore, on both Berkeleian and Platonic premises, there is no real inner hierarchy within the realm of sensory qualities.

Finally, in *S.* 316, the author endorses, at least partly, Plato's reference (in *Timaeus* 61E) to 'the figure and motion of the particles of fire' which 'dividing the parts of our bodies produce that painful sensation we call heat'. Plato's reference to the origin of the 'secondary qualities' is used by Berkeley in order to argue that 'the corpuscularian philosophy' shows that 'neither sensible things' nor things 'clothed with sensible qualities' are 'independent of the soul' (ibid.). His argument here is certainly far from being consistent; for example, he makes a tactical move which allows for the existence of non-spiritual real things as distinct from that of 'sensible' ones.[83] Nevertheless, such polemical moves have to be understood as *ad interim* steps only, and examined against the actual background of Berkeley's late theory of the primary and secondary qualities. Thus, he does *not* say that one may not ascribe 'secondary qualities' to particles, nor that particles are efficient causes of, and somehow more real than, 'secondary qualities'. He only says that, even on the assumption that the corpuscularian realm is 'independent of the soul',[84] what can be observed are sensible occurrences only. But, on his own corpuscularian theory, particles are either hypothetical entities or real new series of ideas.

10. THE ANTI-CARTESIAN TREND AND BERKELEY'S DEFENCE OF EMPTY SPACE

The anti-Cartesian remarks made in several sections of *Siris* (e.g. 232, 243, and 246) are not only instances of Berkeley's general criticism of Descartes's concept of the infinitely divisible material extension. They also refer to, and criticize, more specific tenets of Descartes and the Cartesians, as expounded within the framework of their particular brand of the corpuscularian philosophy.[85] In addition, it is perhaps also noteworthy that Berkeley's attack in *Siris* on the Cartesian concept of the corpuscularian *plenum* is launched under the banner of his own full-fledged corpuscularian theory elaborated on a Newtonian[86] basis. In fact, his endorsement of many Newtonian[87] tenets, and the rejection of the corresponding tenets of Descartes, recall a dictum on Locke and the Cartesians in *Phil. Com.* 811. Berkeley says there that 'Locke is in ye right in those things wherein he differs from ye Cartesians'. In a similar vein, one may say that, in the view of the author of *Siris*, Newton is right in respect to many issues, and especially in cases where 'he differs from the Cartesians', in spite of his errors concerning some other problems, such as the assumption of absolute space and infinite divisibility, the existence of matter, and physical causes. As I have already mentioned above Berkeley's general rejection of Cartesianism, I shall deal now with various details of his anti-Cartesian criticism.

Berkeley's criticism of Descartes is very prominent in *S.* 232 and 246, where he rejects two fundamental tenets of the Cartesians: (*a*) their concept of 'circular motion' (cf. *S.* 232), and (*b*) their classification of the assumed particles into three basic kinds. The crucial explanatory concept of the Cartesians, namely 'the nisus of a subtle element' in the assumed *plenum*, is completely rejected in *S.* 246. The rejection of (*a*), is, in fact, connected with the rejection of (*b*), and vice versa, at least within the framework of an anti-Cartesian criticism, because, on Descartes's view, the 'subtle elements' had been formed by 'grinding' of the original particles due to the 'circular motion' in one continuous *plenum*, and gravity and the propagation of light alike are explained by vorticular vibrations and displacements of variegated particles of extension.

In addition, in *Siris* Berkeley explicitly says that Descartes is wrong in assuming 'that merely from a circular motion's being impressed by the supreme Agent on the particles of extended substance, the whole world, with all its several parts, appurtenances, and phenomena, might be produced by a necessary consequence from the laws of motion' (*S.* 232). He seems to think that Descartes is wrong (on the issue of explanation of all motion and of diversification of particles by means of circular motion in a *plenum*) for two different reasons. The first reason is, on my view, that he prefers explanations by various 'idiosyncrasies' of particles (and, especially, those of the corpuscles of aether) to explanations by means of the 'mechanical principles of size, figure, and the like' (*S*. 243). On his view, the 'idiosyncrasies' of various particles (which are not to be hypostatized as 'forces') provide a better explanation for various phenomena (see again *S*. 239) than the circular motion of the three kinds of corpuscles of the Cartesians (and the corpuscularian 'real essence' of Locke, rejected by Berkeley on epistemological and 'existential' grounds as yet another abstract general idea).

The second reason for Berkeley's rejection of the Cartesian 'corpuscularian philosophy' is Descartes's *horror vacui*. According to Descartes, there is no empty space since he identifies matter and extension. A. G. van Melsen, a historian of atomistic theories, summarizes in the following way Descartes's attack on the concept of absolute vacuum:

Only that which is clear and perspicuous is declared worthy of a place in Descartes' system. By his methodic doubt he decides what is clear and perspicuous, that namely which it is impossible to doubt. These fundamental traits which dominate his entire philosophy had also a decisive influence upon his philosophy of nature. The only thing which is perspicuous in matter are mathematical proportions. Therefore the only thing which is real in matter is extension. Matter and extension are the same. Consequently mathematics, the science of extension, is the only science which can teach us something about matter and its properties. Descartes' doctrine of smallest particles also bears the marks of the fundamental principles outlined above. It was utterly impossible for him to think along the atomistic lines of Democritus, Epicurus, and Gassendi. For if matter and extension are identical, indivisible atoms do not make sense. The same holds for the 'void' which is the second basis of Democritus' system. As far as Descartes is concerned, the concept 'void' is a contradiction in terms. Where there is space, there is by definition extension and matter.[88]

Descartes condemned both major tenets of Democritus' doctrine, according to which *indivisible atoms*, or parts of extension, exist in *empty space*; whereas Berkeley accepted both. It is true that Berkeley attacks 'the Democritic hypothesis' (cf. *S*. 251) and rejects some tenets of 'Leucippus, Democritus, and Epicurus' (cf. *S*. 273). But he criticized only those opinions of the ancient atomists which are involved in their endorsement of *matter*. The atomistic, or 'finitist', thesis that the 'tangible extension', and empty space relative to it, are not infinitely divisible is endorsed by him throughout almost all his writings (from *Phil. Com.* to the *Analyst* and *A Defence of Free-thinking in Mathematics*). But in *Siris* he scarcely deals with the problem of infinite divisibility;[89] whereas his defence of the second tenet of the atomists, i.e. of the existence of a vacuum,[90] is very conspicuous in many sections.

Berkeley's concept of *pure* or *empty space* is defined in *PHK* 116: 'When I excite a motion in some part of my body, if it be free or without resistance, I say there is *space*; but if I find a resistance, then I say there is *body*; and in proportion as the resistance to motion is lesser or greater, I say the *space* is more or less *pure*.'
And he adds:

So that when I speak of pure or empty space, it is not to be supposed that the word *space* stands for an idea distinct from, or conceivable without body and motion . . . When therefore supposing all the world to be annihilated besides my own body, I say there still remains *pure space*: thereby nothing else is meant, but only that I conceive it possible, for the limbs of my body to be moved on all sides without the least resistance . . .[91]

But 'to denominate a body *moved*, it is requisite . . . that it change its distance or situation with regard to some other body' (*PHK* 115). It seems, therefore, that on the Berkeleian view, a *change of place* is only possible where there are, *at least* two bodies (particles, etc.). On the other hand, the very existence, and indeed definition, of *pure or empty space*, as expounded by Berkeley, means rather less than *change of place*, being equated with the lack of 'the least resistance'.[92] Obviously, motion in any material, or tangible, *plenum* would always encounter some resistance, although that resistance may be considered as quite negligible to the extent that one speaks of subtle elements (e.g. consisting of 'splinter-matter' and finely ground particles assumed by the Cartesians), and, in particular, of aether. Thus, Berkeley's definition of *empty space* and the Cartesian *plenum* are incompatible.[93]

Berkeley prefers, therefore, Newton's gravity, and, generally speaking, 'attractions and repulsions',[94] i.e. action from a distance, to the geometrical explanations of motion endorsed by the Cartesians, not only because 'idiosyncrasies' of particles seem to him less fictitious than a 'mechanical' uniformity of nature, or because of his admiration of the Newtonian science, but also in compliance with logical demands of his theory of space,[95] as developed, for instance, in the *Principles*. Gravity assumes action[96] from a distance. Now action from a distance can, of course, be effected through various media. But it is equally true that gravity had sometimes been assumed to bind all, or most, bodies, even in the absence of any media whatever. Berkeley's references to gravity are, accordingly, based on the model of movements of bodies (supposed to exert influence on each other) in *empty space*. Gravity, and other 'attractions' alike, are not, in his view, explainable by the elasticity, or density, of the Cartesian *plenum* and its three kinds of particles. All the variety of 'attractions and repulsions' of particles cannot be explained by 'the mechanical principles' (cf. *S.* 237 and 243) of one continuous medium. Moreover, in his view, even gravity itself, which is regarded by him as an instance only of the observed and assumed 'idiosyncrasies' in the *rerum natura*, is not derivable from the Cartesian aether, nor, for that matter, from other kinds of aether suggested by Newton and by himself (see also my Sections 6 and 7 above). The theoretical reason—in addition to the empirical reasons manifest in the spectacular success of Newtonian science—for this assumed impossibility to explain gravity by means of the two Cartesian 'subtle elements', i.e. (1) the 'celestial matter', or aether, and (2) the sidereal splinter-matter, which was supposed to exert a pressure on it, is precisely the assumption of empty space. Thus in *S.* 244–5, movements, and especially instances of a relative rest, of the corpuscles of aether are explained not by assuming a mechanical impact in a *plenum*, but by postulating 'attraction', or 'the attraction of gravity', inside the empty 'pores' of bodies. In the same vein, Berkeley suggests in *S.* 194 and 222 that the corpuscles of aether, or 'the substance of light', are 'introduced', or freely enter, into the 'pores' of gold which had not previously been occupied by that 'subtlest' and most 'volatile' element. In general, aether, or 'the substance of light', is considered by him as 'attracted and repelled' by, or as 'attracting and repelling', other particles, from a certain distance (see, for instance, *S.* 191), and not only as moved by, or moving, them, due to an actual impact.[97]

Berkeley's assumption of micro-spaces inside medium-sized bodies (which seems to be modelled on certain suggestions of Newton in *Opticks* ii. 3, Prop. 8), is accompanied by the assumption of empty space among stars and planets. In a similar vein, he not

only assumed that fluctuations in the reflection and refraction of
light (see *S.* 224–5) are due to vibrations and attraction of bodies,
which may be partly explained, following some of Newton's
suggestions, by 'attractions and repulsions' of particles,[98] but also
seems to indicate that the path of motion of light in *empty space* may
be changed and its transition slowed down, by gravity (cf. *S.* 227).[99]
The assumption of movement of particles in empty space is very
prominent in *S.* 209, for instance, where he refers to various
proportions between the corpuscles of ('the substance of') light and
'the void'. He also explicitly speaks there of 'the empty space'
(relatively to which the particles of light are 'exceeding small').
Similarly, the rays of corporeal light referred to in *S.* 225 (and
identified by him with aether) are obviously assumed to move *in
vacuo*; and he also speaks there approvingly of 'those ancients who
took *vacuum* [*my italics*], atoms, and the gravity of atoms, for the
principles of their philosophy'. Finally, it is also noteworthy that in
S. 270–1 where he again condemns the concept of *absolute space* as a
source of metaphysical bewilderment, he does not say that there is
no empty space, but only that space is always relative to various
frames of reference, and, accordingly, that there is no pure space, or
'space alone', abstracted from all bodies and instances of 'resistance'.

   In addition to the rejection of (1) the Cartesian concept of aether,
and of (2) Newton's tendency in *Opticks* to accept the mechanical
explanation of gravity via the density and elasticity of aether (cf.
S. 223–4, 237, and 246,[100] and my Section 7 above), he maintains in
S. 225 that the Cartesian-like hypothesis of continuous aether,
expounded by the author of *Opticks* is not necessitated by the
relevant observations, nor by Newton's other theoretical suggestions concerning various problems in optics. The relevant lines of
S. 225 are:

But, in the philosophy of Sir Isaac Newton, the fits (as they are called) of
easy transmission and reflection seem as well accounted for by vibrations
excited in bodies by the rays of light, and the refraction of light by the
attraction of bodies. To explain the vibrations of light by those of a more
subtle medium seems an uncouth explication.

In brief, he criticizes Newton's explanatory hypothesis of aether to
the extent that it substitutes 'the mechanical principles' of motion
in a *plenum* for gravity, or for 'attractions' and 'idiosyncrasies'

effected *in vacuo*. This criticism is applied to the role of the Cartesian-like aether in physics and optics alike.

Against that background of anti-Cartesianism and the rejection of various concepts of *plenum*, it is clear that even phrases like 'the general ocean of aether' (*S*. 192), or 'the invisible elementary mass' (*S*. 198), do not refer to a *continuous* all-pervading medium. Aether was regarded by Berkeley as consisting of heterogeneous particles of 'different shapes or figures' (cf. *S*. 162 and 281), and, accordingly, could hardly be considered as leaving no room for *vacuum* (if only because of 'the difference of the angles' of particles).[101] But even homogeneous particles of aether could not be regarded by him as one continuous 'mass' (or as one continuous 'general ocean') because of explicit reference to *vacuum* (and see again *S*. 209). Therefore, phrases like 'the general ocean of aether', etc., have to be understood, against the background of Berkeley's theories in *Siris*, as referring not to a *plenum*, but to all aggregates and particles of aether *in vacuo*, e.g. in the macrocosmic space between stars and planets where, *ex hypothesi*, they are neither 'arrested' nor individually 'brought into view' (cf. *S*. 197) by any other observed or assumed particles, media, or bodies.

II. 'MICROCOSM' AND 'MACROCOSM'; 'ANIMAL SPIRITS'

Despite Berkeley's anti-Cartesian trend in *Siris*, there is one issue concerning which he accepts a crucial Cartesian *terminus technicus*. That issue is an explanation of very many processes in organic bodies by the 'animal spirits' within the framework of a general comparison of the 'macrocosm' with the 'microcosm'. Therefore I shall first refer briefly to that comparison, and then turn to the status of the 'animal spirits' in Berkeley's theories in *Siris*.

Berkeley partly accepts in *Siris* some supposedly scientific hypotheses of various Neoplatonists and Stoics, as expounded in Antiquity, and as referred to, in an eclectic manner, by 'Hermetic' and Renaissance writers (see, *inter alia*, *S*. 136, 166, 177, 211, 266, 276, 282, and 328). Amongst those old hypotheses the most prominent are (1) the peculiar emphasis laid on light, or fire; and (2) the assumption that certain parallelisms obtain between the universe ('the macrocosm') and human, or presumably any living bodies ('the microcosms'). Berkeley refers to the human body as 'the microcosm' in *S.* 145, 154, 261, and 361. In *S.* 166 'the microcosm' means any living body;[102] in *S.* 86 his usage of this term ('the microcosms of high livers') verges on its modern meaning (or, at least, on reference to microscopic data).

However, the parallelisms between 'the macrocosm' and 'the microcosm' do not, and indeed cannot, on Berkeley's view, mean that the universe is 'an animal', i.e. one living entity whose spirit is equated with the Supreme Being. He certainly did not endorse such vitalistic metaphysics (see, for instance *S.* 153, 172, and 289). The parallelisms between the world and the human body are, on his view, as follows: (*a*) one can discern in both certain rules of 'harmony', or generally prevailing regularities (*S.* 261, 279, and 361); (*b*) some of those regularities are common to, or reveal certain analogies between, both realms (*S.* 154 and 261); (*c*) both realms are explained by a corpuscularian hypothesis, and, indeed, assumed to consist of particles interspersed with the void (*S.* 157, 164–5, 209); (*d*) both realms are activated by spirit alone, of which aether and the 'animal spirits' are but instruments (cf. *S.* 153, 154, 156, and 161). 'The macrocosm' is, in Berkeley's view in *Siris*, moved by God, and 'the microcosms' are moved partly by finite spirits. In 'the macrocosm' aether is the main instrument, and 'the animal spirits' play the same role in 'the microcosms'. Both these activities, being conceived of as (1) primarily spiritual, and (2) effected mainly by various 'attractions and repulsions', may be regarded as equally non-mechanical, whereas many human[103] motions, e.g. those which are an outcome of impact, or even of gravity, were regarded by Berkeley as mechanical, or, in any case, as 'involuntary'; and, in any case, all motions explained by impact, or even gravity, may be, on his premises, 'deemed mechanical'; (*e*) finite and 'limited' spirits 'act by an instrument necessarily' (*S.* 160) 'with limited power and skill' (*S.* 154). The infinite 'Mind presiding in the world, acts by an instrument freely' (ibid.).[104] (*f*) Berkeley says that 'the animal spirit in man is the instrumental or physical cause both of sense and motion' (*S.* 153).[105] However, he certainly regards the 'animal spirit' as a species only of particles, and sometimes seems to regard it as a brand of the corpuscularian aether (see, for instance, *S.* 154 and 156); (*g*) the 'animal spirits' are regarded by him (and he follows on that issue the then prevailing Cartesian notions) as the instrumental cause of both 'voluntary' and some 'natural' motions in the human body (*S.* 156). If so, man may be regarded as activating the 'animal spirits' in the 'voluntary' cases only. The activation of the 'animal spirits' in cases of the 'natural' motion in the human body has, on his premises, to be brought under the heading of the 'stated rules' of the 'macrocosm', or of the divine activity in the microcosmic realm; (*h*) both aether in general, and the 'animal spirits' in particular, are hypothetical, since they are 'inconceivably small' (*S.* 261), 'imperceptible to all our senses' (*S.* 169), and, in any case, 'hitherto' unperceived by humans (*S.* 159). In addition, Berkeley sometimes reveals a tendency to argue by analogy from the assumption of the 'animal spirits' in 'the microcosm' to the assumption of aether in 'the macrocosm' (e.g. in *S.* 156 and 161).

Now it might be maintained that all this notion of the 'animal spirits' and their function in 'the microcosm' is ultimately derived from the *pneuma*-physiology of the Stoics (cf. *S.* 151 and 153). But there is also no doubt that the old concept had been incorporated by Descartes and his followers as a new technical term within the framework of their metaphysics and philosophy of perception; and Berkeley certainly derived his notion of the 'animal spirits' not only from the ancients, but also (and even primarily) from the Cartesians. (Cf. *S.* 161 where he says: 'In the human body the mind orders and moves the limbs; but the animal spirit is supposed the immediate physical cause of their motion.') I have already mentioned above that he accepts this Cartesian hypothesis in its broadest sense, and regards it as a 'secondary' explanation 'both of sense and motion' (cf. again *S.* 153). It seems that he accepted Descartes's view that it is impossible to detach the 'mechanical explanation' of sensations from that of inner and outer motions of the human body. Now, on both Berkeley's and Descartes's views, the activity of the 'animal spirits' in sensation, and in cases of some ('involuntary' and 'inner') motions, does not depend on human will; whereas their activity as the efficient, or at least, 'secondary' cause of the 'voluntary motions'[106] certainly does. In both 'voluntary' and 'involuntary' processes, the 'animal spirits' are assumed as 'flowing, or rather darting, through the nerves' (*S.* 166; and see also *S.* 86 and 171), and, presumably, also through other 'capillaries'. But as 'vehicles' of sensations and 'involuntary motions' they have, on Berkeley's view, and in compliance with the assumption of the general passivity of 'the understanding', to depend on God's laws only, whereas in their capacity as the 'secondary' cause of the 'voluntary motions' they depend, according to him, on our own decisions.

In addition, Berkeley also seems to assume (*a*) that besides the 'animal spirits', the living body depends (for breathing) on yet another kind of particles of aether contained in the air (i.e. he ascribed to aether the role of oxygen, and cf. also *S*. 143); and (*b*) that even the 'animal spirits' equated with a species of the aethereal element, or the 'enclosed aether', have to be aided by grosser particles (e.g. of air) in order to 'swell the muscles and cause a contraction of the fleshy fibres' (*S*. 200), because the 'extremely minute' particles of aether have to be assumed to 'pass through the membranes, and consequently not swell them' (ibid.) by impact, nor even by attraction.[107]

It is also noteworthy that, according to *S*. 200, the activation of limbs, muscles, and fibres by aether and grosser particles may be interpreted in two ways, of which the first has already been referred to above. The second way would be to understand Berkeley as saying that the 'animal spirits' are aether mingled with grosser particles.

In the same vein, he seems to assume in *S*. 214–15 that particles of the heterogeneous aether, which are smaller than 'the fine capillaries and exquisite strainers' of the living bodies, are 'imbibed' and 'attracted', and also 'secreted', by them, and, furthermore, function as the aethereal 'spirits' in various 'microcosms'. The 'animal spirits' of each species may accordingly be regarded either as consisting of aethereal particles only, or as a mixture of aethereal and grosser particles.

The same contention (that the aethereal 'spirits' are 'attracted' and 'imbibed' by various bodies) is applied by him to vegetables as well (ibid.). But he does not, of course, refer to particles of aether in vegetables, or to their mixture with grosser particles, as 'animal spirits'.[108] Besides, he even emphasizes in a mechanistic vein that plants and trees are 'very nice and complicated machines' (*S*. 35), whereas he certainly would not be willing to say the same of the human body.

Finally, I would like to draw attention to the anti-Malebranchian tendency of Berkeley's theory of the aethereal 'animal spirits', and also to his view that the 'cleansing, healing, and balsamic' influence of tar-water (cf. *S*. 84) may and, indeed, has to be understood against the background of his general views on the 'microcosm' and the 'macrocosm'. The 'animal spirits' are assumed by him to behave in a well-ordered manner, according to various regularities of the 'microcosm'. However, all those regularities 'do not hinder' occurrences of 'particular voluntary motions . . . impressed on the animal spirit' by finite agents (*S.* 261). The activity of finite spirits in the 'microcosm' is regarded by him as a 'limited' counterpart of the Creator's action in the 'macrocosm', which is not hindered, or rendered impossible, by 'laws of nature', but rather revealed by them. It is true that, on the Berkeleian view, finite spirits, being 'limited', cause only some of the motions of their bodies, and, presumably, even in their 'voluntary' motions have to use 'instruments' created by God. Still, he certainly does draw (e.g. in *S.* 261) a distinction between 'voluntary' movements of our bodies effected by us by means of the 'animal spirits', and the 'involuntary' ones effected by the infinite Spirit's activation of the 'animal spirits', and of external 'causes' (impact, gravity, etc.). This argument is not only theistic, it is also thoroughly anti-Malebran- chian (and anti-occasionalist in general). According to Berkeley, our souls move our bodies by means of the 'instrumental causes' (the 'animal spirits'), and we do not have to rely completely on concurrent acts of will of God.[109] Malebranche, on the other hand, thought that even in cases of our 'voluntary motion' God moves parts of extension of our bodies at the very moment when we wish them to be moved (to the extent that our wishes do not contradict his will, e.g. as revealed in the prevailing laws of motion).

I have already mentioned above that Berkeley assumes very many analogies between 'the spirits of a man', or 'the animal spirits' in general, and the heterogeneous aether. In addition, various qualities of the 'animal spirits' are, in a way similar to those of all bodies, regarded by him as depending on various kinds, and quantities, of aether; and, moreover, various 'idiosyncrasies', i.e. 'attractions and repulsions', prevail, in his view, between all bodies (the animate ones included) and aether (and see, for instance, *S.* 214–17). It is, however, a pity that what he wants to explain by the theory of the 'animal spirits' are, in many cases, completely obsolete conjectures. Thus, for instance, he refers to the 'congenial, friendly . . . and benign' influence of tar-water as explicable by the 'animal spirits' and aether (*S.* 216–17). The 'luminous spirit' of aether detained in tar-water has a good influence on, and does not cause 'irregular motions and subsequent depressions' in 'the animal

spirits' (ibid.; see also second *Letter to Thomas Prior*, sect. 24).
Berkeley even thinks that the 'experience' of healing by tar-water[110]
proves, once and for all, his theory of aether. He says in *S.* 216–17:

as different kinds of secreted light or fire produce different essences,
virtues, or specific properties, so also different degrees of heat produce
different effects . . . In like manner, one kind or quantity of this aethereal
fiery spirit may be congenial and friendly to the spirits of a man, while
another may be noxious . . . And experience sheweth this to be true. For
the fermented spirit of wine or other liquors produceth irregular motions,
and subsequent depressions in the animal spirits; whereas the luminous
spirit lodged and detained in the native balsam of pines and firs is of a nature
so mild, and benign, and proportioned to the human constitution, as to
warm without heating, to cheer but not inebriate, and to produce a calm and
steady joy like the effect of good news, without that sinking of spirits which
is a subsequent effect of all fermented cordials. I may add, without all other
inconvenience, except that it may like any other medicine be taken in too
great a quantity for a nice stomach; in which case it may be right to lessen
the dose, or to take it only once in the four and twenty hours, empty, going
to bed (when it is found to be least offensive), or even to suspend the taking
of it for a time, till nature shall seem to crave it, and rejoice in its benign and
comfortable spirit.[111]

This supposedly empirical proof of the theory of 'animal spirits' by
the use of tar-water is certainly rather curious. But one of its actual
purposes was, no doubt, to emphasize the corpuscularian 'idiosyncrasies' (e.g. 'attractions and repulsions') obtaining between the
'instrumental causes' of the 'macrocosm' and the 'microcosm'.

3.

Siris (II): Particles as Undoubtedly Real

I. REFERENCES TO PARTICLES AS REAL 'IDEAS OF SENSE'
ON WHAT WE WOULD LABEL TODAY AN 'ATOMIC
(OR SUB-ATOMIC) LEVEL'

In many sections of *Siris* Berkeley does not confine himself to the theoretical use of the concept of particle: time and again, he seems to speak of particles as if they were real constituents of the *rerum natura*. Such unqualified references to particles as real entities, whose existence is a well-known matter of fact, may be subdivided into those which deal with what we would name today the 'molecular' level (discussed in Section 2 below) and other ones which deal with the 'exceedingly minute' particles (discussed in this section). However, it would be very difficult to draw a clear-cut boundary between Berkeley's references to particles (1) as real, and (2) as theoretical entities, if only because in many places he begins to speak of theoretical entities, and gradually slips into a widely different usage of terms which implies that the assumed entities are undoubtedly real. Moreover, the subject-matter of Section 2 below is rather more clearly defined than the present one, because in those sections of *Siris* in which Berkeley refers to supposedly molecular particles it is sometimes much easier to decide whether he means real or hypothetical entities than in cases of reference to very small ones. (A case in point would be any instance of his recurrent references to, or rather of his use of the concept of, particles of water, which, verging on the terminology which had then been used in actual observations, and being independent of any particular corpuscularian theory, may, no doubt, be interpreted as meant to indicate real entities.) In addition, it is sometimes difficult to classify particles mentioned by Berkeley according to their assumed sizes, because, instead of a basic Boylean distinction between *minima naturalia* on the one hand, and their concretions, or concretions of concretions, on the other, he introduced in *Siris* a whole gamut of corpuscularian magnitudes, ranging from the most minute corpuscles of aether to 'parts of water'. For all these reasons, various references classified in the present section might perhaps be relegated either to Chapter 2 above or to Section 2 of this chapter below. However, sometimes it is obvious that references cited in the present section reveal aspects different from those mentioned in Chapter 2 and in Section 2 below, and their classification may contribute something to an evaluation of various shifts of meaning and vacillations in Berkeley's treatment of particles as 'candidates-for-reality'.

Berkeley's reference to the 'extremely minute' particles as real constituents of compounds and elements is very conspicuous in *S.* 71 and 145. Thus, in *S.* 71, he does not even mention any process of inference from the observed qualities of mercury to 'the extreme minuteness' of its parts. He speaks of these 'minutest parts' in the indicative mood, as if describing well-known facts. He also completely blurs the boundaries between references to particles and references to the observed data (such as the observed weight and velocity). What is assumed by him as hypothetical are only some *effects* of the movement of particles of mercury (which, in his view, may be widely different from those achieved by the use of tar-water). In the same vein, he speaks in *S.* 145 as if the existence of 'small particles', and even the laws of their motions, were beyond any doubt: 'Small particles in a near and close situation strongly act upon each other, attracting, repelling, vibrating.'

Particles of air, 'abraded and sublimated from wet and dry bodies', 'cohere', in his view, with the even smaller corpuscles of aether (cf. *S.* 150–1). He certainly speaks of the corpuscularian structure of air (the minute corpuscles of aether included) as a matter of fact: 'Air therefore *is* [*my italics*] a mass of various particles, abraded and sublimated from wet and dry bodies of all sorts, cohering with particles of aether' (*S.* 151).[1] Such references to various particles in general, and to the corpuscles of aether in particular, as undoubtedly real, are rather different from Berkeley's way of speaking in *S.* 222, in which he proceeds by analogy from the existence of items on a more or less molecular level, i.e. of 'acid particles' and 'particles of earth', admitted by all sides, to the assumption of the 'exceedingly minute' 'particles of light or fire'.

S. 225 is also pertinent to the classification of particles on a supposedly atomic level, since Berkeley refers in it to particles as *atoms*. He assumes there that there are no smaller, or 'subtler', particles than those of light, and, in order to defend his view, explicitly mentions the atomistic theories of Antiquity. *S.* 225 is the only place in *Siris* in which references to atoms and corpuscles are, for all practical purposes, interchangeable. According to that section, (*a*) the corpuscularian composition of 'the substance of light' seems to be accepted by all sides,[2] and (*b*) 'the substance of light' is characterized by extremely small particles which may be regarded as identical with, or similar to, atoms.[3]

The 'exceedingly minute' particles of aether, or 'the substance of light', seem also to be spoken of as undoubtedly real in *S*. 227 ('The particles of aether fly asunder with the greatest force', etc.). In this last section, Berkeley only (1) expresses his doubts concerning any derivation of the behaviour of the particles of light from the composition of aether, or from one set of general and well-known laws of motion, and (2) rejects the actual usefulness of the hypothesis of 'hamate atoms'; but he does not question the reality of the particles of light.

'The minute particles of bodies' are also assumed as real beyond any doubt in *S*. 232 and 235. What are put in doubt in those sections are only the precise characteristics of 'various laws of motion' and the continuity of extension within the corpuscularian realm (*S*. 232). In fact, the author rejects the hypothesis of a corpuscularian *plenum* on the physical level, and the ascription of real forces to particles on the metaphysical one (*S*. 235). But 'the minute corpuscles' themselves are referred to as undoubtedly real: 'The minute corpuscles are impelled and directed, that is to say, moved to and from each other, according to various rules or laws of motion.' But 'we are not therefore seriously to suppose, with certain mechanic philosophers, that the minute particles . . . have real forces or powers, by which they act on each other' (ibid.). It is also noteworthy that Berkeley does not reject in *S*. 232 the notion of the less-than-molecular level suggested by the Cartesians. He only denies there that the 'heterogeneous particles', whose existence he himself assumes throughout *Siris*, necessitate the assumption of the continuity of the 'extended substance', and of 'a circular motion' supposed to diversify it.

It seems that particles on an atomic level are also referred to in *S*. 236. In that section, Berkeley tries, among other things, to decide whether Newton is justified in the application of the laws of attraction and repulsion to all bodies whatever (e.g. within the corpuscularian realm). In addition, he rejects the very concept of *corporeal forces*. But he does not there call into doubt the existence of 'particles of air and vapours', nor even that of '*the most minute particles*' (my italics). According to that section, too, one may well think that the existence of 'particles of air and vapours' and 'the most minute particles' alike is universally admitted.

In the same vein, he explicitly includes, in *S.* 238, at least some particles of 'the substance of light' (i.e. on his view, of the heterogeneous aether) in the epistemic index of real entities. As I have already mentioned above, he does not draw a distinction between Newton's optical observations (especially concerning the actual behaviour of light) and his corpuscularian theory of optics, and, arguing from rays to particles, ascribes reality to all those levels of theoretical and empirical discourse. Thus, he says that 'it hath been discovered by Sir Isaac Newton, and an admirable discovery it was, that light is a heterogeneous medium consisting of particles endued with original distinct properties' (ibid.). The only conjectural element, so far as 'the particles of light' are concerned, is, on his view, in that section, the precise scope of their 'secondary causality': 'And upon these [*i.e. on the 'original distinct properties' of the minute corpuscles of aether*] if I may venture to give my conjectures, it seemeth *probable* [*my italics*] the specific properties of bodies . . . may depend.'

The silent transition from references to particles as 'candidates-for-reality' only (which even on that level of candidacy for existence cannot be regarded as a mere instrumentalist device) to a way of speech according to which they are undoubtedly real is also very prominent in *S.* 239–40. In those two sections Berkeley refers both to the smallest particles (of light) and to all other 'fine insensible parts'. He asserts that 'the particles of acids' attract other bodies, without calling into doubt the reality of both. The same procedure, an unqualified reference to particles, is applied by him also to relations of magnitude between the smallest and 'grosser' particles in general (cf.*S.* 244). He does not there call in question the existence of, at least, those two basic kinds of particles; but rather tries to evaluate the role of attraction and geometrical proportions in respect to their location. One may of course maintain that, in the absence of relevant observations, even the existence of particles is, after all, only *assumed* in those sections. But the crux of the matter is that the general explanatory trend in those two sections (and in all other references mentioned here) is to regard as hypothetical not the status of particles, but rather the status of various laws and relations

in the corpuscularian realm. Such an outlook is also characteristic of
S. 248, and of the very crucial claims in *S.* 250 (which has already
been mentioned in Chapter 2, Sections 1 and 3).

In *S.* 248 Berkeley says: 'Nor are they natural agents or corporeal
forces which make the particles of bodies to cohere'; and the
interactions between the 'minute' particles of various bodies and
the smallest particles of ('the substance of') light are examined in
S. 250. Because of the importance of this last section, I quote it here
in its entirety:

Nor, if we consider the proclivity of mankind to realise their notions, will it
seem strange that mechanic philosophers and geometricians should, like
other men, be misled by prejudice, and take mathematical hypotheses for
real beings existing in bodies, so far as even to make it the very aim and end
of their science to compute or measure those phantoms; whereas it is very
certain that nothing in truth can be measured or computed beside the very
effects or motions themselves. Sir Isaac Newton asks, Have not the minute
particles of bodies certain forces or powers by which they act on one
another, as well as on the particles of light, for producing most of the
phenomena in nature? But, in reality, those minute particles are only
agitated according to certain laws of nature, by some other agent, wherein
the force exists and not in them, which have only the motion; which motion
in the body moved the Peripatetics rightly judge to be a mere passion, but in
the mover to be ἐνέργεια or act.

I have already emphasized in Section 3 of Chapter 2 above the
implications of the words 'in reality' in the text above. But, in
addition, I would like to mention here that the corpuscularian
theory is not considered by Berkeley in this or any other section of
Siris as one of those 'mathematical hypotheses' (e.g. of absolute
space, equilibrium of forces, etc.; cf. also *S.* 271), which 'mechanic
philosophers' are inclined 'to realise'. In other words, the concept
of particles is *not*, in Berkeley's view as presented in the section
under discussion, one of those 'notions' which are wrongly
'realised', but a basically explanatory term which may at least be
supposed to refer to real entities. It seems, therefore, that *S.* 250 is
not less important than *S.* 228. In *S.* 228 Berkeley draws a sharp
line of distinction between reticular 'laws of nature' and 'hypotheses'; and in *S.* 250 he distinguishes purely 'mathematical' terms
from explanatory ones. 'Forces', for example, are regarded in
S. 250 as terms in purely 'mathematical' hypotheses,[4] but 'particles'
are considered as explanatory terms, or even as names of new sorts

of real entities. In addition, it should be noted that both kinds of particles referred to in *S*. 250 as undoubtedly real (i.e. 'the particles of light' and 'the *minute* particles' of various bodies) differ from the 'gross' particles of water, earth, etc., mentioned in many other sections, and, may, accordingly, be considered as representatives of entities on a less-than-molecular level.

In a similar vein, the existence of particles is not doubted at all in *S*. 277[5] where Berkeley does not mention the need for confirmation of their hypothetical standing. In his view, even 'the *minutest* particles [*my italics*] are governed in their natural motions according to the several laws of attraction, gravity, electricity, magnetism, and the rest'; and the principles of their motions may well be similar to (but he does not say that they are, or should be considered as, identical with) those of 'the great masses' which 'are held together in their orderly courses'. Also in that section he seems to endorse a view according to which separation and attraction of particles of 'elementary fire' by 'leaves and cortical vessels' of plants is one of the well-known *matters of fact* that need themselves to be explained.

Finally, it should be noticed that the progress from the examination of 'the outward form of gross masses' to research into 'the inward structure and minute parts' is described by Berkeley in *S*. 295 as a general tendency of science. It is also noteworthy that in that section Berkeley refers again to hypotheses, and says that they are formed not instead of, but side by side with, the empirical progress into the realm of the *minutiae* and the formulation of laws of nature: 'From the outward form of gross masses . . . a curious inquirer proceeds to examine the inward structure and minute parts, and, from observing the motions in nature, to discover the laws of those motions. By the way, he frames his hypothesis and suits his language to this natural philosophy.'

2. REFERENCES TO PARTICLES AS THE SMALLEST PARTS OF DIVISION OF CHEMICAL COMPOUNDS ON WHAT WE WOULD TODAY LABEL 'A MOLECULAR LEVEL'

In many sections of *Siris* corpuscles are referred to not as (1) either theoretical or (2) real and *extremely minute* entities, but rather as (3) parts, or quasi-molecules, of chemical compounds which seem to be just beyond the range of the then possible microscopic observations.[6]

Thus, at the very beginning of *Siris* (in sects. 8 and 11), even before the exposition of various more involved aspects of Berkeley's corpuscularian hypotheses, mention is made of particles of tar and 'balsamic particles' which, for instance, 'impregnate the air'. These last particles are characterized in *S.* 38 as small parts of oil, water, and salts whose assumed 'natural history' is, on Berkeley's view, in accordance with that of the observed parts (e.g. of water, resin, and bark) and processes (e.g. 'the economy of the plant and action of the sun'), and provides an explanatory basis for the physiology of plants as conceived of by scientists in the first half of the eighteenth century (such as Nehemiah Grew). Such 'oily, aqueous, and saline particles' seem to be just on the verge of a possible microscopic discovery. Moreover, it even seems to me that in *Siris* Berkeley actually speaks of the process of 'dissolution' of such 'molecular' particles in due course of chemical reactions within the plants. It seems that such an explanation of the first sentences in *S.* 38 is in accordance with, or may even be regarded as demanded by, the logic of the syntax. The sentence begins as follows: 'The alimentary juice taken into the lacteals, if I may so say, of animals or vegetables, consists of oily, aqueous, and saline particles, which being dissolved, volatilized, and diversely agitated, part thereof is spent and exhaled into the air . . .'. Now it seems that not only from the physical but also from the syntactical point of view, it is easier to assume that 'which' refers to 'particles' than to 'the alimentary juice' as a whole. In any event, the line of reasoning I am expounding here does not depend on the exact meaning of only one sentence; and, moreover, even the alternative interpretation of that sentence (according to which 'which' would refer to 'the alimentary juice' as a whole) still leaves room for regarding particles of oil, water, salts, etc., as being compound corpuscles on a 'molecular' level.

In addition, Berkeley argues in *S.* 46 that the separation of the fine 'juice of olives or grapes' from grosser compounds is well explained by an analogy from the observed parts to the corpuscles of the juice, i.e. by assuming 'that the finest, purest, and most volatile part is that which first ascends in distillation' on observed and unobserved levels alike. Corpuscles of 'juice of olives or grapes' have, of course, to be regarded as smaller (and, accordingly, on

Berkeley's view, as 'more active') than the seen parts, but they have
to be also regarded as much grosser and more compound than, for
instance, the particles of the 'subtle acids', and of aether, or 'the
substance of light' (cf. also *S.* 209).

In regard to the compound nature of such grosser particles (of oil,
of some salts, of various 'juices', etc.), it is not clear whether they are
conceived in *Siris* as aggregates even apart from any reference to the
corpuscles of aether, or whether Berkeley maintains that they are
aggregates of medium-sized particles and the corpuscles of aether.
His explanatory theory, according to which the heterogeneous
corpuscles of aether 'specify' all other bodies, or analogies from the
observed phenomena employed by him in various sections, do not
help to clarify this last issue. Thus, for instance, he says in *S.* 37–8
that 'various specific qualities' of cells in plants and trees depend on
'the peculiar texture' of the grosser compounds and their 'pre-
existing juices', on the one hand, and on the 'solar influence' of 'the
substance of light', on the other. But it is far from obvious (*a*)
whether the specified compounds are not assumed to include some
corpuscles of light even prior to their last specification; and (*b*) what
is the assumed organization of particles of compounds after the
specification. Accordingly, it is difficult to evaluate what was
Berkeley's explanation of connections between the dissolution of
compounds and the actual behaviour of their particles. Are we to
assume that, on his view, the grosser particles of the compounds are
actually dissolved by the separation of the 'most active' corpuscles
of aether? Such an explanation seems very natural in the light of
many sections (e.g. 38, 46, and 49, and, especially, 127 and 128
referred to in n. 9 below). However, it is not the only possible one.
Be that as it may, it is obvious that particles of water, or of the grape-
juice, or of tar itself, may, or even have, to, be regarded as pretty
close to the surface, or boundary, as it were, of the observed parts of
the phenomena.

For instance, 'the fine[7] particles of tar' are described as follows in
S. 52: '[They] are not only warm and active, they are also balsamic
and emollient, softening and enriching the sharp and vapid blood,
and healing the erosions occasioned thereby in the blood-vessels
and glands.' Now all this description (and, especially, reference to
particles as 'warm' and 'balsamic') is certainly a far cry from the
descriptions of the most minute particles of aether, or 'the
substance of light',[8] or even of acids, in other sections of *Siris*, or

from a cautious theoretical approach to particles of gases in *S*. 228. The particles of tar, water, etc., seem to be close to the then actually observed level of *minutiae* (e.g. of the 'fine capillary tubes and vessels', cf. *S*. 29).[9]

'The saline particles' which, according to *S*. 58, 'insinuate themselves into the small ducts with less difficulty and danger' when their 'corrosive acrimony' is 'softened by the mixture of an unctuous substance', were certainly considered in *Siris* as being on the verge of the detected realm of physical parts of division. After all, particles which have to be 'insinuated' into 'the small [*and at least partly observed; cf*. S. *29*] ducts', and sometimes even encounter *difficulties* in that process of 'insinuation', are certainly a long way both from the 'indefinitely small' particles of light (cf. *S*. 207–9, and Chapter 2, Section 8, and Section 1 of this chapter above), and the assumed *uniform* particles of gases (cf. *S*. 228, and Chapter 2, section 2 above). The same contention seems to be applied by Berkeley to 'fine particles of essential oil' (*S*. 59) assumed to 'serve as a vehicle for the acid salts'. The same line of reasoning may also by applied to 'particles of mercury' mentioned in *S*. 71.[10] I also take it that the whole of the following passage (in sect. 127) which deals so prominently with the 'old science', may be most naturally understood as referring to particles on the 'molecular' level:

But earth itself is not soluble in water, so as to form one vegetable fluid therewith. Therefore the particles of earth must be joined with a watery acid; that is, they must become salts, in order to dissolve in water, that so, in the form of a vegetable juice, they may pass through the strainers and tubes of the root into the body of the plant, swelling and distending its parts and organs, that is, increasing its bulk. Therefore the vegetable matter of the earth is in effect earth changed into salt. And to render earth fertile is *to cause many of its particles to assume a saline* form [*my italics*].

Berkeley also endorses (in *S*. 130) the Newtonian hypothesis (*Opticks* iii, Qu. 31) according to which particles of salt are regarded as compounded of heterogeneous constitutents: 'He [*Newton*] supposeth the watery acid to flow round the terrestrial part, as the ocean doth round the earth, being attracted thereby; and compares each particle of salt to a chaos, whereof the innermost part is hard and earthy, but the surface soft and watery.' Particles on the same (i.e. obviously molecular, or even more-than-molecular) level are also referred to in *S*. 134 which deals again with Newton's corpuscularian hypothesis: 'Sir Isaac Newton accounts for the watery acid's making earthy corpuscles soluble in water, by supposing the acid to be a mean between earth and water, its particles greater than those of water and less than those of earth, and strongly to attract both.[11]

The air, which is regarded in *Siris* as the 'general seminary' of particles of all 'natural' bodies, seems also to include, on that view, among its other constituents, the grosser particles of earth, water, etc. (*S*. 139–40, 145). The same contention is also expounded in *S*. 147, where Berkeley explicitly speaks of '*grosser* particles' (my italics), and also says that the less subtle 'particles of antimony,[12] of themselves not volatile, are carried off in sublimation and rendered volatile by cohering with the particles of sal ammoniac'. Parts of 'moist vapours and dry exhalations' 'heated' and 'agitated' by 'fire', which certainly are, or include, 'grosser' particles, are mentioned also in *S*. 149. Berkeley's general theory of the air, as expounded in *S*. 150–1, clarifies his distinction between 'grosser' and extremely 'fine and subtle' particles. The 'more gross' part of the air consists, on this view, of corpuscles of various bodies, whereas the 'fine' and 'subtle' one is assumed to be aethereal. One may, therefore, sum up as follows: on the whole, Berkeley tends to assume that the 'grosser' and more 'passive' corpuscles are parts of the observed bodies, whereas the 'exceedingly minute' ones are parts of aether. However, he sometimes speaks also of very minute particles of non-aethereal compounds and elements, such as mercury (cf. again *S*. 71), 'pure acids', and 'animal spirits', though one may well argue that the 'subtlest parts' of 'animal spirits' were *identified* by him with the corpuscles of aether.

The 'grosser' particles of 'wet and dry bodies' are not, in his view, 'a pabulum' whose function is 'to nourish' the 'subtler' corpuscles of aether, but 'a vehicle' which 'arrests' them. The 'subtlest' particles (i.e. those of aether) penetrate the *vacua* among particles of all grosser bodies whose corpuscularian structure may be regarded as very minute, or as being at the threshold of the observed realm. Thus, the corpuscles of aether are described in *S*. 200 as 'permeating all bodies', and also as 'in some part fixed and arrested by the particles of air'. That process of penetration and the subsequent partial 'imprisonment' of the corpuscles of aether are described as follows in *S*. 201:

Although this aether be extremely elastic, yet, as it is sometimes found by *experience*[13] [*my italics*] to be attracted, imprisoned, and detained in gross bodies (Sect. 169), so we may suppose it to be attracted, and its expansive force diminished, though it should not be quite fixed, by the loose particles of air[14] which combining and cohering therewith may bring it down, and qualify it for intercourse with grosser things.

Air, on the whole, is regarded here as mediating between 'grosser particles' of various bodies and the minute corpuscles of aether. The corpuscularian structure of water, characterized, according to *S.* 222, by a certain numerical proportion between 'solid parts' and 'pores', seems also to be closer to what is labelled today 'the molecular level' than to other realms of micro-entities. In the same section Berkeley also distinguishes the 'grosser' particles, e.g. 'those of earth', from the smaller ones, e.g. of acids, and refers to them in an 'existential' fashion.

The relations between attraction, gravity, and sizes of 'heterogeneous' particles, examined in *S.* 225 and 227, have, too, a close bearing on the differentiation of particles into 'grosser' and smaller ones, and on the ascription of existence to some of them. One of Berkeley's contentions, for instance, is that 'attractions' within the corpuscularian realm do not become stronger whenever bigger particles are involved, but rather depend on various 'idiosyncrasies' of the 'minutest parts'. This contention is regarded by him as applicable to 'atoms' in the hypotheses of Antiquity (*S.* 225), to the small corpuscles of the heterogeneous aether, and to the 'grosser' particles alike. Thus, particles of oil and water, mercury, iron, and light are all considered in *S.* 227 as endowed with their proper 'idiosyncrasies'. He seems, therefore, to imply that (1) particles on *all* levels have certain characteristic features which cannot be simply explained by reference to 'idiosyncrasies' of other particles, and (2) that the 'grosser' particles are not endowed with greater 'forces' of attraction.

After having rejected (in *S.* 232) the Cartesian doctrine of the 'circular motion' and its reference to three kinds of particles (the 'grosser' kind included), Berkeley proceeds in *S.* 235 to expound some important aspects of his own theory of corpuscularian compounds. Most of the particles mentioned in this last section are certainly on what we would now call 'the molecular level'. In fact, it seems that, in this section, arguing by analogy, he is inclined to blur the line of distinction between observed minute parts of bodies on the one hand, and unobserved relatively 'gross' particles on the other. 'When salt of tartar flows *per deliquium*, it is visible that the particles of water floating in the air are moved towards the particles of salt, and joined with them. And when we behold vulgar salt not to flow *per deliquium*, may we not conclude that the same law of nature and motion doth not obtain between its particles and those of the floating vapours?' In a similar vein, he argues there from other known phenomena (movements of parts of a drop of water) to partly assumed ones (movements of particles of oil, etc.) which, again, verge on the observed realm.

Similarly, in *S.* 236, he refers to both (1) 'most minute particles', and (2) particles of 'air and vapours', and explains motions of both by analogy with motions of observed bodies. In *S.* 237 he refers both to particles of acids, regarded by him as more 'active' and 'subtler' than many others, and to particles of water, and even of 'common salt', which were considered by him as 'grosser' than those of 'pure acids' and mercury, and much more so than the corpuscles of 'the substance of light'. 'Heterogeneous' particles, or 'particles of different bodies', are mentioned also in *S.* 238, which seems to refer to micro-entities on all levels whatever; and the distinction between aether, or 'the substance of light', and its corpuscles on the one hand, and 'the fine insensible parts of minerals or vegetables' on the other, is referred to in *S.* 239. (But since in this last case he places emphasis on the smallness and 'insensibility' of even the non-aethereal particles, it is dubious whether that reference may be regarded as completely similar to references to particles of 'common salt', etc.)

In *S.* 240 Berkeley applies again his theory of 'attractions and repulsions' to various kinds of particles, be they the 'most minute' corpuscles of aether, to the non-aethereal ones; and in *S.* 244 he mentions particles of 'a very gross kind'. It is true that in this last section he rejects an hypothesis according to which the particles of light are to be included among that grosser kind. But he does not deny the very assumption, or even existence, of particles of such 'a very gross kind', or of other 'grosser' particles[15] mentioned in the second half of the same section. The corpuscular 'formation' of tissues of plants and animals is mentioned in *S.* 255.[16]

The 'idiosyncrasies' of particles of plants (and of parts of plants in general) in regard to other particles (e.g. those of air) are assumed in *S.* 277. Not only the particles of the 'elementary fire', but also those of the 'heterogeneous' air are supposed to be 'separated' and attracted by, and to penetrate, 'the leaves and cortical vessels' of plants (ibid.). Accordingly, the magnitude of the particles of air has to be regarded as being between that of the 'exceedingly minute' corpuscles of aether and the diameters of the apertures of various 'capillaries'. The gradation of particles throughout a considerable scale of extended magnitudes, and the formation of relevant hypotheses on each corpuscularian level, are explicitly mentioned in *S.* 283 and 295. 'It is a vulgar remark, that the works of art do not bear a nice microscopical inspection, but the more helps are used, and the more nicely you pry into natural productions, the more you discover of the fine mechanism of nature, which is endless or inexhaustible; new and other parts, more subtle and delicate than the precedent, still continuing to offer themselves to view . . .' (*S.* 283). Similar remarks in *S.* 295 have already been mentioned at the end of Section 1 above. Berkeley's references to the gradual epistemic progression into the realm of the *minutiae* (e.g. by means of microscopes), and to the heterogeneity (of sizes, etc.) of particles, clearly assume the existence of various levels of 'insensible parts' discoverable in due course of scientific research. And, as I have tried to show in the present Section, the 'insensible parts' assumed by Berkeley in *Siris* range from the 'indefinitely small' corpuscles of 'the subtance of light' (cf. *S.* 209) to the 'grosser' particles on what we would now call 'the molecular level',[17] and most of those 'grosser' particles are referred to as undoubtedly real.

4.

Siris (III): Particles as of Old

I have already mentioned above in Chapter 2 (cf. Section 6) that in *Siris* Berkeley uses the term 'spirit' in two different senses: (1) as indicating the existence of non-sensible realities and powers; and (2) as referring to the 'secondary causes', i.e. to certain subtle *bodies*, in the *rerum natura*. Now this second (and metaphorical) meaning of 'spirit' has nothing to do with 'spiritual' entities or states of affairs (as God and thought are, or are said to be, spiritual). However, D. Davie is certainly right in saying that the very use of the term 'spirit' in English philosophy and literature in the first half of the eighteenth century in general, and in Berkeley's works in particular, manifests a tendency to employ 'spiritual' terms when referring to physical occurrences, and vice versa[1] (the very tendency condemned by Berkeley in regard to references to forces).

For Berkeley's warnings against an incautious reliance on metaphors, in ordinary and technical languages alike, see, for instance, *Phil. Com.* 176 and 176a, and *M.* 3 and 42; *M.* 42 deals explicitly with various uses of the term 'spirit'. But in *Siris* he sometimes refers to the aethereal particles as 'active *souls*'(!) and 'spirits of life', and does not always take pains to warn the reader that terms like 'spirits', or 'vital spirits', are 'equivalent', and must be taken with a grain of salt. In the same vein, he sometimes seems to speak in a rather loose way of the 'activity' of aethereal 'sensitive souls', etc.; although he emphasizes the 'equivocality' of such a use in other sections, those metaphors create a climate of a spiritualized physical reality, imbued with the aethereal light and its glowing 'souls' and 'forms'.

For instance, he explicitly refers to 'particles of light or fire' as 'souls' (although 'vegetable' ones) in *S.* 165. In addition, he calls aether itself 'the vital spirit of the world' (*S.* 147), and the boundaries between the respective meanings of 'a fine subtle spirit' (*S.* 150), which is only the most 'tenuous' corporeal 'substance', and of 'vital spirits', 'sensitive' souls, and 'virtues' (cf. *S.* 140) of bodies get so blurred in *Siris* that an unwary reader may well interpret Berkeley in an eclectic Neoplatonic[2] sense.[3] 'Virtues' can be understood not only as particles which are concomitant 'causes' of various secondary qualities and healing 'powers', nor even only as those qualities and 'powers' themselves, but also as unperceivable and sublime quintessences of things inherent in various semi-alchemical 'spirits' and elixirs. See, for instance, references to the *ens primum*, or the 'native spirit', in *S*. 136, and to the 'great cordiac elixir' of Stoughton in *S*. 53. He even speaks, in *S*. 50, of the unobserved 'spirit' as 'the very flower of specific qualities' of any given body.

Similarly, a flight of imagery like 'these native spirits or vegetable souls [*sic*!] are all breathed or exhaled into the air' (*S*. 137) is, as it were, double-faced, because it seems not only to indicate physical processes in inanimate chemical 'substances', or in plants, but also nearly to converge (via the 'animal spirits') on Berkeley's explanation of basic functions of *living*—and perceiving—organisms (higher animals included). It might of course be maintained that, even on Berkeley's premises, there is nothing wrong with the view that the function of 'native spirits' of inanimate bodies, or of 'vegetable souls' of plants, is just like that of the 'animal spirits' in the higher 'microcosms' (i.e. in the living bodies). However, first, the 'animal spirits' are, on Berkeley's view, a highly special brand of the heterogeneous 'aethereal spirits' which exert their influence on inanimate and animate bodies alike. The function of the 'animal spirits' is, in his view, quite different from that of other species of aether, or from that of other compounds of aether and 'grosser particles'. Thus, according to *Siris*, other aethereal particles, and not the 'animal spirits', are supposed to explain the diversification of various compounds and most chemical reactions in the 'microcosms'. Secondly, if various 'native spirits' and 'vegetable souls' had in *Siris* been viewed as counterparts of the 'animal spirits', they would, *eo ipso*, have been very close indeed to the realm of 'spirits' of animals which, on Berkeley's view (in sharp contrast to Descartes's credo), are endowed with perception. References to such close connections between various links of the 'great chain of beings' are on the one hand an outcome of a general tendency manifest in the very title of Berkeley's last major work; but, on the other hand, they may be regarded as an embarrassment rather than an asset from the point of view of an immaterialist interested in a clear-cut distinction between perception and its absence.

2. PHYSICAL SEEDS OF GENERATION

Besides references to 'native spirits' and 'vegetable souls', Berkeley also reveals in some sections of *Siris* a tendency to identify corpuscularian and genetic explanations. Thus the air, which in his view consists of many kinds of particles, of which the corpuscles of aether are an instance only, is also described by him in *S*. 141 as 'a common seminary' of 'the seeds of things':[4]

The seeds of things seem to lie latent in the air, ready to appear and produce their kind whenever they light on a proper matrix. The extremely small seeds of fern, mosses, mushrooms, and some other plants are concealed and wafted about in the air, every part whereof seems replete with seeds of one kind or other. The whole atmosphere seems alive. There is everywhere acid to corrode, and seed to engender. Iron will rust, and mould will grow in all places. Virgin earth becomes fertile, crops of new plants ever and anon shew themselves; all which demonstrates the air to be a common seminary and receptable of all vivifying principles.

It seems that this section identifies, for all practical and theoretical purposes, some species of the minute particles of air, and of the 'proper matrices' of all bodies, with the genetic code itself. In addition, it is noteworthy that Berkeley seems to imply that even the genetic 'forms' of plants and animals, and not only their growth or activities, partly depend on particles and 'seeds' 'latent in the air'. The very lack of definite demarcation between inorganic and organic realms as in *Siris*[5] facilitates an ascription of similar qualities to 'seeds' and acids, and a corpuscularian explanation of both.[6]

The genetic role of particles is ascribed by Berkeley via air to the heterogeneous corpuscles of aether. Aether, sometimes mentioned by Berkeley even apart from its corpuscularian structure, is described as a receptacle of various seeds of generation. 'The element of aethereal fire or light seems to comprehend, in a mixed state, the seeds of . . . things' (*S*. 164). 'Distinct essences' of things, which, according to *Siris*, depend on the corpuscles of aether, are accordingly identified not only with 'qualities and properties' of various chemical compounds and elements, but also with those of all 'generated' and 'corrupted' bodies, plants and animals included.

In a similar vein, he tries to show that the Heraclitean concept of fire as the vehicle of generation may be identified with his own concept of generative aether: 'Aggreeably thereto an aethereal substance or fire was supposed by Heraclitus to be the seed of the generation of all things, or that from which all things drew their original' (*S.* 166).

The identification of certain features of the corpuscularian composition of aether with genetic codes of species is most clearly expounded in *S.* 281:

The living fire, the living, omniform seminary of the world, and other expressions of the like nature, occurring in the ancient and Platonic philosophy, how can they be understood exclusive of light or elemental fire?— the particles of which are known to be heterogeneous, and, for aught we know, may some of them be organised, and, notwithstanding their wonderful minuteness, contain original seeds which, being formed and sown in a proper matrix, do gradually unfold and manifest themselves, still growing to a just proportion of the species.

It is particularly noteworthy that *S.* 281 refers to the 'unfolding' of 'seeds' of species which are included in the corpuscularian structure, despite its 'wonderful minuteness', and 'manifest them-selves' in due course of generative processes. This Aristotelian, and, one may say, biological approach,[7] which is rather different from Neoplatonic and Stoic references to 'spirits', 'souls', and *pneuma*, is also reinforced by reference to 'forms' (cf. for instance, *S.* 165 and 167; and see Section 3 below, concerning 'forms of all sublunary things'). In *S.* 282 Berkeley also identifies the corpuscularian 'seeds' and 'animalcules' with some new data discovered by microscopists of the second half of the seventeenth and the first half of the eighteenth century:

May not this aethereal seminary, consistently with the notions of that philosophy which ascribed much of generation to celestial [*sic*] influences, be supposed to impregnate plants and animals with the first principles, the stamina, or those animalcules which Plato, in his *Timaeus*, saith are invisible for their smallness, but, being sown in a proper matrix, are therein gradually distended and explicated by nourishment, and at length the animals brought forth to light? Which notion hath been revived and received of late years by many who perhaps are not aware of its antiquity, or that it was to be found in Plato.

Plato's 'theory or hypothesis' is regarded by the Berkeley of *Siris* as very 'agreeable to modern discoveries', i.e. to 'microscopical observations', and, in fact, as 'confirmed' by them (*S.* 283).

The sections mentioned above clearly exhibit Berkeley's tendency in *Siris* to blend corpuscularian and genetic explanations within the general framework of his unified theory of aether.[8] The 'idiosyncrasies' of the heterogeneous corpuscles of aether are supposed to explain chemical, physiological, and biological phenomena alike. However, it should also be noticed that this genetic-cum-corpuscularian explanation is sometimes accompanied and complicated by references to even more ancient theories of *homoiomeriae*, *logoi spermatikoi*, and 'forms', to which we have now to turn our attention.

3. 'FORMS OF ALL SUBLUNARY THINGS', *LOGOI SPERMATIKOI, HOMOIOMERIAE*

Berkeley uses in several sections of *Siris* the term 'forms' as indicating those parts of aether, or 'the substance of light', which endow various 'substances' with their 'specific properties', or 'make' their 'distinct essences' (cf. *S.* 164). This assumed process of 'information' is described as follows in *S.* 43:

It should seem that the forms, souls, or principles of vegetable life subsist in the light or solar emanation (Sect. 40), which in respect of the macrocosm is what the animal spirit is to the microcosm—the interior tegument, the subtle instrument and vehicle of power. No wonder, then, that the *ens primum* or *scintilla spirituosa*, as it is called, of plants should be a thing so fine and fugacious as to escape our nicest search. It is evident that nature at the sun's approach vegetates, and languishes at his recess; this terrestrial globe seeming only a matrix disposed and prepared to receive life from his light;[9] whence Homer in his *Hymns* styleth the earth the wife of heaven . . .

These references to 'forms', combined with descriptions and theories of processes of generation and corruption, seem to reveal a tendency to identify, in a very eclectic manner, (1) the Stoicized Neoplatonic, and (2) Aristotelian concepts in regard to the actual ways of specification of 'subtances'. The Stoicized Neoplatonic explanation of various empirical processes (which relies mainly on the aethereal *pneuma* identified with the soul of the universe) has already been referred to in Chapter 2, Sections 6 and 8 above. The use of Aristotelian terms in a somewhat fantastic genetic-cum-corpuscularian theory is accentuated in *S.* 43 which has already been mentioned above, in *S.* 47, and also in *S.* 137, 152, and 167.

Thus in *S.* 137 he says that

These native spirits or vegetable souls are all breathed or exhaled into the air, which seems the receptacle as well as source of all sublunary forms, the great mass or chaos which imparts and receives them. The air or atmosphere that surrounds our earth contains a mixture of all the active volatile parts of the whole habitable world, that is, of all vegetables, minerals and animals. Whatever perspires, corrupts, or exhales, impregnates the air, which, being acted upon by the solar fire, produceth within itself all sorts of chemical operations, dispensing again those salts and spirits in new generations, which it had received from putrefactions.

It is true that the formal causes are interpreted in *Siris* as the *corpuscularian concauses.*[10] Nevertheless, the very use of the Aristotelian nomenclature in several sections of *Siris* is not purely coincidental, especially as it is related to references to generation by seeds, and does not characterize Berkeley's earlier writings.

Berkeley's use of some Aristotelian concepts is also very conspicuous in his reference in *S.* 137 to '*sublunary*[11] forms' (my italics). It seems that he considers the arrangements, the sizes, and the shapes of the corpuscles of aether as the 'forms' which the earthly bodies get from the general 'ocean' of light via the heterogeneous air. The same tendency reveals itself, for instance, in *S.* 140–2: 'And numberless instances there are of salts produced by the air, that vast collection or treasury of active principles, from which all sublunary [!] bodies seem to derive their forms, and on which animals depend for their life and breath' (*S.* 142). In addition, the 'vegetative souls or vital spirits' of various species are identified with 'forms' in *S.* 152. Berkeley even calls the 'pure invisible fire' itself the common 'vegetative soul or vital spirit of the world', since it is 'pregnant with forms which it constantly sends forth and resorbs'. 'Seeds', 'natural causes', and 'forms' seem to be regarded by him as identifiable, at least in some cases, with each other (cf. *S.* 164). Moreover, in *S.* 167, he quotes in his support Peripatetic authorities[12] who, in his view, confirm his own suggestions as propounded in *S.* 43:

According to the Peripatetics, the form of heaven, or the fiery aethereal substance, contains the forms of all inferior beings (Sect. 43). It may be said to teem with forms, and impart them to subjects fitted to receive them. The vital force thereof in the Peripatetic sense is vital to all, but diversely received according to the diversity of the subjects. So all colours are virtually contained in the light; but their actual distinctions of blue, red, yellow, and the rest, depend on the difference of the objects which it illustrates. Aristotle, in the book *De Mundo*,[13] supposeth a certain fifth essence, an aethereal nature, unchangeable and impassive; and next in order a subtle flaming substance, lighted up or set on fire by that aethereal and divine nature.

Berkeley tries to reconcile in *Siris* some remnants of the Aristotelian concept of *form* and the new scientific discoveries and theories (for example of the microscopists, and of Newtonian optics), presumably because of his tendency to incorporate biological explanations within the hypothesis of the corpuscularian aether. But he seems, *en route*, to elaborate his own classification of the Aristotelian causes, and also to develop an application of Peripatetic concepts of potentiality and actuality to the corpuscularian and physiological theories of *Siris*. In respect to causes, the final and the efficient ones are ascribed by him to the non-corporeal realm of God's (and other spirits'[14]) forces and designs. 'Principles', 'virtues', and 'spirits' (in a metaphorical sense of 'spirit'), i.e. various aggregates of the minute corpuscles of aether, are supposed to endow bodies with their 'forms' (and are themselves labelled 'forms'). Those 'virtues', or 'principles' and 'secondary' agents, are supposed to function as formal causes which explain the processes of generation and the very formation of species. The 'material' causes would be, on this view, all non-aethereal bodies whose corpuscularian structure is penetrated by aether. (But even those 'material' and 'formal' causes exist, of course, on Berkeley's view, as correlates of perception only.) In respect to the concepts of potentiality and actuality, as applied to states of affairs in the organic and inorganic realms alike, it seems that the corpuscularian structures of all bodies are regarded by him as physical patterns for the absorption of the actualizing aethereal 'forms'. And in most relevant sections of *Siris* (e.g. 43, 141, 281) the genetic role of the 'informing' aether is even more stressed than in *S*. 167.

On Berkeley's view in *Siris*, metals, acids, plants, animals, etc., are all related as links in the 'great chain of beings'[15] (cf., for instance, *S*. 303), and reveal their potentialities of change under the influence of the 'invisible fire'. The actual development (e.g. growth) of various bodies depends, in his view, on chemical interactions between their particles and those of aether, rather than on their own corpuscularian structure. All this rather fantastic mixture of Aristotelianism, Stoicized Neoplatonism, and the scientific developments of the first half of the eighteenth century is presented in *S.* 181 (quoted in its entirety in Chapter 2, Section 9 above), in which Berkeley claims that 'The heaven is supposed pregnant with virtues and forms, which constitute and discriminate the various species of things'; and that 'the light, fire, or celestial aether, being parted by refracting or reflecting bodies, produceth variety of colours' (and also 'the tastes, and odours, and medicinal virtues so various in vegetables').

The contentions of *S.* 181 are also reinforced in *S.* 229, in which the 'forms' are explicitly equated with the 'spermatic reasons' (*logoi spermatikoi*). Berkeley refers there approvingly to the Stoic tenet that fire 'comprehends and includes' 'the spermatic reasons or forms (λόγους σπερματικους) of all natural things', and adds that 'as the forms of things have their ideal existence in the intellect, so it should seem that seminal principles have their natural existence in the light'. Incidentally, in *S.* 229 Berkeley also emphasizes two other major tenets of his theory of the corpuscularian aether. Firstly, he says that this theory may be supposed to account for phenomena in widely different realms: 'The phenomena of light, animal spirit, muscular motion, fermentation, vegetation, and other natural operations, seem to require nothing more than the intellectual and artificial[16] fire of Heraclitus, Hippocrates, the Stoics, and other ancients.' Secondly, he maintains that, even within the framework of one unified and unifying theory of aether, one still has to make allowances for (*a*) heterogeneity of corpuscles, and (*b*) variety of 'attractions and repulsions' (especially of the corpuscles). In addition, he explicitly says, in sharp contrast to his more 'realizing' utterances, that both the 'nature' of particles of aether and the 'laws' of their changes and motions are only assumed *ex hypothesi*. The aethereal light is, in his view,

A medium consisting of heterogeneous parts, differing from each other in diverse qualities that appear to sense [*i.e. in their effects*], and not improbably having many original properties, attractions, repulsions, and motions, the laws and natures whereof are indiscernible *to us* [*my italics*] otherwise than in their remote effects. And this animated heterogeneous fire should seem a more adequate cause, whereby to explain the phenomena of nature, than one uniform aethereal medium.

Berkeley complicates his theory of semi-Peripatetic 'forms' and *logoi spermatikoi* by an introduction of yet another concept, namely that of preformed genetic animalcules, or *homoiomeriae* (e.g. seeds which 'contain their solid organical parts in miniature'; cf. *S*. 233). Here I shall mention only that *homoiomeriae* (1) are the main subject-matter of *S*. 233, 267, 281, 282, and 283; (2) are regarded in *Siris* as at least one of the alternative explanations of the generation of species; (3) are assumed to be discovered by the microscopists;[17] and (4) cannot be considered, on the view put forward in *Siris*, as an argument in favour of a once-for-all act of Creation which does not leave room for God's interference in nature. The concept of *homoiomeriae* plays an important role in Berkeley's vacillations between the *minima*-theory and 'the corpuscularian philosophy' proper during the formative period of his thought, i.e. in early entries of the *Philosophical Commentaries*, where it is applied to problems involved in the immaterialistic account of the Creation. For a more detailed discussion of Berkeley's reliance on *homoiomeriae* see my 'Particles and *Minima* in George Berkeley's Immaterialism',[18] where I point out that Berkeley seems to be indebted to a certain extent to Aristotle's discussion of Anaxagoras' *homoiomeriae* and his own *elachista* in *Physics* i, 4.

4. PARTICLES AS THE SMALLEST PARTS OF TRADITIONAL 'ELEMENTS'

Some of Berkeley's references to particles assume the existence of 'elements' in a traditional (medieval or spagyrist) sense. It is not always easy to evaluate the precise location of boundaries between his references to the Boylean and Newtonian corpuscularian hypotheses on the one hand, and his use of ancient, medieval, and Renaissance terms on the other. Thus, the 'invisible fire' itself is, no doubt, spoken of in many sections of *Siris* as a theoretical entity in a modern sense, whose characteristics are, in many important respects, based on the corpuscularian models of Boyle and Newton. However, it should also be noticed that the 'invisible fire' seems many times to be identified by Berkeley with the traditional 'element' which bears the same name.

For instance, the general explanatory trend of his arguments in *S*. 147 and 150–1 is to describe the air as consisting of two main ingredients: (1) 'various particles, abraded and sublimated from wet and dry bodies of all sorts', and (2) 'particles of aether'. Now this hypothesis, which refers to various analogous levels of observation and theory, certainly sounds quite modern, regardless of its truth or falsity; it is also influenced by the methodic approach of Boyle and Newton. Even Berkeley's identification of aether with 'the substance of light', or the 'invisible fire', in sharp contrast to Newton's distinction between aether and light (cf. *S.* 223–6, and also Chapter 2, Sections 6–8 above), may be considered as a shrewd theoretical move which shows how to use Occam's razor in hypotheses. But, rather unfortunately, Berkeley's 'fire' sometimes seems to be Janus-faced. One aspect is theoretical, and, one may say, quite modern; but the other reveals a tendency to rely on the ancient 'element' 'fire' which is so manifest in the many references in *Siris* to the relevant Stoic tenets. The assumption of theoretical entities as in *Siris* was clearly a progressive step in Berkeley's philosophy of science, especially as he tries, in some places, to clarify Newton's usage of relevant terms (such as 'force', 'quantity of matter', and even 'hypothesis' itself). But, on the other hand, some of his theoretical terms bear rather obsolete features of ancient Neoplatonic (cum Stoic) origin, and have to be considered, at least in some respects, as retrogressive rather than progressive. The case in point would be 'fire' itself. Berkeley relies so heavily on 'ancient philosophers' (cf. *S.* 151) in identification of 'pure aether, or light, or fire' (ibid.) that one may well be afraid that he does not in fact explain actual observations by quite modern theoretical assumptions, but rather proceeds by analogy from the observed 'vulgar culinary' fire to its traditional and semi-mythical 'elemental' namesake. The departure from the purely observational realm may, in many sections of *Siris*, be interpreted as a move in either a modern and theoretical, or a traditional direction.

The same tendency to refer to fire as an 'element' is discernible in *S.* 162–3. In *S.* 163 an attempt is made to provide a scheme of things which, despite being corpuscularian, would take into account the frame of reference of the four traditional 'elements'. Alternatively, one may say that the corpuscularian scheme is imposed in *S.* 163 on an ancient explanatory pattern of four 'elements'. Particles of 'water and earth' of 'wet and dry bodies' (cf. *S.* 151) constitute, 'in a mixed state' (cf. *S.* 147 and 164), the 'passive parts' of the air. But the air in its supposedly actual and 'active' form also includes, on this view, the 'element' of pure 'fire'.

Therefore, air can be derived from the other three 'elements', i.e. from earth, water, and fire; and is supposed to be 'more volatile than water or earth, and more fixed than fire'.[19] Although all those references to the four ancient and medieval elements are equivocal, and may be understood as indicating observed compounds, tentatively characterized by assumed corpuscularian structures, the interplay of relatively new and ancient meanings is very prominent in this group of sections (162–4, and also 165).

Besides references to the *four* ancient and medieval 'elements' (and, especially, 'fire'), Berkeley seems also to have been influenced by the spagyrist theory of the *three* 'elements' (sulphur, mercury, and salt), as expounded for example by Paracelsus' disciple, Van Helmont;[20] salt and mercury, for instance, are mentioned respectively in *S.* 58 and 71. It is perfectly true that Berkeley might well refer to observed compounds, or elements, when using terms with traditional antecedence. But it seems that he also tried to combine Van Helmont's assumptions with the Boylean and Newtonian corpuscularian theories. Such a view is certainly made plausible by the ascription of special 'virtues' to mercury in *S.* 56, 71, and 100. Thus, following Boerhaave, Berkeley approves of this remedy of the alchemists and explains its special 'virtues' by 'the extreme minuteness' mobility, and momentum of its parts', conceived as 'grosser' only than those of aether itself (cf. *S.* 71). In the same vein, he endorses Homberg's view (derived from the alchemists and the early spagyrists) that 'the pure salt, salt the principle' is 'in itself similar and uniform, but never found alone' (*S.* 126). And *S.* 126 is, in fact, devoted in its entirety to the exposition of Homberg's theory of the hypothetical salt, and its adaptation to the theory that acids are 'the cause of fermentation in . . . liquors', and to Berkeley's description of the air. Now there is clearly a difference between (1) hypothetical entities like various particles, 'pure acids', 'animal spirits', and even aether, which have constituted useful parts of new apparatuses of scientific theories, some of them at least (i.e. some particles) having actually been transferred from the hypothetical index to the index of observed items, and (2) fantastic 'elements' like 'pure salt' (supposed to be 'the great principle' of 'vegetation', solubility and solidity).[21] The difference between (1) and (2) is (*a*) that 'elements' like 'salt' were assumed, *ex hypothesi*, to indicate 'principles' of qualities, rather than constitutive parts; and (*b*) that, in most, if not all, cases, the theory of 'elements' was not connected with the corpuscularian hypotheses. Boyle's opposition to the elements-theory of the spagyrists was most important for the development of science, although he was wrong in being sceptical of the very existence of elements. On the other hand, Berkeley adopted in *Siris* a rather cautious policy of incorporating many spagyrist premisses within the framework of his corpuscularian philosophy.

It is also very characteristic of the eclectic approach in *Siris* that the theory of the corpuscularian aether, the three elements theory, and the four elements theory are all variously combined in many sections (or at any rate are apparently considered by the author of *Siris* as non-contradictory, or even as supplementary). For instance, 'salts' seem to be regarded by him as consisting of the 'elementary' earth and water, and as including, on this view, 'watery acids'; and they are supposed to be 'active', since the corpuscles of aether present in acids make them so. (The presence of the corpuscles of aether is regarded by him as the explanation also of 'activity' of 'subtle parts' of air and 'animal spirits'.) Accordingly, 'salts' are regarded by him as very important co-agents in chemical reactions (cf. the group of sections 126–36).[22]

Tensions characteristic of Berkeley's attempts to incorporate at least some factors of the three elements theory within the hypothesis of the corpuscularian aether are conspicuous in *S.* 191–2. In *S.* 191 Berkeley says (after trying to clarify relations between various tenets in the four elements theory):

Acid salts are a menstruum, but their force and distinct powers are from sulphur. Considered as pure, or in themselves, they are all of the same nature. But, as obtained by distillation, they are constantly joined with some sulphur, which characterizeth and cannot be separated from them. This is the doctrine of Monsieur Homberg. But what is it that characterizeth or differenceth the sulphurs themselves? If sulphur be the substance of light, as that author will have it, whence is it that animal, vegetable, and metallic sulphurs impart different qualities to the same acid salt? Can this be explained upon Homberg's principles? And are we not obliged to suppose that light, separated by the attracting and repelling powers in the strainers, ducts, and pores of those bodies, forms several distinct kinds of sulphur, all which, before such separation, were lost and blended together, in one common mass of light or fire, seemingly homogeneous?

In a similar vein, he is inclined (in *S.* 194) to explain the composition of gold by mixture of mercury[23] and light; and the

Neoplatonic ancestry of the three elements theory is described by him in the following words:

it appears that gold is only a mass of mercury penetrated and cemented by the substance of light, the particles of those bodies attracting and fixing each other. This seems to have been not altogether unknown to former philosophers; Marsilius Finicus, the Platonist, in his commentary on the first book of the second *Ennead* of Plotinus, and others likewise before him, regarding mercury as the mother, and sulphur as the father of metals; and Plato himself, in his *Timaeus*, describing gold to be a dense fluid with a shining yellow light, which well suits a composition of light and mercury.

One may therefore sum up this section of the chapter by saying that Berkeley's corpuscularian philosophy in *Siris* was influenced not only by the theory of parallelism of the microcosm and macrocosm, but also by many other ancient Neoplatonic and alchemistic tenets. However, all this mixture of antiquated views and pseudo-insights, inherited from various periods in the history of philosophy and 'old science', is not simply blended in *Siris* with Berkeley's relatively modern hypothetico-deductive theories. The two explanatory tendencies—the old and the relatively modern— seem rather to coexist peacefully, and the modern part can be in most cases disentangled from its ancient and bizarre background.

Berkeley's Early Atomism as Expounded in His Theory of *Minima*

I. THE 'FIXITY' AND INDIVISIBILITY OF *MINIMA*

Berkeley's view that bodies (and visual extension) are composed of *minima sensibilia*, i.e. of indivisible units of extension, is one of the main pillars of his approach to geometry and to some branches of physics, and he also considered it as one of the basic tenets and foundations of his immaterialism. Now, one of his first queries about *minima* is whether they 'be fixt' (see, for instance, *Phil. Com.* 65–6, where the problem is raised with regard to *minima visibilia*). His answer is that the smallest parts of any given extension (on his view, there exist the tangible extension and the visible one) must obviously have 'fixt' value, i.e. be always identical with one another in so far as extension is concerned, if they are to be considered as universal units of numerical measurement in the *rerum natura*. (By 'universal' I mean here 'common to, i.e. at least identifiable by, all human and non-human observers'.[1]) The 'greatness' or 'smallness' of any (e.g. tangible) bit of extension composed of *minima* would be, of course, relative to various observers (e.g. to their sizes, or to the sizes of their perceptual fields), and may, accordingly, be regarded as quite independent of the numerical value itself, i.e. of the number of 'sensible atoms' countable in any given bit of extension.[2] But the measurement of the actual size of any extension would, on the above-mentioned atomistic premises, depend on the universally valid 'fixity' of its countable units. Berkeley emphasizes that 'tangible extension is a continuity of tangible points' (*Phil. Com.* 78a). It follows, therefore, that, on his view, the very concept of common numerical measurement of physical objects would be mere verbiage unless different observers could refer to tangible 'continuities' as composed of 'fixt' units. In brief, there would be 'no stated ideas of length without a minimum' (*Phil. Com.* 88). The question whether the *minima* 'be fixt' is raised by the young Berkeley near the very beginning of his philosophical notebooks (cf. *Phil. Com.* 65–6; but also 11 and 29), and answered by him in the affirmative: the real (i.e. non-mathematical) units of extension are equal to each other. This affirmative answer is already implied by *Phil. Com.* 88, and explicitly given in 116.[3]

Berkeley's assertion in *Phil. Com.* 88, which refers to 'stated length' and *minima sensibilia* in general, is afterwards applied all through *Phil. Com.* and *An Essay Towards a New Theory of Vision*[4] to more specific problems of composition and measurement of heterogeneous (i.e. tangible and visible) extensions. Above I have already referred to *Phil. Com.* 78a, which deals with 'continuities' of 'points' whose 'fixity' is a necessary and sufficient condition for the possibility of any objective measurement. Thus the real size of physical bodies and spatial intervals may, on Berkeley's premises, only be measured by taking into account 'continuities' of 'tangible points'. In the same vein, visible extension is regarded by him as composed of indivisible minima[5] equal to each other. These basic quanta of 'light and colours' are not subdivided, on Berkeley's view, in any visual state of affairs. Thus, for instance, he says that the fixed atomic composition of light and colours[6] is not to be doubted in spite of an ever-increasing perfection of microscopes which reveal to us new and varying visual landscapes. 'The visible point of he who has microscopical eyes will not be greater or less than mine' (*Phil. Com.* 116). This contention that the units of the visible extension[7] are 'fixt' is basic to him, and is also expounded in *Phil. Com.* 272, 324 (presumably also in 333), and 464. The same contention (i.e. the positive conclusion in regard to the 'fixity' of *minima*) is also applied to the common measurement of the tangible extension in *Phil. Com.* 324 where Berkeley says: 'Qu. why may not the Mathematicians reject all the extensions below the M. as well as the dds. . . as well as the quantitys next below the m?' Now 'm' is apparently *minimum*, 'M.' means *moment* (Newton's term for differential, applied to computations of volume, path, and velocity of moving bodies); and 'dds' means differentials of the second order. The rejection of the 'dds' and 'quantitys next below the m', and, in brief, of 'all the extensions below the M.', is based here on the assumption of 'fixt' *minima*. Although Berkeley refers in the same entry to the visible extension (if 'the dds etc., . . . are allow'd to be something' they 'consequently may be magnify'd by glasses'), it is clear that, on his own premises, the rejection of 'all the extensions . . . below the m' may, and has to be, applied to the tangible extension as well, which he regarded as the real basis of geometry whereas visible points, lines, and surfaces may, on his view, only function as a symbolical notation of their tangible counterparts.[8]

    In the first place, all the applications of analytic geometry and calculus to the visible extension have, of course, to be relevant with regard to moving *bodies* in order to be considered as useful in various branches of mechanics. Secondly, reference to instances, or parts, of the tangible extension, i.e. to bodies, is, on his view, a necessary condition for regarding rules of calculus as geometrical theorems applicable to kinematics, optics, etc., and not merely as mathematical games.[9] According to this line of reasoning, geometry is based on the tangible extension whose two- and three-dimensionality and finite divisibility enable us, in their turn, to apply analytic geometry and calculus to kinematics and mechanics. Therefore it is not surprising that the finite divisibility of the *tangible* extension and its composition of 'fixt' *minima* are also Berkeley's main arguments against the 'logic' of the Newtonian (and Leibnizian) calculus. He rejected the logic of the new calculus (i.e. the ascription of existence to infinitesimals), but accepted its practical 'conclusions' (cf., *inter alia*, *An.* 19–20). He asserts the 'fixity' of *minimum sensibile* in general, but applies this somewhat abstract assumption to the two concrete examples of 'Continuities', i.e. to the two 'extensions' whose heterogeneity manifests itself in many different ways. Thus, for instance, only the tangible extension is regarded by him as the real basis of geometry, presumably because he thinks that geometrical measurement may not be detached from the kinaesthetic space and extension.

Berkeley himself specifies that the very use of the term '*minimum sensibile*' is to be understood as referring to *visibilia* and *tangibilia* alike (*Phil. Com.* 441). *M.v.* and *m.t.* may only be mentioned after showing 'the Distinction between visible and tangible extension' (ibid.). Meanwhile, he says, he 'must not mention M.T. and M.V. but in general M.S.' (ibid.). The general characterizations of *minimum sensibile*, such as its indivisibility and 'fixity', do not seem, therefore, to depend upon 'the Distinction'. All references to the indivisibility and 'fixity' of *m.s.* will therefore be considered by the present writer as legitimately applicable to *m.t.* and *m.v.* alike. Furthermore, in many cases where Berkeley speaks of 'fixity' and indivisibility of *m.v.* (and especially in cases in which he does not refer to special problems of vision), it seems quite reasonable to regard *m.v.* as an example of *m.s.* in general (*m.t.* included). *M.v.* are mentioned by Berkeley more than *m.t.* because many entries in *Phil. Com.* (especially in Notebook B) form part of the preliminary work for the *Theory of Vision*.

Another reason for the abundance of Berkeley's remarks with regard to *m.v.* seems to be the general and vivid interest which was so characteristic of the second half of the seventeenth and the first half of the eighteenth century. (The then prevailing preoccupation with new optical instruments is reflected in Berkeley's very numerous references to 'glasses', 'microscopical eyes', 'Xtallines', etc.) But most considerations which have bearing on *m.v.* may be applied to *m.t.* as well. Thus, for example, Berkeley himself very clearly indicates in *Phil. Com.* 464 that the reference to *visibilia* is sometimes only an instance of a more general argument whose range of application is definitely wider, and may therefore be employed when dealing with *m.t.* The line of reasoning in *Phil. Com.* 464 is as follows: the hypothesis that the *minimum*, or the 'sensible atom', is composed of insensible parts is (*a*) unnecessary; (*b*) unprovable; and (*c*) includes a contradiction in terms. It is unnecessary because instead of explaining an appearance of a sensible atom by 'coming together' of its 'insensible parts', one may well maintain that one of the basic units of the *rerum natura*, which had not been observed before, is now observed (or 'perceived') under certain (e.g. spatio-temporal) conditions. In this spirit, Berkeley says, *inter alia*: 'a great number of insensibles, or thus, two invisibles say you put together become visible therefore that *m.v.* contains or is made up of Invisibles. I answer, the *m.v.* does not comprise, is not composed of Invisibles, all the matter amounts to this viz. whereas I had no idea a while ago I have an idea now' (ibid.).

The hypothesis of 'insensible parts' is also regarded by him as unprovable, because, by definition, the *explanans* is never allowed to be observed. The 'insensibles' are regarded as put altogether beyond the scope of human knowledge. He says, therefore, in a quite ironic vein: 'It remains for you to prove that I came by the present idea because there were 2 invisibles added together' (ibid.). Such an unnecessary and unprovable hypothesis is, on Berkeley's view, one of those metaphysical and useless 'speculations' which obscure 'the study of Nature', and must accordingly, be discarded. (Cf. also *PHK* 102 where he refers to the Lockean doctrine of the real essence.)

After arguing that the hypothesis of insensibles is useless, being (*a*) unnecessary (i.e. matters of fact may be convincingly explained by, and confirm, other hypotheses, such as the theory of *minima*), and (*b*) unprovable, Berkeley also tries to indicate that it is logically invalid. Unperceivable parts are, in his view, 'nothings', and addition of nothings cannot give something. In any case, it is noteworthy that 'invisibles' stand in this entry for 'insensibles'; and 'visibles' indicate all 'sensibles' whatsoever. Berkeley uses at the beginning of entry 464 the more general *terminus technicus* ('A great number of *insensibles*' (my italics)) and the term 'idea' also stands throughout the entry for *m.v.* and *m.t.* alike. But he decides to exemplify his contention by referring to one species of *minima*, namely, to *m.v.* (cf. the following part of the argument: 'or thus, two invisibles', etc.). An almost identical argument is used in *Phil. Com.* 343 with regard to *minimum sensibile* in general, without any exemplification by means of *m.v.* ('To suppose a M.S. divisible is to say there are distinguishable ideas where there are no distinguishable ideas'.) The real existence, or, at least, the possibility of real existence, of indivisible and 'fixt' *minima*, whose features are relatively immune to logical contradictions, in contrast to mathematical points and *momenta* of calculus, is also vindicated in *Phil. Com.* 344.[10] This last entry, along with *Phil. Com.* 346, indicate, among other things, that *minima tangibilia* may be considered as a real basis of computations (e.g. of movements of bodies), whereas *mathematical points* (and *infinitely divisible particles,* and *momenta* of calculus as well), may, at most, be purely instrumental devices.

Phil. Com. 345 indicates, among other things, that a *minimum tangibile* is indivisible, but is not a mere mathematical point (presumably because it may be really discerned); and *Phil. Com.* 346 sheds light on its predecessors because of its reference to Cavalieri.[11] Both Berkeley and Cavalieri maintained that geometrical lines consist of real indivisible units ('simplest, constituent parts or elements', as Berkeley puts it in *Phil. Com.* 70). However, according to Cavalieri, any given line may be, and, indeed, is, composed of an infinite number of indivisible material parts, whereas Berkeley maintains that no finite line may include an infinite number of 'sensible atoms'. His 'new method of indivisibles', which is consistently finitist, is regarded by him as 'easier perhaps and juster than that of Cavallerius' (*Phil. Com.* 346). The indivisibility of the *minima* necessitates, on Berkeley's view, the division of any given extension into a *finite* number of observable atoms. These 'sensible atoms' in a remarkable contrast to the corpuscles of the Lockean 'real essence', or to the three kinds of particles in the Cartesian *plenum*, are regarded as consisting neither of sensible nor of insensible parts. It is perhaps worthwhile to point out that Berkeley tries to immunize his concept of *minima sensibilia* against antinomies inherent in the very concept of the least unit of extension by indicating that, on his view, extension is neither matter nor absolute space, and its atomic composition depends, therefore, directly on actual or potential limits of epistemic givenness. He seems to indicate that it is no use to engage in a search for constituents of a *minimum sensibile*, because a *m.s.* is regarded as an epistemic point, an 'idea' without parts, an ultimate atom of perceivable extension.[12] He summarizes his ultra-atomist approach as follows: '*M.S.* is that wherein there are not contain'd distinguishable sensible parts. Now how can that which hath not sensible parts be divided into sensible parts? if you say it may be divided into insensible parts. I say these are nothings' (*Phil. Com.* 439). His argument in favour of real sensible *atoms* which are literally indivisible may also be exemplified as follows: Let us assume that the extension of the universe, i.e. of what he calls the *rerum natura*, includes 10^n *minima tangibilia*. One can, of course, ask whether this extension (which consists of 10^n 'sensible atoms') may be subdivided into 10^{n+1} parts. But the crux of the matter is that, on the Berkeleian premisses, terms which appear in mathematical calculi (e.g. in division, or in computation of *momenta*), and provide us with a satisfactory machinery of quantitative notation, need not have real (i.e. physical) counterparts. One may, of course, divide any given number into 10^{n+1} (instead of 10^n) parts, obtaining $x/10^{n+1}$ instead of $x/10^n$, and regard this result as significant in respect of non-mathematical realms, such as cosmology and physics. However, from the point of view of philosophy of science (and epistemology as well), it would be perfectly legitimate to maintain that such a division may have a non-mathematical significance[13] only on the assumption that (1) there are 10^{n+1} real (i.e. physical) units of measurement (e.g. atoms) in the universe. (1) has perhaps to be accompanied by yet another assumption (2) according to which such units may be co-ordinated in a spatial context which can be divided into 10^{n+1} parts, or 'intervals'. (I assume here for the sake of simplicity that units of measurement are identical (a) in respect to kinematics, on the one hand, and relatively static bodies, on the other; and (b) with regard to (1) space and (2) material bodies, or 'tangible extension'.)

It should also be noticed here that the rejection of infinity of indivisibles in a finite line on the one hand, and the assumption of the 'fixity' of *minima* on the other, are closely connected and both complete the thesis of finite divisibility. Indivisible atoms may be yet smaller than any given epistemic point. If so, a number of indivisibles in any given extension may always be greater than any number of points enumerated by any given observer. In this case, i.e. if every epistemic *minimum* may be subdivided into real points of extension which constitute, in the last account, lines, surfaces, and volumes, there is no bottom, as it were, to the progression downwards in the realm of the *minutiae*, although the hypothesis of indivisibles is not completely discarded. The hypothesis as it stands before the stipulation of two provisos, (1) the universal 'fixity' of sensible *minima*, and (2) the finite divisibility of finite lines, is, therefore, on Berkeley's view, unhelpful, and also unduly metaphysical, if only because it is by definition unprovable. Cavalieri's indivisibles are too similar to mathematical points (cf. the cluster of entries 341–7 in *Phil. Com.* where 'the Mathematicians' points' and 'indivisibles . . . of Cavallerius' are both rejected, together with 'unperceivable perception'). Moreover, the 'old method' of indivisibles, as Berkeley calls the theory of the Italian mathematician, does not provide an atomist with 'fixt' and real *minima* which are (or, at least, can be) common to, i.e. identifiable by, all observers. The unqualified indivisibility, being still too abstract, does not satisfy the demands of Berkeleian theory of real and concrete *minima*. According to the inner logic of Berkeley's particular brand of atomism, the units of enumeration, e.g. *minima tangibilia*, must be not merely indivisible but also 'fixt' in regard to all observers, and not infinitely small. He of course supports Cavalieri against the then prevailing theories of infinite divisibility, according to which lines are composed of mathematical, i.e. non-physical, points. However, he certainly maintains that the thesis of indivisibles has to be strengthened and completed by the two above-mentioned provisos which support each other: the 'fixity' of 'sensible atoms' and the finite divisibility of finite extension.[14]

We have seen that the 'sensible atoms' are not composed, on Berkeley's view, of insensible points or parts, and reference was made to his three arguments against the theory of insensible parts ((a) insensible parts of a *minimum* are not necessary from a theoretical point of view; (b) their existence is unprovable; (c) they involve us in logical muddles). Now, in the context of Berkeley's references to Cavalieri, he also relies on two other arguments against insensibles. Firstly, *minima* have no parts, according to their very definition (but the explanatory powers of the concept of *minimum* may not be based, of course, on a mere definition, but rather have to depend on the framework of an atomistic theory). Secondly, there are no insensible parts in the entire *rerum natura*. But this last contention is regarded by Berkeley as valid, i.e. as logically deduced from his general immaterialistic premisses, only if 'insensible' means 'unperceived by any observer', or even 'unperceivable by any finite observer whatsoever', and not merely 'unperceived by finite (e.g. human) observers', or 'unperceived by myself'. His rejection of unperceivable parts of extension (cf., *inter alia*, *Phil. Com.* 347, an entry which comes just after the entries on the infinite divisibility and Cavalieri's indivisibles) logically follows from the rejection of unperceived parts, and from the assumption that whatever is perceived by one observer (a God, an angel, a human, a non-human alien, etc.) may in principle also be perceived by other observers who are, or may be, endowed with identical faculties, or 'inlets' of perception (cf. *PHK* 77 and 81). If everything in the *rerum natura*, i.e. every physical thing, is perceived, and the objects of perception of any given observer may, in principle, be discovered by all other observers endowed with the same perceptual faculties, it certainly follows that in the entire *rerum natura* there is nothing which is in principle unperceivable, i.e. any single item may be perceived by any single observer endowed with suitable senses. (But the very notion of perceivability, as opposed to actual perception, is, of course, applied here to finite observers only.)

I have already mentioned above that, in addition to his other arguments in favour of finite divisibility, Berkeley also points out (e.g. in *PHK* 101–2) that the assumption of existence of unperceivable parts is a useless, and what one may call 'purely metaphysical', hypothesis.[15] Moreover, such a metaphysical hypothesis undermines belief in the progress of science and the possibility of our acquaintance with the physical universe, and makes 'the *sceptics* triumph' (ibid.). If 'the real essence, the internal qualities, and constitution of every the meanest object, is', forever, 'hid from our view', and 'something there is in every drop of water, every grain of sand, which it is beyond the power of the human understanding to fathom or comprehend', we are doomed to be eternally 'bantered . . . by our senses and amused only with the outside and shew of things' (ibid.). It is noteworthy that Berkeley maintains not only that every existing smallest part of extension is actually perceived, e.g. by God or 'other intelligences', but also that every existing smallest part of extension, i.e. every 'sensible atom', *minimum tangibile* etc., is *in principle*, perceivable, i.e. may be discovered, by human, or indeed, any other, observers who do not at present have any empirical evidence with regard to its existence. This last contention, which sounds so optimistic, may, of course, be considered (and, presumably, endorsed) even apart from Berkeley's more general theological and metaphysical assumptions, such as the permanence and ubiquity of Divine perception, and the identification of physical objects with actually 'perceived ideas'.

Thus, for instance, the contention that elementary particles may well be observed can be incorporated, without any internal inconsistencies, within the framework of a materialist approach to physics, as it is not necessarily connected with Berkeley's immaterialistic ideism nor with any other metaphysical outlook (materialism included). It may certainly be endorsed also by positivists who (1) reject extreme versions of instrumentalism, and (2) maintain that unperceivable entities are of no avail in explanatory hypotheses (i.e. in hypotheses which are neither purely metaphysical assertions nor sets of mathematical equations with possible present or future use in physics, cosmology, etc.). I am endeavouring in this Appendix (see also n. 6 below) to substantiate my claim that Berkeley, when speaking of human, and indeed of any finite, perception, tends sometimes (in some crucial entries in *Phil. Com.* and also in *TV*) to regard *minima* as perceivable units of division rather than as actually given epistemic 'points', which are immediately revealed to any observers whatever. But it should also be noticed that, instead of drawing a distinction between ontic and epistemic states of affairs, he prefers to speak of the difference between the infinite (Divine) epistemic standpoint, i.e. God's all-encompassing perception, on the one hand, and finite (e.g. human) epistemic standpoints on the other. The ontic differentiation is identified by him with an actual (and, presumably, infinite) variety of ideas perceived by God.[16] Therefore he freely speaks of the actual existence of objects[17] unknown to various finite 'perceiving spirits', but this actual existence depends, according to him, on God's permanent and omnipresent perception. The distinction between the actual existence of 'points', or *minima* (which depends on God's perception), and their observation by human, or other, 'spirits' is emphasized, *inter alia*, in *Phil. Com.* 445–6. Berkeley uses there the concept of 'points' as an actually existing limit of division, which is not necessarily perceived by any given finite observer, in order to reconcile (1) his atomistic approach to physics and geometry, and (2) his contention that ideas are completely revealed in an immediate perception. If every object of an immediate perception is, as it were, given to us in its entirety, in what sense does a perceived line consist of unperceived points? Strictly speaking, says Berkeley, an idea of a whole and ideas of its parts are not identical (cf. also the remark on 'two kinds of visible extension', one 'successive' and the other perceived at once 'by a confus'd view', in *Phil. Com.* 400, and n. 7 below). Thus, 'the idea of a Circle' may often be had 'without thinking' of *minima*, or 'points', 'whence it should seem' also that it 'is not made up of the ideas of points' (*Phil. Com.* 445). Berkeley's tentative answer to his own query (e.g. 'mem: nicely to discuss wt is meant when we say a line consists of a certain number of . . . points', ibid.), is that an idea of extension does *not* have to immediately include the 'constituents' into which it may be subdivided (see also *Phil. Com.* 400 and 443). This answer seems to refer even to cases in which a whole—e.g. a line, a surface—and its parts can be simultaneously seen or touched,[18] and, *a fortiori*, to cases in which they cannot be seen or touched in such a manner (e.g. to situations in which a part of an object occupies an entire field of vision, or in which 'the more we fix our sight on any one object, by so much the darker and more indistinct shall the rest appear'; *TV* 83). I have already indicated above that Berkeley's answer to his own query seems to refer not only to what he labels 'proper objects of sight', but also to 'proper objects of touch'. In fact, he does not specify in *Phil. Com.* 445–6 whether he refers to visible or tangible points (lines, circles, etc.), and prefers to cover both under common labels of 'perception' and 'thought'.[19] He emphasizes in *Phil. Com.* 445–6 his contention that real units of division may be distinguished in any given line, figure, or bit of extension, but does not refer in detail to the different extensions, which are mentioned in other entries of *Phil. Com.*, and regarded as opposed to the general abstract idea of extension, according to the nominalist and phenomenalist tendencies of his theory of perception. In brief, he says that the 'fixt constituents' of any given (i.e. on his premisses, sensible[20]) extension may be perceivable, and not actually perceived, from any finite epistemic point of view. From any finite epistemic point of view it may well be maintained that a geometrical figure (e.g. 'the idea of a Circle'), or a bit of extension, 'is not made up of the ideas of points, square inches, etc.'. Nevertheless, he says, it may be maintained that 'squares or points *may* be perceived in or made out of a Circle etc.', or even that 'they are actually in it' (as presumably perceived from the supposed infinite epistemic point of view). 'Points' 'are *perceivable* in a Circle',[21] and in other figures and bodies, from the respective points of view of various lesser 'spirits' and actually perceived by higher spirits and God. In a similar vein, he assumes that 'Tis a perfection we may imagine in superior spirits that they can see a great deal at once with the Utmost Clearness and distinction whereas we can only see a point' (*Phil. Com.* 835).

I shall proceed now to examine Berkeley's application of the above-mentioned closely connected theses, (*a*) that *minima sensibilia* are 'fixt', and (*b*) that no finite line may be subdivided *in infinitum*, to the various possible relations between physical bodies and their atoms (brought by him under the common denominator of 'tangible extension' and *m.t.*) on the one hand, and the arrangements of *visible minima* on the other. The Berkeleian analysis of haptic–optic co-ordinations is based on atomistic theory. His basic contention is that the 'fixt' 'elements and constituents' of tangible extension (which, incidentally, he also regards as fundamental and final units of geometrical measurement; e.g. instead of mathematical points) may not be dismantled into yet smaller parts. The young Berkeley's rejection of the prevailing corpuscularian hypotheses of his time had nothing in common with the rejection of the atomic composition of 'tangible extension',[22] nor with the rejection of existence of quanta of 'light and colours'. On the contrary, he was a convinced atomist in regard to both tangible and visible extensions. His reasons for his rejection of Locke's and Descartes' corpuscularian hypotheses[23] were twofold:

(*a*) Most of those hypotheses (e.g. the theory of real essence as expounded in Locke's *Essay*) represent a peculiar brand of corpuscularianism: namely, corpuscularianism blended with a theory of infinite divisibility.[24] Berkeley was in fact a much more orthodox atomist than those who held that there exist limits of division due to empirical difficulties, but still assumed that every physical and mathematical object (be it a particle of matter, a segment of extension, a number, etc.), and every unit of spatial and temporal measurement, may, at least in principle, be infinitely subdivided.[25]

According to the thesis of infinite divisibility every particle is, in a certain sense, infinite, having an infinite number of parts (cf., *inter alia*, Berkeley's criticism of this contention in *PHK* 47, and my Chapter 1, Section II above, which, however, does not analyse the relevant entries of *Phil. Com.* mentioned in this appendix). In his view, this supposedly absurd conclusion is entailed by (1) the 'matterist' premiss, and (2) the premiss of infinite divisibility which is made possible by the 'matterist' concept of unperceived 'non-epistemic' parts. He maintains, therefore, that the absurd conclusion invalidates the premisses.[26] He also relates this last argument to the discussion of *minima* and 'reasoning about infinitesimals'. His general standpoint in the cluster of entries 351–5 of *Phil. Com.* is that *minima sensibilia* are not involved in the paradoxes revealed in the concepts of (1) particles with 'an infinite number of parts', and of (2) 'infinitesimals' (to the extent that the infinitesimals indicate 'evanescent or nascent quantities' which lack any fixed value). Thus *Phil. Com.* 354, 354a, and 355 refer to infinitesimals, and the problem of 'an infinite particle' is dealt with in *Phil. Com.* 352: 'Evident yt wch has an infinite number of parts must be infinite'. In regard to infinitesimals, he says that we cannot meaningfully 'reason about' them to the extent that they are simultaneously supposed to be, and not to be, 'ideas'. (See also *Of Infinites*, vol. iv, pp. 235–6). On the other hand, the infinitesimals are, on his view, 'words, of no use, if not suppos'd to stand for Ideas' (*Phil. Com.* 354a). However, this last contention (the assumption that only 'reasoning about ideas' is useful) was finally discarded by Berkeley, as can be gleaned from the later entries of *Phil. Com.* onwards. In *Phil. Com.*, *Of Infinites*, and the *Analyst*, Berkeley consistently rejects the 'logic' of allegedly metaphysical premisses which accompany the new calculus. But this criticism of the 'logic' of the infinitesimal calculus must not be confused with the rejection of the entire relevant apparatus of mathematical notation, its techniques of computation and the correct 'conclusions' made possible by it. (The distinction between the 'logic' and the useful 'conclusions' of the infinitesimal calculus is also mentioned in *An*. 49.) In brief, Berkeley's criticism of the infinitesimal calculus is an attempt to purge mathematics of the 'nihilarianism' of infinite divisibility rather than a condemnation of the new mathematical machinery. Infinite divisibility, on Berkeley's view, is intimately connected with other incorrect metaphysical assumptions (e.g. 'matterism'[27]), and cannot, therefore, be accepted as one of the basic concepts of mathematics.[28]

(*b*) Berkeley's second reason for attacking the prevailing corpuscularian hypotheses of his age was the matterism of his opponents. Elementary particles, i.e. basic constituents of physical bodies, were considered by the corpuscularians (e.g. by Boyle and Locke on the one hand, and by the Cartesians on the other) as minute divisions of a supposedly *unperceived* extension, or *matter*. Now Berkeley discards not only an unperceivable (object of) perception,[29] but also an unperceived one as a mere *flatus vocis*, and, moreover, as a contradiction in terms. Accordingly, he holds that extension is nothing if not an object of perception.

2. CO-ORDINATION BETWEEN ATOMS OF TANGIBLE EXTENSION AND THEIR VISUAL *SIGNIFICANTIA*

I have tried to argue that Berkeley does not attack the 'corpuscularian philosophy' *per se*. Moreover, I have tried to show that the theory of minute parts is endorsed by him in *Phil. Com.* in its extreme atomist version, and incorporated within the framework of his immaterialistic ideism. He in fact criticizes and rejects there only the matterist and infinitist tenets blended with the 'corpuscularian philosophy' in general, and with atomism in particular. I have also pointed out that Berkeley's particular brand of atomism is characterized, among other things, by a tendency to regard *minima* as 'sensible atoms' which may be perceived by any given observer(s). However, on Berkeleian premises, there are no unqualified 'sensible atoms'. *Minima tangibilia* are different from *minima visibilia*, just as the tangible extension is different from the visible one. Accordingly, some problems arise in regard to the logical co-ordination between the applications of the concept of 'fixity' to *m.t.* on the one hand, and to *m.v.* on the other.

(*a*) *On interdependence of the 'fixity' of* minima visibilia *and* minima tangibilia

One of the crucial questions in this context, which in addition has a bearing on the status of visible extension in Berkeley's more general arguments, concerns the 'fixity' of *minima visibilia* that he continually emphasizes. Is this 'fixity' a theoretical premiss independent of any assumption with regard to *minima tangibilia*, or is it ultimately based on the 'fixity' of *m.t.*?

It can be maintained that the 'fixity' of *minima visibilia* is introduced by Berkeley not simply because of its own merits, but as an implication of the hypothesis of the atomic composition of the tangible extension. One reason for such an argument may be that Berkeley himself tends sometimes to argue that any given bit of visible extension is already blended[30] not only with this or other colour, but also with 'tangible ideas'. At times he says things that seem to indicate that without tangible extension there would be no visible one, the proper and immediate objects of sight being only light and colours (cf. *TV* 129–30; and also nn. 32 and 33 to this appendix). According to this 'stronger' thesis[31] with regard to (1) differences between visual and tangible extensions, and (2) the characteristic features of visual extension (Berkeley's 'weaker' thesis concerning (1) and (2) is simply that the tangible extension and its visible counterpart are heterogeneous), even bi-dimensional, and not only three-dimensional, visual manifolds are conditioned and 'mediated' by kinaesthetic and tactual information. It would seem, therefore, that the 'constituents and elements' of the 'secondary'[32] and 'mediated' extension, i.e. *minima visibilia*, also require to be 'mediated' by the 'constituents and elements' of the 'primary' one, i.e. by *minima tangibilia*. According to this line of reasoning, the atomic composition of the 'secondary' extension will only be made possible by the atomic composition of the 'primary' one. In a similar vein, it may well seem that the 'fixity' of the constituents of the derived extension has to be based on the 'fixity' of the constituents of its more elementary, immediate and stabler counterpart (see also n. 32 below). However, these last suggestions do not necessarily follow from the premisses of Berkeley's atomism, and, moreover, contradict his theory of the atomic composition of visual extension.

First, it is not really clear whether he employs the concept of *m.v.* when speaking of visual *extension* only (i.e. when referring to bi-dimensional manifolds which appear in the ordinary visual experience and have to be regarded as different from mere luminescence, or darkness). It seems sometimes that even 'proper objects of light', i.e. 'light and colours', are regarded by him as composed of *minima*. The very constitution of bi-dimensional visual manifolds may be explained by referring to correlations between quanta of light and colours (*m.v.*) and physical atoms (*m.t.*) only in so far as light and colours are considered as composed of the smallest units of *intensity*, or of the smallest units of visual extension which as yet are *not* organized and arranged within one continuous and comprehensive context. That is to say, according to Berkeley's 'stronger' thesis concerning visual extension, even the constitution of bi-dimensional manifolds of 'light and colours' depends on optic–haptic correlations; but *minima* of 'light and colours' are regarded as epistemically prior to their arrangement in an extension (see especially *Phil. Com.* 59). Berkeley tries to co-ordinate in *Phil. Com.* 59 his answer to the 'Molyneux problem'[33] (and the epistemic and linguistic clarifications—e.g. of the term *extension*—which are embedded in, and follow, this answer), with a completely theoretical assumption concerning the existence of *minima*. However, the crux of the matter is that he co-ordinates these two contentions not by indicating that there are no *minima visibilia* prior to the constitution of the visible extension, but rather by assuming that the constitution of the visible extension depends on co-ordination between basic units of light and colours (*m.v.*) and *m.t.* In other words, he assumes that it depends on 'how *m.t.* would look'. He says: 'Blind at first sight could not know yt wt he saw was extended, until he had seen and touch'd some one self something. Not knowing how *minimum tangibile* would look.' Here he applies to the 'Molyneux problem' his 'stronger thesis' on extension: the congenitally blind would not know 'at first sight that what he saw was *extended*' (my italics). 'A person blind from infancy' (cf. *TVV* 71) would not know 'at first sight' that what he sees is extended, or that geometrical figures appear in his visual field (e.g. in a 'sphaera visualis'), not only because the tangible and visible extended figures are heterogeneous (this last contention has been labelled above the 'weaker thesis'), but also because visible extension has to be constituted and organized by mediation of touch, i.e. to be ultimately based on tangible manifolds. The basic 'extensional' co-ordination and lack of co-ordination between *m.v.* and *m.t.* represent here the parallel co-ordination and lack of co-ordination of their medium-sized counterparts. In the same vein, Berkeley sometimes assumes even when not speaking of geometry that various visible events or relations (say, changes of distance, and estimates of location) cannot be differentiated in total absence of bodies and kinaesthetic measurement. However, he does not say, even in cases where he applies the 'stronger thesis' that there are no minimal visual data prior to the constitution of visible extension. Thus, for instance, it is clear that on his view the intensity of light may not be infinitely diminished.[34] He maintains rather that the minimal units of light and colours have yet to be correlated with the corresponding *tangibilia* in order to constitute an orderly visible manifold. This theoretical assumption logically completes Berkeley's partly empirical premiss that the congenitally blind given sight have first to learn the mutual correlations of visible data, or of bits of visible extension, and also their correlations with their tangible counterparts.[35] The very same assumption concerning correlations of *m.v.* and *m.t.* also provides a theoretical basis for co-ordination of visible figures (say, lines and circles) with their tangible counterparts. The contention that the 'visible extension is a *continuity* [*my italics*] of visible points' (*Phil. Com.* 78a) need not be understood as relegating the *visibilia* to the realm of the ordered extension only, i.e. to the realm of unified visible manifolds. Even a flickering havoc of light and colours may yet consist, on these premisses, of discontinuous visible *minima*, or sets of *minima*[36] (but in this last case it seems that one must avoid any reference to the visualization of 'gaps' between the seen 'parts', or, at least, *not* consider them as *extended* dark *stretches*). A *minimum visibile* may, on this view, be compared to 'a sound so small that it is scarce perceiv'd' (*Phil. Com.* 710). This assumption of *minima audibilia* would not in itself necessitate any hypothesis in regard to the arrangement of such minimal units within a unified framework of audible *extension*, or *space*. In a similar vein, the assumption concerning the existence of *m.v.*, the basic quanta of light and colours, does not necessitate any hypothesis with regard to their arrangement within a unified context, be it of extension or space.

To sum up: the argument that the existence and 'fixity' of *minima visibilia* have to depend on the existence and 'fixity' of *m.t.* is based on the contention that the visible extension is 'secondary' only, being 'blended' with, and initially organized by means of reference to, the 'primary' tangible extension. However, this argument seems to be rather unconvincing. Even if the visible extension were always 'blended' with the tangible one (but this is a very spurious contention, and Berkeley himself had second thoughts about it—see, among other references, nn. 31 and 32 below), it would not automatically follow (*a*) that *m.v.* may only exist as parts of visible extension, i.e. within a framework of a well-ordered and continuous bi-dimensional manifold; and (*b*) that units (e.g. *m.v.*) of an orderly extension (or, for that matter, of discontinuous presentations) have to be always correlated in the same manner as fixed tangible *minima* within any simultaneously perceived and static frame of reference.[37]

However, there is another argument in favour of the dependence of *m.v.*'s existence and 'fixity' on the existence and 'fixity' of *m.t.*, which should be taken into account. Space, or three-dimensional manifold, is relegated by Berkeley to the realm of 'tangible ideas' both on the 'stronger' and 'weaker' view concerning the visual surfaces, or visual two-dimensional manifolds.[38] Space, or distance, is always considered by him as primarily tactual, or kinaesthetic, whereas he constantly wavers (and, indeed, is not able to be consistent at all) in respect to the rejection of the primarily visual bi-dimensional extension (see also nn. 31 and 32 below). Space is, on his view, (1) a kinaesthetic datum which is identified with the idea of motion without resistance, and may accordingly exist even in cases when there exists only one moving body, or, indeed, only one moving *m.t.*, and (2) a relative frame of reference between two, or more, *tangibilia*.[39] *M.t.* which are, on his view, basic units of three-dimensional bodies and kinaesthetic measurement, have, accordingly, to be more closely related to what he considered as the only real space, and also to what he did sometimes consider as the 'primary' extension, than their visible counterparts whose extended arrangements are regarded by him mainly as well-ordered sets of *significantia* corresponding to authentically spatial *significanda*.[40] This contention (with regard to the priority of non-visual space, and of non-visual measurement and its units of division) is endorsed by Berkeley in *PHK* and *TV* alike.

It is true that the status of *minima tangibilia* in *TV* is rather doubtful, because the theory of indivisibility, and presumably also the thesis of 'fixity', of *m.t.*, as introduced for instance in sect. 54, seem to be inconsistent with Berkeley's *ad interim* contention in *TV* that physical objects exist 'without the mind' (see, for example, sect. 55). According to this contention, physical objects may be regarded not only as existing in three-dimensional 'ambient space', be it relative or 'absolute', but also as different from 'sensible extension' (sect. 54), be it tangible or visible, and, accordingly, as not necessarily divisible into ultimate epistemic units. Berkeley sometimes tries in *TV* to blur and minimize the above-mentioned distinction between tangible extension, composed of *m.t.*, and matter. On the one hand, he certainly may be understood as referring to unperceived physical objects, whose existence was assumed by his 'matterist' opponents when saying: 'The magnitude . . . which exists without the mind, and is at distance, continues always invariably the same' (*TV* 55), although the very expression 'without the mind' is systematically ambiguous because it refers to three-dimensionality and matter alike. (See n. 44 below.) In a similar vein, Berkeley himself admits (in *PHK* 44) that the 'vulgar error' of conceding the existence of material objects had been *temporarily* accepted in *TV*, where he reminds the reader that that 'vulgar error' had not been an inherent part of his doctrine, and also explicitly asserts that what had been assumed in *TV* to exist 'without the mind' was, in fact, 'tangible object'. Nevertheless, in many sections of *TV* he identifies, for all practical purposes, material and tangible objects. Thus in *TV* 55 he identifies 'the tangible object' which one recedes from, or approaches to, with 'the object which exists without the mind, and is at a distance'. But, in spite of this confusion, it is quite clear that extension 'without the mind', and 'particles of matter' which are mentioned in *TV*,[41] may not be simply identified with the tangible extension and *m.t.*

According to Berkeley's exposition in *TV* 54, the two 'sensible extensions' are composed of *minima*. This atomic composition of both 'sensible extensions' is the real basis of any reference to absolute magnitude, that is of the possibility of objective measurement. 'Each of these magnitudes are greater or lesser, according as they contain in them more or fewer points, they being made up of points or minimums' (ibid.). However, Berkeley does not say in *TV* that physical objects in space are bits of tangible (and, *ipso facto*, *perceived*) extension, since he wants to refer there to *material* bodies as well. Accordingly, his reference to *m.t.* has to be understood as applied in *TV* to epistemic points of 'sensible extension' only, and not as necessarily indicating units of division of physical objects. Therefore it is not surprising that he says in *TV* that the tangible extension consists of *m.t.*, whereas the physical 'things' are composed of 'particles of matter'.[42] It also follows that, according to *TV*, space and real physical objects may well be infinitely divisible (since Berkeley connects matter with infinite divisibility), and, in any case, are not to be divided into *m.t.*, because it is not explicitly asserted that the tangible extension is the only extension of external bodies. The hypothesis that physical bodies are identical with tangible ones, or, at least, composed of particles in one-to-one correspondence with *m.t.*, is not actually discarded in *TV*; but *m.t.* are certainly relegated to the inferior realm of epistemic differentiation and 'sensible' measurement[43] (in a sharp contrast to ontic and 'insensible' existence of matter and its presumably divisible and heterogeneous particles). 'Particles of matter', the concept of which seems to be employed in *TV* as a didactic device, are introduced at this period of half-way materialism as a sort of *ad interim* candidate for the basic units of objective measurement.[44] In *TV* even the sensible tangible-cum-kinaesthetic three-dimensional manifolds have to be regarded only as epistemic indications of physical space; and the visual three-dimensionality had to be, as it were, doubly removed from reality. It had then to be considered as an analogue of tangible three-dimensionality, based in its turn on physical bodies and space.

In any case, the contention that space is non-visual, or that there is no visual space, was not abandoned by Berkeley even within the framework of his full-fledged immaterialism, from *PHK* onwards, according to which the kinaesthetic three-dimensionality *is* the physical space (in all cases when there is no resistance to be met), and visible ideas are as real as bodies.[45] But after the *TV* period he explicitly commits himself to the views that space is not an absolute frame of reference, and that spatial relations and their bodily terms may not exist unperceived. His view in *TV* that space is not immediately revealed by sight,[46] because it is *'without the mind'*, is represented (and remodelled) in *PHK* and later texts as an assertion that space is related to tangible bodies and their movements, and not to sight. This contention that there is no visual space seems also to be endorsed by him much more strongly than the parallel view with regard to bi-dimensional manifolds (cf. references above to the 'blended' extension, and also n. 32 below). Accordingly, the 'fixity' of *m.v.* seems to be more problematic than the 'fixity' of *m.t.* *M.t.* function, on Berkeley's premises, as units of extension and (kinaesthetic) space alike, whereas *m.v.* are detached, as it were, from any immediate reference to space, and have to be 'mediated' by *m.t.* whenever (three-dimensional, and perhaps even two- and one-dimensional) motion and spatial measurement are involved. *M.t.*, 'tangible inches', etc., were always regarded by Berkeley as more valuable and objective units of measurement than their visible counterparts (cf., for instance, his arguments in *TV* 61 which do not seem to be made null and void by the explicit rejection of the concept of matter in *PHK*).

However, it seems to me that Berkeley's rejection of the immediacy of visual space, or of visually achieved concepts of space, and subsequent hesitations as to whether arrangements of *m.v.* may have a status equal to that of arrangements of *m.t.*, are both unfounded for two different reasons, of which one is empirical, and the other deals with the logical coherence of Berkeley's own theory.

First, the epistemic primacy of kinaesthetically achieved spatial concepts, which Berkeley assumes as a premiss, and sometimes tries to validate by arguments from perception, is far from being established (see n. 35 below). Secondly, even on the Berkeleian premisses, there is no need to assume that space, or spatial concepts, are exclusively, or primarily, kinaesthetic, as there is nothing in the thesis of heterogeneity of 'proper objects' of sight and touch which *necessitates* such a conclusion. Moreover, the thesis of heterogeneity may even be regarded as being in favour of visual space. The 'argument from kinaesthetic space' (in favour of the dependence of 'fixity' of *m.v.* on 'fixity' of *m.t.*) may, therefore, be discarded. The thesis of 'fixity' of *m.v.*[47] may be directly based on Berkeley's general atomistic premisses, not as an outcome of the 'fixity' of *m.t.*, but as a theoretical assumption which corresponds to, while being independent of, its counterpart within the realm of kinematics[48] and mechanics. In brief, the 'fixity' of *m.v.* may be directly derived from the atomistic and finitist premisses of Berkeley's immaterialism, without any reference to *m.t.* And this, in fact, is what Berkeley does in spite of his reservations with regard to the visual space and 'blended' extension. See, for instance, *TV* 80–1 where he argues, *inter alia*, that the '*minimum visibile* is exactly equal in all beings whatsoever that are endowed with the visive faculty.' Thus, every finite visible extension is regarded as composed of a finite number of *minima* which may be enumerated with equal results by 'all beings whatsoever'. Moreover, such an enumeration is conceived of as independent of any tactile and kinaesthetic faculties or activities. (Cf. also *TV* 54.) The highly theoretical thesis of 'fixity' is, accordingly, applied by Berkeley to (1) *m.v.* and the visual manifolds, and (2) *m.t.* and 'bodies', without interpreting the suggested atomic structure of (1) as dependent on the suggested atomic structure of (2).[49] The mutual independence of different manifolds and their respective *minima* is summarized as follows in *TV* 54:

> It hath been shewn there are two sorts of objects apprehended by sight; *each whereof hath its distinct magnitude, or extension.* The one, properly tangible, *i.e.* to be perceived and measured by touch, and not immediately falling under the sense of seeing: The other, properly and immediately visible, by mediation of which the former is brought in

view. *Each of these magnitudes are greater or lesser according as they contain in them more or fewer points, they being made up of points or minimums* [*my italics*].

(*b*) *On numerical relation between* minima visibilia *and* minima tangibilia

The assumption that *minima* (the 'simplest, constituent parts or elements' of extension) are 'fixt' is, of course, not to be understood as indicating that *minima tangibilia* have to be, or are, uniformly correlated with *minima visibilia*.

According to Berkeley, *minima tangibilia*, the 'simplest, constituent parts or elements' of the tangible extension, are not always signified by the same number of *minima visibilia*. (I of course refer here to any *given* number of *m.t.*). Let us assume that a tangible object X is composed of Y 'sensible atoms'. Now, in one state of affairs, X (i.e. Y) would be visually signified by W *minima visibilia*, i.e. by a certain purely visual magnitude. However, in another state of affairs, X (i.e. Y) may well be represented by Z *minima visibilia* (Z may, of course, be either greater or smaller than W), i.e. by another purely visual magnitude. (The purely visual magnitude is defined in two alternative, but not necessarily exclusive, ways in *Phil. Com.* 256: (1) as 'relation to the Sphaera Visualis', or (2) as 'relation to the M.[inimum] V:[isibile]'.[50] Berkeley says that such relations are 'all that I would have meant by our having a greater picture' (ibid.).) In a similar vein, the same number of visual quanta, i.e. of *minima* of light and colours, may, in different times and situations, stand for widely different physical objects, or particles (be they 'continuities' of *m.t.*, or 'particles of matter' mentioned in *An Appendix* to *TV*). Moreover, says Berkeley, there is no necessary correlation between (1) an increase in the tangible size (e.g. as considered not in its relative 'greatness' or 'smallness', but as an absolute magnitude enumerated by its own atoms), and (2) an increase of its visible counterpart. Berkeley even emphasizes that 'Tis possible (and perhaps not very improbable that it is sometimes so) we may have the greatest pictures from the least objects' (*Phil. Com.* 256). A great visible extension 'might possibly have stood for or signify'd small tangible extensions' (ibid.). The empirical example he gives there is as follows: 'Certainly the *greater* relation to S.V.: and M:V. does [*i.e. does 'signify small tangible extensions'*] frequently in yt men view *little* objects near the Eye' [*my italics*]. His conclusion is, therefore, that (1) 'no necessary connexion' obtains between visible and tangible magnitudes, and (2) in many instances there is, in fact, no fixed connection between these two magnitudes in the *rerum natura* (ibid.). Berkeley's epistemological analysis indicates, first, that correlations between visual and (what one may call) physical magnitudes should not be regarded as necessarily constant (even in absence of any examples of lack of constancy). However, he adds, the lack of constancy of the above-mentioned correlations is also an empirical feature of many occurrences in the universe. 'Visible magnitudes' and 'tangible objects' *might*, of course, be correlated in unchanging proportions. But such fixed correspondence need not be regarded as necessary. Moreover, while it occurs in nature, its occurrence is not universal. The again, the actually shifting correlations between, say, physical stars and towers and their 'pictures' (for 'pictures' cf., *inter alia, TVV* 52–8) are much more complicated than they might be in another (and simpler, e.g. stabler) universe. (These last considerations are very intimately connected with the first two divisions—on distance and magnitude—in *TV*; and, in fact, the relevant entry in *Phil. Com.* (256) is accompanied by the marginal signs *1 × 2* which refer to mathematics in a broad sense, and to the discussion of distance and magnitude in *TV*. In addition, Berkeley's references to 'pictures' are pertinent to his discussion of situation and heterogeneity of sight and touch.)

Now one may certainly agree with Berkeley that the existence of any given physical object, whose magnitude is fixed, may be, and sometimes is, indicated by *various* 'visual magnitudes'. (Consider, for instance, two observers whose visual fields are organized in different ways, all other conditions being equal; or, again, consider one observer, looking consecutively at a star, or a tower, from increasingly remote spatial locations, etc.) Moreover, even the correlations between increasing distances (e.g. when one is being driven away from a star, or a tower) and decreasing visual magnitudes lack a complete uniform (e.g. an inversely proportional) correspondence. In addition, in some cases, greater visual magnitudes do *not* indicate changes of distance. And this is also what Berkeley argues concerning the 'Moon Illusion' and other cases unsolved by the Geometrical Theory of Vision which depended too much on fixed angular measurement. However, it should be mentioned that, on Berkeley's view, the lack of necessary, or, for that matter, factual, constancy characterizes not only correlations between heterogeneous extensions, but also correlations between heterogeneous *minima* (*visibilia* and *tangibilia*).

It should also be noted that the contention concerning varying correlations between *extensions* is partly an empirical, and partly an epistemological analysis of actual states of affairs; whereas the ascription of lack of constancy to correlations between heterogeneous *minima* is a purely theoretical move, to the extent that *minima* are hypothetical constructs rather than empirical phenomena 'noticed', or discovered, by human observers.[51] It is true that, according to Berkeley, the assumption of a one-to-one correspondence between *m.v.* and *m.t.* is the most convenient hypothesis (which, in regard to limits, or 'thresholds', of perception of humans, and of certain animals, may also be based on correlations of actual abilities of visual and tactual differentiation of 'points'). On his view, 'it is convenient the same thing which is *M.V.* should also be *M.T.*' (*Phil. Com.* 869). But, nevertheless, he assumes that a one-to-one correspondence between heterogeneous *minima* may well be impaired by certain asymmetries. *M.v.* may just be 'very near' *m.t.* in absence of a one-to-one correspondence (ibid.). In brief, Berkeley emphasizes that the assumption of a one-to-one correspondence of the heterogeneous *minima* is only the most convenient hypothesis (or, in the same vein, the most convenient correlation between various epistemic units, or 'points' of human differentiation). But he also most explicitly stipulates that 'it might have been otherwise' (ibid.). Moreover, in *TV* 62 he even says that the lack of constancy in relations between the 'two distinct extensions' may be explained by the lack of constancy in relations between heterogeneous *minima*, and speaks neither of empirical asymmetries between visual magnitudes and bodies, nor of a purely epistemic analysis, e.g. as employed in the solution of the 'Moon Illusion', which does not refer to *minima*. He says that the correspondence between the 'two distinct extensions' might be less symmetric and constant than it is at present,[52] or even disappear, because, for instance, we might 'be able to see nothing but what were less than the *minimum tangibile*'. This example brings matters to the extremes. However, he did not really need to have recourse to a model of a state of affairs in which there would be no haptic–optic correlations. It would have been sufficient for him merely to point out that varying numbers of *m.v.* may correspond to one *m.t.*, just as he indicated in many entries and sections of *Phil. Com.* and *TV* that various 'visible extensions' may, and sometimes do, signify one physical (i.e., on his view, tangible) object.

In any case, the main features of this theoretical move (i.e. the ascription of lack of constancy to correlations between *m.t.* and *m.v.*) are not to be regarded as logically or empirically connected with any observations, experiments, or descriptive generalizations of perceptual evidence. The lack of constant correlations between sight and touch (or between bi-dimensional visual magnitudes and three-dimensional physical objects in space, etc.) does not necessitate the very assumption of quanta and atoms. In addition, human epistemic 'points', limits, or 'thresholds' of perception may be regarded as completely different from quanta and atoms, or, indeed, from any real *minima* (that is to say from the least and last units of measurement in the *rerum natura*). Therefore the ascription of lack of constancy to correlations within the realm of *minima* is neither an empirical assertion, nor is it necessitated by what I have previously called Berkeley's 'stronger' and 'weaker' theses concerning differences between 'proper objects of sight' and 'proper objects of touch'. The ascription of lack of constancy to the realm of *minima* may only be deduced from the conjunction of two premises which do not refer to empirical evidence concerning 'points': (*a*) tangible and visible magnitudes are heterogeneous, and not necessarily correlated in constant manner; and (*b*) both hetero-geneous extensions are characterized by an atomic composition. Obviously, (*a*) means that one-to-one correlation between the physical size of an object and its visual magnitude is sometimes not to be found; and if a conjunction of (*a*) *and* (*b*) is assumed, i.e. if, in addition to (*a*), both 'extensions' (i.e., the physical size and the visual magnitude) are regarded as not capable of subdivision *in infinitum*, it is also rather difficult to maintain that (*c*) the heterogeneous *minima,* the last and least units of division, are to be regarded as uniformly correlated according to fixed numerical proportions.[53] Therefore, even Berkeley's own cursory remark in favour of the possible 'convenience' of such one-to-one correspondence of heterogeneous *minima* (see again *Phil. Com.* 869) may be regarded as justifiable from the point of view of simplicity only, and not as entailed by the logic of his own theory.

In any event, the direct correlations which, on Berkeley's view, may be said to prevail between heterogeneous *minima* (even without referring to co-existence of various 'extensions') have to be classified as follows: (*a*) one *m.v.* stands for several *m.t.*; (*b*) several *m.v.* stand for one *m.t.*; and (*c*) one *m.v.* stands for one *m.t.* All these correlations do not assume an existence of *two* different and well-ordered *manifolds.* Such manifolds are only possible on the assumption that (*d*)x *m.v.* correspond to y *m.t.*, when $x > 1$ and $y > 1$ (but various values of x/y or y/x need not, of course, be integers). It is also noteworthy that even according to (*d*) one yet may get a multiplicity, or rather two multiplicities, of *minima* instead of two different and well-ordered manifolds. In a similar vein (*c*) certainly does not refer to any manifold whatsoever, and (*a*) and (*b*) refer, at most, to one manifold only.

However, as I have already indicated above, in *TV* Berkeley seems to suggest a provisional semi-materialist scheme for various relations between visual quanta (i.e. *minima* of 'light and colours') and units of division of physical bodies. This alternative scheme refers to *m.v.* and 'particles of matter' and to the lack of constancy in their relations. Accordingly, the problem of constancy of correlations between visual quanta and their non-visual *significanda* has to be examined not only against the background of *m.t.*, but also within the frame of reference to material particles. Here, too, one has to take into account four subdivisions: (*a*) one *m.v.* stands for several particles of matter[54]; (*b*) several *m.v.* stand for one particle of matter; (*c*) one *m.v.* stands for one particle of matter; and (*d*) x *m.v.* stand for y particles of matter when $x > 1$ and $y > 1$. The *minima* of 'light and colours' mentioned in *TV* have to be correlated not only to the tangible *minima* but also to *material particles* whose existence had then been admitted by Berkeley. He speaks in *TV* of *minima tangibilia* (see, for instance, sects. 54 and 62). Now these tangible *minima* may be regarded as identical with material particles to the extent that he identified in *TV* to all purposes the 'tangible object' and the 'object without the mind',[55] and, as I have already mentioned above, 'without the mind'[56] means not just 'in real space', but also 'independent of perception' (see G. J. Warnock, *Berkeley*, 2nd edn. pp. 57–8). An alternative move would be to regard *m.t.* as representative *ideas*, i.e. as representations, or, at least, analogues, of material particles. In this last case, each *m.t.* has to be conceived as an indivisible representation of a material particle which, in its turn, would be subjected to all the queries about the infinite divisibility. And the evaluation of the status of divisible material particles as compared with that of indivisible *m.t.* has an obvious bearing on estimates of numerical proportions between them and *m.v.*

Berkeley agrees with the vast majority of the 'corpuscularians' that an *unperceived extension*, or *matter*, has to be infinitely divisible.[57] He therefore assumes that the rejection of the concept of *matter* (which is, on his view, a logical monstrosity) has to be accompanied by a devastating attack on the concept of the infinite divisibility. If the 'tangible extension' were really identified in *TV* with *material* objects in real[58] space, it would follow, on Berkeley's own premisses,[59] that the 'tangible extension' and distance are not only 'without the mind', but also infinitely divisible. However, such a conclusion would be in sharp contrast to his basic contention that 'sensible extension is not infinitely divisible', which is maintained by him not only in *Phil. Com.* and *PHK*, but even during the 'as-if' half-materialist period of *TV* (e.g. in sect. 54). He could not, accordingly, assume that *m.t.* are identical with particles of matter, nor simply identify numerical proportions obtaining between *m.v.* and *m.t.* with those obtaining between *m.v.* and particles of matter, despite various references to 'tangible objects without the mind' which might, no doubt, create an opposite impression. The only alternative move open to him, by which he could attempt to defend his assumption of *m.t.* in the half-materialist context of *TV*, was obviously to regard *m.t.* as Lockean-like[60] epistemic points that exist separately from, but which, presumably, represent, particles of matter. And, indeed, despite partial and quite confused identifications of the *tangible extension* and its parts with *matter* and its parts, Berkeley develops in *TV* a more consistent *ad interim* line of reasoning, according to which particles of matter are mentioned quite independently of *m.t.* In other words, he tries to eliminate certain inner inconsistencies, inherent in his use of the concepts of *m.t.* and 'tangible objects' in *TV*, by referring to particles proper, i.e. to material corpuscles assumed by Gassendi and Boyle, Newton and the Cartesians. In addition, he also refers to various (for example, numerical) correlations between these material corpuscles (or their tangible analogues) and *minima visibilia*.

As I have already mentioned, Berkeley refers to particles of matter in a highly interesting passage in *An Appendix* to the second edition of *TV*. This passage in *An Appendix* is of great importance, so I quote it in its entirety:

Thirdly, against what is said in Sect. 80 [*where Berkeley assumes the 'fixity' of m.v.*] it is objected that the same thing which is so small as scarce to be discerned by a man may appear like a mountain to some small insect; from which it follows that the *minimum visibile* is not equal in respect of all creatures. I answer, if this objection be sounded to the bottom it will be found to mean no more than that the same *particle of matter* [*my italics*], which is marked to a man by one *minimum visibile* exhibits to an insect a great number of *minima visibilia*. But this does not prove that one *minimum visibile* of the insect is not equal to one *minimum visibile* of the man. The not distinguishing between the mediate and immediate objects of sight is, I suspect, a cause of misapprehension in this matter.

It is perhaps noteworthy that, besides introducing the concept of 'particle of matter', Berkeley here also emphasizes again the 'fixity' of *m.v.* It is also very conspicuous that he does not reject a corpuscularian hypothesis of Gassendi, mentioned in *An Appendix* few lines before the passage quoted above, although he does reject a geometrical part of Gassendi's solution to the 'problem of magnitude' as exemplified by the appearance of the horizontal moon (and sun). (Berkeley refers to Gassendi's *Epist. I de apparente Magnitudine solis humilis et sublimis.*)

In addition, he also mentioned rather grosser particles in *TV* 68 ('the particles which compose our atmosphere') and 72 ('the particles of the intermediate air and vapours'). But terms like 'the particles of . . . air', etc., almost verge on reference to the chemical composition of known compounds, whereas the above-mentioned passage in *An Appendix* deals with corpuscularian hypotheses on a more general and theoretical level. Besides, *An Appendix* is the only place in *TV* where particles are explicitly referred to as 'material'.

It seems, therefore, that the lack of constancy in relations between (1) quanta of 'light and colours', and (2) atoms, or particles, which 'exist without the mind', may be, and, in fact, is, spoken of in *TV* in two different senses, or presented in two different versions. According to both versions the tangible frame of reference has to be considered as 'primary', and its visible counterpart as 'secondary' only. However, according to the first version, *m.v.* are correlated to *m.t.* which, in their turn, may be considered either as identified with parts of 'tangible objects without the mind',[61] or as representing, and epistemically existing (say, at intermittent intervals) side by side with, matter and its particles.[62] On the other hand, according to the second version, one may also refer to direct correlations between *m.v.* and particles of matter (see, especially, *An Appendix* to *TV*).

Both these versions are completely superseded by the logical conclusions of Berkeley's full-fledged immaterialism in *PHK* which are, on the whole, identical with his initial arguments in *Phil. Com.* Moreover, the very contention that visual magnitudes in general, and *m.v.* in particular, are mere signs of *significanda*, whose tangible existence is somewhat more real than that of 'light and colours', does not survive in Berkeley's later writings, and is radically changed and reformulated from *PHK* onwards. Thus, according to the consistent version of immaterialism held in *PHK* , the tangible extension is not more real than any other 'ideas of sense'. Every *significans* may now function as 'a thing signified', and vice versa. The four above-mentioned possibilities of correlations between *m.v.* and *m.t.* may accordingly, be rewritten as follows: (*a*) several *m.t.* stand for one *m.v.*; (*b*) one *m.t.* stands for several *m.v.*; (*c*) one *m.t.* stands for one *m.v.*; and (*d*) *y* *m.t.* stand for *x m.v.*[63]

The above analysis shows that Berkeley's contention (1) that 'sensible atoms' and visual quanta, the least and last units of division in the *rerum natura*, may be identically enumerated by any observers whatever is accompanied by (2) an emphatic rejection of a fixed (e.g. one-to-one) correspondence between the heterogeneous units of visible and tangible extensions; i.e. between the visible and tangible *minima* (which are considered as independent from one another, despite Berkeley's contention that visual space, and perhaps even visual extension, depend on their tangible counterparts). However, it should also be noted that Berkeley develops, within the framework of his early atomism in *Phil. Com.* and *TV*, yet another thesis (3), namely that each observer (or each kind of observer) 'perceives at all times' an *equal number* of *minima*. Thus, for instance, Berkeley says in *TV* 82, after having referred to *m.v.* in *TV* 81, that 'of these visible points we see at all times an equal number'. And his argument in favour of this rather unexpected contention seems to indicate that it is applicable to the tangible *minima* as well. Now, in my view, Berkeley's thesis (3) on *minima* is not implied by his theses (1) and (2) as above, although it is very ingenious. However, I am not able, because of limitations of space, to deal with it here, and I hope to devote a separate essay to it.[64]

Did Popper Misunderstand Berkeley?

I

Berkeley's philosophy of science, so Karl Popper has been telling us time and again, is simply an early example of Machian instrumentalism. In his essay *A Note on Berkeley as Precursor of Mach and Einstein*[1] (hereafter referred to as *A Note*) he tells us that the most fashionable conception of science today is a Berkeleian or Machian positivism, or instrumentalism.[2] Similarly, in his 'Replies to My Critics' (1974) Popper asserts that 'Berkeley and Mach regarded "atom" and "corpuscle" as metaphysical terms'. And in *The Demarcation between Science and Metaphysics* he asserts: 'Most of the concepts with which physics works, such as forces, fields, and even electrons and *other particles* [*my emphasis*], are what Berkeley (for example) called "*qualitates occultae*".'[3] It seems, therefore, that, in Popper's view, Berkeley is a convinced instrumentalist and opposed to any realist interpretation of 'the corpuscularian philosophy'.

Popper continually ascribes to Berkeley an extreme form of instrumentalism. I simply do not have the space to quote all his utterances on this subject; however, I cannot resist quoting the following passage from his essay in *Conjectures and Refutations*:

> Today the view of physical science founded by Osiander, Cardinal Bellarmino and Bishop Berkeley has won the battle without another shot being fired. Without any further debate over the philosophical issue, without producing any new argument, the *instrumentalist view* [*original italics*] (as I shall call it) has become an accepted dogma (pp. 99–100).

Such an interpretation of Berkeley's views on corpuscularianism was put forward also by other Berkeleian scholars and is quite characteristic of the traditional image of Berkeley as a convinced anti-corpuscularian. Thus Dawes Hicks says (in his *Berkeley* (London, 1932), p. 115 n. 1): 'I am not, *of course*, implying that Berkeley would have admitted the existence of atoms and molecules . . .' [*my italics*]. It seems, therefore, that Popper's misinterpretation of Berkeley's evaluation of the 'corpuscularian philosophy' was foreshadowed by some previous research. Thus, according to Dawes Hicks and Popper, even molecules cannot be considered as real on Berkeley's supposedly 'Machian' view. But Dawes Hicks does not, at least, mention Berkeley's corpuscularianism in *Siris*, whereas Popper mentions and misinterprets it.

Moreover, in *Unended Quest: An Intellectual Autobiography*, (London and Suffolk, 1976), p. 152, Popper asserts anew that Mach and Berkeley alike were vehement opponents of atomism and the 'corpuscular' theory of matter, which they regarded as metaphysical (and here he refers again to his Machian interpretation of Berkeley in *A Note*). Now Berkeley certainly considered *matter* as a metaphysical term with neither use nor reference; but, in sharp contrast to Mach's views, he did *not* consider *particles, corpuscles*, etc., as metaphysical, or unnecessary terms. And in *Postscript to the Logic of Scientific Discovery* (London, 1985), p. 105, Popper says: 'Hume . . . followed Berkeley who had dismissed atomic theories as meaningless, and he was in his turn followed by Mach'. But Berkeley's early *minima*-theory *is* atomistic, and his corpuscularian theories in *Siris* are not anti-atomistic. In regard to Mach's rejection of the reality of atoms and his doubts whether corpuscularian theories were of much use, cf., *inter alia*, *The Analysis of Sensations* (English trs., La Salle, Ill., 1960), p. 599.

[For the rejection of the contention that Mach finally accepted the reality of atoms after having been shown alpha-ray scintillations, see J. T. Blackmore, *Ernst Mach, His Work, Life and Influence* (University of California Press, 1972), pp. 319–23. For an analysis of Lenin's view in his *Materialism and Empiriocriticism* that Mach was a Berkeleian instrumentalist, and that Berkeley was a proto-Machian in the philosophy of science (although much more honest than his Austrian follower), see my 'Lenin, Mach and Berkeley', *Proceedings of the Israeli Association for Studies of Marx and Socialism* (Haifa, 1983), 165–78 (in Hebrew). And see also D. Flamm's article, 'Boltzmann: His Influence on Science', *Studies in History and Philosophy of Science*, 14/4 (1983), 255–78, and especially p. 273: 'On the continent the spiritual leader of the movement against atoms was Ernst Mach. He declared that atomistics is pure metaphysics. Even after radioactive decay and Brownian movement had provided strong support for atomistics he would not accept it.' Flamm, a grandson of Boltzmann, tries in his article, among other things, to describe the historical background of the Boltzmann-Mach controversy. See also P. K. Feyerabend, 'Mach's Theory of Research and its Relation to Einstein', *Studies in History and Philosophy of Science*, 15/1 (1981), 1–22. Feyerabend says (sect. 6: 'Atoms and Relativity', p. 19), 'There is no doubt that Mach counted atoms among the monsters that had arisen because scientists had wandered away from the instinctive basis of the science of their time. Atoms, for Mach, were not merely idealizations, but "pure objects" of thought which from their very nature cannot impinge upon the senses.']

Incidentally, one finds in Popper's references to Berkeley other curious mistakes. Thus, in *Conjectures and Refutations* (third edn. rev., 1969), on p. 104 he claims that the 'Berkeleian' instrumentalists' concept of description may be deployed only when dealing with the observed ordinary world, and this assertion does not seem to take into account Berkeley's corpuscularian theories in *Siris*. He claims too that 'neither Bacon nor Berkeley believed that the earth rotates' (ibid., p. 114), an assertion which certainly appears not to take into account sects. 58–9 (and presumably also sect. 114) of *PHK* , and the *Third Dialogue between Hylas and Philonous* (vol. ii, p. 238). To cap it all, Popper asserts that 'Berkeley's idealism' can be expressed 'by the following thesis: "The empirical world is my idea"' (*Conjectures and Refutations*, p. 193). Now this assertion is simply untrue to facts, for it does not take into account Berkeley's views on God and other spirits. And in *The Logic of Scientific Discovery* (English trans., London, 1959), p. 18, he claims that 'the new way of ideas . . . was used by Berkeley and Hume chiefly as a weapon for harrying their opponents. Their own interpretation of the world . . . which they were anxious to impart to us was never based upon this method.' Now this last assertion, too, seems to me to be without any foundation in Berkeley's writings. And in *Postscript to the Logic of Scientific Discovery*, p. 116, he wrongly ascribes to Berkeley the view that the Copernican theory is a purely instrumentalist view.

Now while there are some views on the nature of science that Berkeley and Mach held in common, Popper's assertion that Berkeley's treatment of 'corpuscles' and 'particles' is Machian, or instrumentalist, is simply false. This point should be obvious to anyone who has read Berkeley's writings, especially *Siris*. Why it is not obvious to Popper is in itself an interesting question; it is not, however, this question with which I shall be concerned here. My aim is simply to point out that the instrumentalist interpretation Popper puts on Berkeley's corpuscularianism finds no real support in Berkeley's writings, and sometimes is even quite obviously untrue to facts. Moreover, the influence of Popper's views makes the critical task of the present Appendix most pertinent in the context of contemporary Berkeleian research. Therefore, in what comes below, I will gather together several tenets of my anti-Popperian criticism, some of which have been already mentioned above in various parts of the main body of this book.

II

The prime source for Berkeley's corpuscularian theory is *Siris*.[4] Indeed, in *A Note* Popper refers directly to *Siris* thirteen times. But, although particles are regarded as 'candidates-for-reality' in tens of sections of *Siris*,[5] Popper is adamant in his claim that Berkeley conceived of particles as Mach did, namely as purely mathematical constructs. He attempts to substantiate this claim by concluding *A Note* with a long quotation from *S*. 228. Popper's reference to *S*. 228 runs as follows:

At the same time we can now admit, without becoming instrumentalist, what Berkeley said of the nature of hypotheses in the following passage (*Siris*, 228) . . . 'It is one thing', Berkeley writes, 'to arrive at general laws of nature from a contemplation of the phenomena; and another to frame an hypothesis, and from thence deduce the phenomena. Those who suppose[d] epicycles, and by them explain[ed][6], the notions and appearances of the planets, may not therefore be thought to have discovered principles true in fact and nature. And, albeit we may from the premises infer a conclusion, it will not follow that we can argue reciprocally, and from the conclusion infer the premises. For instance, supposing an elastic fluid, whose constituent minute particles are equidistant from each other, and of equal densities and diameters, and recede one from another with a centrifugal force which is inversely as the distance of the centres; and admitting that from such supposition it must follow that the density and elastic force of such fluid are in the inverse proportion of the space it occupies when compressed by any force; yet we cannot reciprocally infer that a fluid endowed with this property must therefore consist of such supposed equal particles.'[7]

Popper claims that although the author of *S*. 228 reveals an 'admirable understanding of the logical structure of hypothetical explanation', he none the less expresses in this section, and in *Siris* at large, an instrumentalist conception of particles (and, in addition, 'fails to realize the conjectural character of all science').[8] In Popper's view, 'we' 'can now admit' Berkeley's 'admirable understanding of the logical structure' of hypo-thetico-deductive theories, as exemplified by the corpuscularian theory of *S*. 228, but must reject Berkeley's instrumentalism which mars his otherwise valuable insights. According to this line of reasoning it would seem that in Berkeley's view theories and theoretical terms, e.g. *particles*, are only 'mathematical hypotheses, that is nothing but instruments for the prediction of appearances'.[9]

In other words, Popper ascribes to the author of *Siris* the following view: while 'particles' or 'corpuscles' have a use, i.e. are useful terms, in mathematical-cum-predictive theories, they do not, and indeed cannot, have any counterparts in reality. Popper claims that in Berkeley's 'Machian' view 'structures of corpuscles, absolute space and absolute motion, etc. are eliminated . . . because we know that the words expressly designating them must be meaningless. *To have a meaning, a word must stand for an "idea"*.'[10] The implication is that for Berkeley the terms 'particle', ('corpuscle', etc.) can no more stand for an idea than the terms 'absolute space' and 'absolute motion'. Now it seems to me that I managed to show in Chapter 2 above that this claim is not made by Berkeley himself. It is to be found neither in *S*. 228 (a section to which I referred in some crucial passages of my analysis of Berkeley's corpuscularianism), nor in other sections of *Siris*. I shall try below to sum up again the relevant evidence with particular reference to Popper's arguments.

III

As I have mentioned before, Popper's claim is that for Berkeley the phrase 'the structure of corpuscles' is devoid of meaning. It is, first of all, unclear just what Popper means by 'the structure of corpuscles'. The phrase can refer to either (*i*) the structure (e.g. geometrical qualities) of particles proper, or (*ii*) the corpuscular structure of phenomena. But whichever reading we select, Popper's claim is incorrect.

(*i*) In *S.* 162 Berkeley refers to the differences between 'shapes or figures' of various particles, and mentions 'the difference of their angles'. He maintains, for example, that 'the different modes of cohesion, attraction, repulsion and motion (of particles) appear to be the source from whence the specific properties are derived, rather than different shapes or figures'. In this section, and also in other sections (e.g. 134, 165, 194, 222, 235, 238, and 239) of *Siris*, Berkeley speaks of corpuscularian shapes, figures, and angles, although he does not consider them as the main source, or 'concause', of the secondary qualities. And, in *S.* 132 ff., he specifically mentions the figures and magnitudes of particles of salts and acids. He there clearly speaks of shapes, figures, and angles of particles as characterizing the structure of existing things, i.e. of real items in the sensible universe, or *rerum natura*. In a similar vein, he speaks in *S.* 239 not only of 'certain idiosyncrasies . . . with regard to the fine insensible parts', but also of 'the different size, figure, number, solidity or weight of those particles' (of solids, fluids, 'animal spirits', and light).

These, as he goes on to point out, may be real in the sense that 'the density or elasticity of a medium' is real, although they are not the real causes, nor even the viable 'concauses' of various qualities of medium-sized objects. These realistic views concerning the specific figures, angles, etc., of particles surely do not encourage us to endorse Popper's instrumentalist interpretation of Berkeley's references to corpuscles.

(*ii*) Now let us turn to the corpuscular structure of phenomena as propounded in *Siris*, i.e. to Berkeley's references to the very existence of particles as real constituents of bodies, in distinction from reference to their specific shapes, angles, etc. I have already pointed out in my Chapters 2–3 above that there is ample evidence that in many cases Berkeley is, in *Siris*, inclined to endorse moderately realistic views concerning the corpuscular structure of all physical bodies. For instance, in *S.* 250 Berkeley states:

Sir Isaac Newton asks, Have not the minute particles of bodies certain forces or powers by which they act on one another, as well as on the particles of light, for producing most of the phenomena in nature. But, *in reality* [*my italics*], those minute particles are only agitated according to certain laws of nature, by some other agent, wherein the force exists and not in them, which have only the motion; which motion in the body moved the Peripatetics rightly judge to be a mere passion, but in the mover to be ἐνέργεια or act.

Here, as I have pointed out in Chapter 2, only the causal powers of 'the minute particles' are treated by Berkeley as fictitious, but 'the minute particles' themselves seem to be considered as real parts of the *rerum natura* a new microcosmic series of ideas of sense. (Berkeley had, in a very similar way, incorporated into the framework of his immaterialistic ideism the new visual data revealed by the microscope; cf. the discussion of the 'eleventh objection', *PHK* 60–6. And see also Tipton's reference to it in his article in Turbayne's collection.) Let me paraphrase here my findings concerning the status of particles as in *Siris*. Particles are regarded in *Siris* as 'candidates for reality'. Force[11] alone remains as a fictitious concept. Particles, or at least some series of particles, are incorporated into the *rerum natura* as real ideas of sense. But, being a new series of sensory phenomena, they of course share, in Berkeley's view, the sheer passivity of all ideas of sense, and are described, therefore, as 'only agitated according to certain laws of nature, by some other agent, wherein the force exists and not in them,[12] which have only the motion'. Particles as theoretical entities are regarded by him as terms in (at least initially) mathematical hypotheses, which may, or may not, acquire the status of real ideas of sense.[13] But if they are new perceptual data, they should behave according to their new status and share, according to Berkeley, the passivity of all ideas of sense, i.e. their motions, mutual 'attractions' and ordered 'idiosyncrasies'[14] are only descriptions of regularities under the rubric of 'laws of Nature',[15] and are not to be considered as revealing causal powers (it must be remembered that Berkeley ascribes powers to spiritual agents only). All this line of reasoning is quite incompatible with Popper's instrumentalist interpretation of Berkeley's corpuscularian theories.

Let us now examine section 228 of *Siris* on which Popper lays so much stress (see the final part of his *Note*, quoted above). The first thing to note is that Popper does not quote the whole of the section. He leaves out the part at the end in which Berkeley compares the hypothetical particles of 'an elastic fluid' with '*constituent particles of air*' [my emphasis].[16] This comparison undermines any interpretation of *S.*228 which construes it as representing an instrumentalist position with regard to particles. Berkeley maintains that from the 'supposition' of 'an elastic fluid whose constituent minute particles are equidistant from each other, and of equal densities and diameters, etc. . . .' it must follow that the 'elastic fluid' is endowed with certain properties (its 'density and elastic force are in the inverse proportion of the space it occupies'). But, adds Berkeley, it does not follow that we can argue 'reciprocally' and from 'the conclusion' (the perceived properties of the fluid) infer 'the premises' (the existence of the above-mentioned particles). Popper interprets this argument as exemplifying Berkeley's instrumentalist, or 'Machian', approach to particles, i.e. a conception of particles as purely fictitious premisses in hypothetico-deductive theories. But, if Popper's interpretation is correct, it would follow that Berkeley relegates to such a fictitious status not only particles in various 'mathematical hypotheses', but even 'the constituent particles of air', which are, in his view, analogous to the hypothetical particles of elastic fluid. But surely it would be rather curious, and, in fact, impossible, to maintain that the author of *Siris* denied the very existence of 'the constituent particles of air'. The existence of the particles of air is asserted time and again in *Siris*; see especially *S.* 147, 150, 151, and 197. Thus in *S.* 151 Berkeley claims that 'air therefore is a mass of various particles, abraded and sublimated from wet and dry bodies of all sorts'; and in *S.* 197 he asserts that 'air is *in reality [my emphasis]* nothing more than particles of wet and dry bodies volatilized and rendered elastic by fire', and argues from the real level of the particles of air to the hypothetical level of the particles of aether.

Be that as it may, no rejection of the status of any particles whatsoever as 'candidates-for-reality' is implied by *S.* 228. We cannot 'from the conclusion [*which refers to medium-sized objects*] infer the [*corpuscularian*] premisses'; but the premisses can, of course, be real on quite independent grounds. In fact, even a casual reading of that part of *S.* 228 which Popper does quote reveals that Berkeley is not claiming that particles do not exist. His claim is only that there is a *possibility* that particles do not exist. After all, the premisses of a hypothetical deduction may simply have no reference. On the other hand, however, they *may* have a reference. This is sufficient to show that Berkeley's 'corpuscularian philosophy' in *Siris* is not Machian or instrumentalist, for Mach's contention was that theoretical terms in various corpuscularian theories ('atoms', 'corpuscles', etc.) do not and cannot refer to real entities. (See also n. 3 below.)

I have already mentioned that Berkeley's contention with regard to theoretical terms, such as 'minute particles', is that they may or may not refer to existents, i.e. it is not sure whether the term 'particles' refers to real micro-bodies. Particles are considered in *Siris* either as theoretical entities in hypothetico-deductive systems or as new series of 'ideas of sense' in the *rerum natura*. They are obviously regarded by Berkeley as bigger than the *minima tangibilia*;[17] and, to the extent that they are real, may be located on the map of 'ideas of sense' somewhere between the *minima* and the *minutiae* dealt with in *PHK* (in the discussion of 'eleventh objection', sects. 60–6). In any case, let me emphasize here again my brief reference to Berkeley's fork and Berkeley's razor in Chapter 2 above. I have already mentioned there that the use of the concept of particle is regarded by the Berkeley of *Siris* as compatible with the general immaterialistic framework of his metaphysics (and also with what seemed to him the correct linguistic analysis of the term 'existence'). He seems to have applied to particles a sort of bifurcating logical approach, or what I have above labelled 'Berkeley's fork'. And, as I have already claimed in Chapter 2, the use of such a label is, to my mind, much more justified than Popper's reference to 'Berkeley's razor'. According to Popper, Berkeley eliminates in an instrumentalist way any possibility of existence in so far as theoretical entities are concerned (be they forces, micro-entities, or absolute space and absolute motion). Berkeley's razor is supposed by Popper to be a rather indiscriminating tool; whereas Berkeley's fork indicates a dual approach, according to which 'particles', and, indeed, any other not purely mathematical terms in hypotheses, may signify real 'ideas of sense' as distinct from terms like 'absolute space' and 'absolute motion'.[18] The same may be said of the application of Berkeley's view to 'the corpuscles of aether', as referred to in *Siris* (e.g. in sects. 147, 150, 151, 162, 163, 165, 194, 202, 207, 209, 222, 224, 226, 227, 238, 244, 248, 281, and 282). This term, too, may, in Berkeley's view, refer to real particles. In fact, what Berkeley did in *Siris* was, among other things, to incorporate the Newtonian brand of 'the corpuscularian philosophy' in general, and the tentative hypothesis of aether in particular, within the framework of (1) his immaterialistic metaphysics; and (2) his qualified positivism (and his admirably modern approach to hypothetico-deductive systems).[19]

IV

Popper's *Note* deals not only with Berkeley's treatment of particles, but also with Berkeley's criticism of Newton's theory of gravitation and forces in general. Popper claims that according to Berkeley's analyses of 'Newton's theory' and of 'corpuscular theory' alike the following must be distinguished:

(*a*) Observations of concrete, particular things.

(*b*) Laws of Nature, which are either observations of regularities or which are proved . . . by experiments, or discovered by 'a diligent observation of the phenomena' (*Principles*, 107).

(*c*) Mathematical hypotheses, which are not based on observation, but whose consequences agree with the phenomena (or 'save the phenomena', as the Platonists said).

(*d*) Essentialist or metaphysical causal explanations, which have no place in physical science.[20]

According to Popper, Berkeley is against moving from (*c*) to (*d*). This is correct; but Popper also claims that, in Berkeley's view, it is impossible, or strictly forbidden, to move from (*c*) to (*a*) or (*b*), because (*c*) is to be interpreted as strictly instrumentalist. Berkeley, however, considers these last moves as perfectly legitimate, and, indeed, does move from (*c*) to (*a*) and (*b*), e.g. in his treatment of particles mentioned above (and, in this context, his move from (*c*) to (*a*) is most important). Other examples of such a 'realist' or 'existential' approach to hypotheses may also be found in Berkeley's discussion of 'various particles abraded and sublimated from wet and dry bodies of all sorts'[21] and in his references to particles of animal spirits and aether. Thus, for instance, Berkeley claims in *S*. 159 that nobody 'could *hitherto* [*my italics*] discern' particles of aether and animal spirits, implying, as I have already mentioned in Chapter 2 above, that there is no principled reason why someone should not perceive them some time in the future. Therefore, Popper is simply wrong in asserting that, in Berkeley's view, (*c*)-terms in initially mathematical hypotheses can never be employed referentially, i.e. transformed into (*a*)-terms (referring to particular existents), and into (*b*)-terms (referring to observed regularities of nature).

V

Popper also cites the *Analyst* as supplying additional evidence of Berkeley's instrumentalism. This work, published in 1734, belongs to the interim period of Berkeley's analysis of, and reference to, the corpuscularian philosophy, flanked as it is by *De Motu* and the *Principles* on the one hand, and *Siris* on the other. However, it seems that Popper has misconstrued that passage of the *Analyst* (50, Query 56) to which he refers specifically.[22] Popper takes Berkeley in this Query to be equating atomism in particular, and corpuscularian theories in general, with 'constructing an invisible world of inward essences'.[23] But it is precisely in this section of the *Analyst* that Berkeley takes his first steps towards reconciling his immaterialism with the then prevailing corpuscularian philosophy (but not, of course, with the concept of material substance). The text of *An*. 50, Qu. 56, runs as follows: 'Whether the corpuscularian, experimental and mathematical philosophy, so much cultivated in the last age, hath not too much engrossed men's attention; some part whereof it might have usefully employed?' The final words in the second part of the Query ('some part whereof it might have usefully employed'), and perhaps even the 'too much' in its first part, indicate quite clearly a new tendency in Berkeley's treatment of the concept of particle, namely an attempt to come to terms with some tenets of the corpuscularian philosophy (but, of course, not with *matter*).

Berkeley deals more explicitly with the same subject-matter (the possible use and limitations of the corpuscularian philosophy) in *S.* 331. There he states that 'the corpuscularian and mechanical philosophy which hath prevailed for about a century . . . might usefully enough have employed some share of the leisure and curiosity of inquisitive persons. But when it entered the seminaries of learning as a necessary accomplishment, and most important part of education, by engrossing men's thoughts, and fixing their minds so much on corporeal objects and the laws of motion, it hath, however undesignedly, indirectly and by accident, yet not a little indisposed them for spiritual, moral and intellectual matters.' Even the very words 'engross', 'usefully', and 'employ' appear in identical contexts in both places. It is, therefore, obvious that the above-mentioned passage in *S.* 331, in which, as in many other sections of *Siris*, Berkeley's own brand of 'corpuscularian philosophy' is developed, dispels any possible doubts in regard to the meaning of *An.* 50, Qu. 56. In any case, I cannot find here an application to the 'corpuscularian theory' of what Popper calls 'Berkeley's razor', not even when this theory 'attempts to explain the world of appearances' (cf. *A Note*, p. 443). Neither *An.* 50, Qu. 56, nor *S.* 232 and 235 to which Popper refers (on p. 443) as rejecting 'the invisible world of corpuscles', are anti-corpuscularian. On the contrary, they reveal Berkeley's coming to terms with corpuscularianism, and even with its most realist interpretations. Everyone would agree, of course, with Popper that Berkeley rejects any physical or metaphysical 'inward *essence*'. But the relevant point (and one may perhaps say as well the real issue) here is that Berkeley (to some extent in the *Analyst* in the 1730s, and especially in *Siris* in the 1740s) was quite ready to admit the 'invisible world', referred to by the 'corpuscular theory', although not as an 'inward essence', but as a new, and perhaps indefinitely (though not infinitely) 'open' series of appearances.

VI

If what I have said is correct, Popper, despite all his references to *Siris*, has misunderstood, or misconstrued, its corpuscularian thesis. But it may be argued that the interpretation Popper gives of *Siris* (1744) is applicable to the *Principles* (1710). However, though it is true that Berkeley reveals instrumentalist leanings in *De Motu* (1721, in which, however, particles are not mentioned) and in *PHK*, G. Buchdahl has conclusively shown that, at least in *PHK*, Berkeley was not espousing instrumentalism, in so far as particles are concerned. Buchdahl rightly asserts that Berkeley had 'to formulate a notion of "explanation" that will eliminate reference not so much to observable entities as to a metaphysical level with which they formerly have become confused'. Therefore, 'it does not follow that . . . Berkeley (and other phenomenalists like him) could not make room for concepts (and "entities") like atoms . . . Too many philosophers (even nowadays) think that a philosophical analysis which "reduces" certain concepts by moving them to some other level must thereby be involved in corresponding *empirical* denials also. All that such misunderstandings show is the difficulty of a demarcation of the realm of "metaphysics".'[24]

I have already shown above (see Chapter 1) that in *PHK* and *Three Dialogues between Hylas and Philonous* Berkeley accepted a sort of 'package deal', according to which (1) the thesis of infinite divisibility; (2) the division into primary and secondary qualities; (3) the assumption of *matter*; (4) the ascription of causal powers to physical entities; and (5) the very assertion of the existence of unperceived minute particles, are identified, or unified, under the name of *the corpuscularian philosophy*. It is, therefore, sometimes quite difficult to evaluate the precise logical force of his attacks on the corpuscularian theory of the Lockean real essence, i.e. to draw clearcut distinctions between various trends in his apparent anti-corpuscularianism. Let me paraphrase, or in fact even quote, again my analysis of Berkeley's apparent anti-corpuscularianism as in *PHK* and the *Dialogues*: in all the relevant passages of *PHK* and the *Dialogues* Berkeley does not say anything in favour of corpuscularian theories of nature, and his attacks on 'the corpuscularian philosophy' of the 'real essence', which is a mixture of theses (1)–(5), can, accordingly, be easily regarded as the rejection of (5), and not only of (1)–(4). However, it seems to me that Berkeley neither rejected (5) in the relevant texts, nor needed to do so on his own premisses. But he certainly did not develop, in that most important period of his philosophy, his own corpuscularian theory (in sharp contrast to *Siris*), nor did he take pains to refer to (5) alone; nor did he then ascribe to particles a purely theoretical role (like that mentioned by him, *inter alia* in *TVV* 43).[25] Berkeley's change of mind in regard to the use and possible reference of the concept of particles dates from the 1730s (the *Theory of Vision Vindicated* and the *Analyst*) and is most conspicuous in *Siris*. But the existence of particles had been rejected neither in *PHK* nor in the *Dialogues*, and it had been, in fact, even endorsed by him (perhaps as a sort of an *ad interim* device) in his first *Essay on Vision*.

VII

It seems to me that I have quite conclusively shown, by reference to Berkeley's writings cited by Popper, that, at least concerning particles and the corpuscularian theories at large, the instrumentalist interpretation of Berkeley's philosophy of science is mistaken.[26] A careful reading of the relevant texts, and especially of *Siris*, would confirm that instrumentalism only plays a limited role in Berkeley's evaluation of corpuscularian hypotheses.

The Corpuscularian Index of *Siris*

THIS corpuscularian index includes the numbers of sections in which particles are mentioned explicitly. Numbers in brackets refer to other sections which have very close bearing on the corpuscularian subject-matter.

8, 11, (12), 38, (42), (43), (44), 46, (47), (48), (50), 52, (54), 58, 59, 71, (86), 110, (113), (120), (121), (126), 127, 128, 130, 134, (136), (137), 139, 140, (141), (142), 145, 147, (149), 150, 151, (152), (159), (161), 162, 163, 164, 165, (166), (167), (181), (189), (191), (192), 194, 197, (198), 200, 201, 202, 207, (208), 209, (221), 222, (223), 224, 225, 226, 227, 228, (229), 232, 233, (234), 235, 236, 237, 238, 239, 240, (243), 244, (245), (246), (247), 248, 250, (251), 255, (259), (261), 267, (273), 277, (280), 281, 282, (283), 295, 316, (331).

Particles are also mentioned by Berkeley in *Three Letters to Thomas Prior*, the subject-matter of which is tar-water and its merits.

First Letter: paragraphs 14, 15, (16), (17), 18, 19
Second Letter: paragraph 24
Third Letter: pp. 195, 196, 197, 198*

Possible division of the index according to different meanings of 'particle' in Siris

(*a*) Particles as hypothetical entities in scientific theories from which we deduce physical—i.e. sensory—phenomena. This subdivision includes corpuscles of the aether, as well as non-aethereal particles.

(*b*) Real atomic (or subatomic) particles (i.e. real ideas of sense).

(*c*) Active 'souls' and 'spirits of life'.

(*d*) Physical seeds of generation.

(*e*) 'Forms of all sublunary things', *logoi spermatikoi, homoiomeriae*.

(*f*) Molecules of real chemical compounds. By 'real' is meant here 'non-fantastic'—i.e. the opposite of 'fantastic' as in (*g*). From another angle, in *S.*, as in others of Berkeley's writings, these real chemical compounds also denote complexes of ideas.

(*g*) Smallest parts of fantastic elements with traditional philosophical antecedence; for instance, like the four Aristotelian elements, or the three elements of the alchemists: salt, sulphur, and mercury.

---

* *Works*, vol. v.

(*h*) Particles of light.†

Some of the sections below are classified simultaneously in different subdivisions because particles are mentioned in them in more than one sense. Particles of aether (i.e., of 'substance of light' and 'invisible fire') are considered mainly in subdivision (*a*) unless they have some bearing on visible light; in this last case they are considered in subdivision (*h*).

(*a*) 134, (137), 147, 150, 151, (152), (159), (161), 162, 163, 165, (166), (167), (181), (189), (192), 194, (198), 202, 207, (208), 209, (221), 222, (223), 224, 225, 226, 227, 228, (229), 232, 236, 238, 239 (243), 244, (245), (246), (247), (251), (261), 267, 277, 281, 282, (283), 295), 316‡

(*b*) (47), 71, 139, 145, 150, 151, (181), 197, (198), 222, 225, 227, 232, (234), 235, 236, 237, 238, 239, 240, (243), 244, (245), (247), 248, 250, (251), 255, 267, 277, 282, 295, 316.

(*c*) 38, (42), (43), (44), (47), (48), (50), (86), (113), (120), (121), (136), (137), 140, (142), 147, 150, 151, (152), (159), 165, (166), (229), (261), (280), and 15, 18, 19 in *First Letter to Prior.*

(*d*) 140, (141), 164, (166), 281, 282, (283).

(*e*) (43), (44), (47), (137), 140, (141), (142), (152), 164, 165, (166), (167), (181), (229), 233, 267, 281, 282, (283).

(*f*) 8, 11, (12), 38, 46, 52, 58, 59, 71, 110, (113), 127, 128, 134, 139, 140, 145, 147, (149), 150, 151, (181), 197, 200, 201, 222, 225, 227, 232, 235, 236, 237, 238, 239, 240, 244, 255, 277, 295.
First Letter to Prior: 14, 15, 18, 19.
Second Letter to Prior: 24.
Third Letter to Prior: pp. 195–8.§

(*g*) 58, 71, 127, 128, 130, 134, 140, 145, 147, 150, 151, (152), (159), 162, 163, 164, 165, (166), (167), (181), (189), (191), (192), 194, 197, (198), 200, 201, 202, (221), 222, 227, (229), 277, 316.

(*h*) (43), 110, 151, 164, 165, 194, 207, (208), 209, (221), 222, 226, 227, 238, 240, 244.
First Letter to Prior: (16–17).

Controversy with 'corporealists' and 'corpuscularians' (to the extent that they are materialists) is to be found in sections 259, 273, and 331.

---

* *Works*, vol. v.

† (*a*) and (*h*) mainly refer to the subject-matter of Ch. 2, Sect. 2 above; (*b*) and (*f*) refer respectively to Ch. 3, Sects. 1 and 2; (*c*) to Ch. 4, Sect. 1; (*d*) to Ch. 4, Sect. 2; (*e*) to Ch. 4, Sect. 3; and (*g*) to Ch. 4, Sect. 4.

‡ (*a*) may be further subdivided into sections dealing with (*a*1) corpuscles not considered as parts of aether, and (*a*2) corpuscles of aether. Corpuscles of type (*a*1) are referred to in sects. 134, 147, 150, 151, 194, 222, 227, 228, 232, 236, 238, 239, 244, 267, 277; corpuscles of type (*a*2) in sects. 147, 150, 151, 162, 163, 165, 194, 202, 207, 209, 222, 224, 225, 226, 227, 238, 244, 277, 281, 282.

§ *Works*, vol. v.

Index of References to *Minima*★ in the
Philosophical Commentaries†

59. 3 × 1‡ Blind at 1st sight could not know yt wt he saw was extended, until he had seen and touch'd some one self same thing. Not knowing how minimum tangibile would look.

65. +Extension if in matter changes its relation wth minimum visibile wch seems to be fixt.

66. +Qu: whether m.v. be fix'd.

70. 3 × 1 Tangible and visible extension heterogeneous because they have no common measure: also because their simplest, constituent parts or elements are specifically distinct viz. punctum visibile et tangibile. N.B. The former seems to be no good reason.

78a. 3 × 1 Why may not I say visible extension is a continuity of visible points tangible extension is a Continuity of tangible points.

88. 2 × 1 No stated ideas of length without a minimum.

116. 2 × 1 The visible point of he who has microscopical eyes will not be greater or less than mine.

132. +Magnitude when barely taken for the ratio partium extra partes or rather for coexistence and succession without considering the parts coexisting and succeeding, is infinitely or rather indefinitely or not at all perhaps divisible because it is it self infinite or indefinite, but definite determin'd magnitudes, *i.e.* lines or surfaces consisting of points, whereby (together wth distance and position) they are determin'd, are resoluble into those points.

★ The theory of the *minima* is also expounded in *TV* 54, 62, 79–86; and in *An Appendix* to the 2nd edn. of *TV*. It is only once mentioned in *PHK* (132). However, it is obvious that the finitist doctrine was upheld by Berkeley in the 1730s (e.g. in *An.*), and in *S.* (208–9, 271) as well.

† This index also includes some references to 'points' (to the extent that they are considered as last and least units of extension, i.e. as *minima*). The three entries put in brackets (296a, 374, and 488) do not directly refer to *minima* or 'points', but deal with divisibility of extension and time.

‡ The multiplication sign is used by Berkeley in *Phil. Com.* to refer to mathematics in general, and to geometry in particular. 1, 2, and 3 refer to the divisions of *TV* planned by him in advance. (1 refers to distance, 2 to magnitude, and 3 to heterogeneity of sight and touch. And 3a—not mentioned in the entries quoted in this Appendix—refers to situation.)

175. 2 × 1 Qu: whether it be possible to enlarge our sight or make us see at once more or more points than we do by diminishing the punctum visibile below 30"?

218. 2 × 1 As long as the same angle determines the minimum visibile to two persons, no different conformation of the Eye can make a different appearance of magnitude in the same thing. But it being possible to try the Angle, we may certainly know whether the same thing appears differently big to 2 persons on account of their Eyes.

219. 2 × 1 If a man could see " objects would appear larger to him than to another: hence there is another sort of purely visible magnitude beside the proportion any appearance bears to the visual sphere, viz. its proportion to the m.v.

250. × Any visible circle possibly perceivable of any man may be squar'd, by the Common way, most accurately, or even perceivable by any other being see he never so acute *i.e.* never so small an arch of a Circle this being wt makes the distinction between acute and dull sight, and not ye m: v: as men are, perhaps apt to think.

256. 1 × 2 Tis possible (and perhaps not very improbable that it is sometimes so) we may have the greatest pictures from the least objects. Therefore no necessary connexion betwixt visible and tangible ideas. These ideas viz. great relation to the Sphaera Visualis or to the M: V: (wch is all that I would have meant by our having a greater picture) and faintness, might possibly have stood for or signify'd small tangible extensions. Certainly the greater relation to S.V: and M: V., does frequently in yt men view little objects near the Eye.

258 × Diagonal of particular square commensurable wth its side they both containing a certain number of M: V:.

272. 1 × 2 Yr M.V. is suppose less than mine. Let a 3d person have perfect ideas of both our M: V:s. His idea of my M.V. contains his idea of yrs and somewhat more, therefore tis made up of parts, therefore his idea of my v.m. is not perfect or just wch diverts the Hypothesis.

273. 2 × 1 Qu: whether a m.v. or T. be extended?

277. 1 × 2 Tis impossible there should be a M.V. less than mine. if there be mine may become equal to it (because they are homogeneous) by detraction of some part of parts, but it consists not of parts. Ergo. etc.

287. × Extension being the Collection or distinct coexistence of Minimums *i.e.* of perceptions intromitted by sight or touch, it cannot be conceiv'd without a perceiving substance.

295 × 13 Visible extension cannot be conceiv'd added to tangible extension. visible and tangible points can't make one sum. therefore these extensions are heterogeneous.

296. 1 × 1 A Probable method propos'd whereby one may judge whether in near vision there is a greater distance between the Xtalline and fund than usual. or whether the Xtalline be onely render'd more convex if the former, then the V.S. is enlargd and ye m.v. corresponds to less than 30″ or wtever it us'd to correspond to.

(296a. 12 × Little extension, by distinction made great.)

321. × Qu: why difficult to imagine a minimum. Ans. because we are not us'd to take notice of 'em singly, they not being able singly to pleasure or hurt us thereby to deserve our regard.

324. × Qu. why may not the Mathematicians reject all the extensions below the M. as well as the dds etc wch are allow'd to be somthing and consequently may be magnify'd by glasses into inches, feet etc as well as the quantitys next below the m?

343. × to suppose a M.S. divisible is to say there are distinguishable ideas where there are no distinguishable ideas.

344. × The M.S. is not near so inconceivable as this Signum in magnitudine individuum.

345. × Mem: To examine the Math: about their point wt it is something or nothing, and how it differs from the M.S.

346. × All might be demonstrated by a new method of indivisibles, easier perhaps and juster than that of Cavallerius.

(374. × Sir Isaac owns his book could have been demonstrated on the supposition of indivisibles.)

438. × That wch is visible cannot be made up of invisible things.

439. × M.S. is that wherein there are not contain'd distinguishable sensible parts. now how can that wch hath not sensible parts be divided into sensible parts? if you say it may be divided into insensible parts. I say these are nothings.

440. × Extension abstract from sensible qualities is no sensation, I grant, but then there is no such idea as any one may try. there is onely a Considering the number of points without the sort of them, and this makes more for me. since it must be in a Considering thing.

441. 1 × 12 Mem: before I have shewn the Distinction between visible and tangible extension I must not mention them as distinct, I must not mention M.T. and M.V. but in general M.S. etc.

441a. × this belongs to Geometry.

442. 1 × 3 Qu: whether a M.V. be of any colour? a M.T. of any tangible quality?

445. × mem: nicely to discuss wt is meant when we say a line consists of a certain number of inches or points etc. A Circle of a certain number of square inches, points etc. Certainly we may think of a Circle, or have its' idea in our mind without thinking of points or square inches etc. whence it should seem the idea of a Circle is not made up of the ideas of points square inches etc.

446. × Qu: is any more than this meant by the foregoing Expressions viz. that squares or points may be perceived in or made out of a Circle etc. or that squares points etc are actually in it *i.e.* are perceivable in it.

464. × A great number of insensibles. or thus. two invisibles say you put together become visible therefore that m.v. contains or is made up of Invisibles. I answer. the m.v. does not comprise, is not compos'd of Invisibles. all the matter amounts to this viz. whereas I had no idea a while agoe I have an idea now. It remains for you to prove that I came by the present idea because there were 2 invisibles added together. I say the invisibles are nothings, cannot exist, include a contradiction.

469. × I say there are no incommensurables, no surds, I say the side of any square may be assign'd in numbers. Say you assign unto me the side of the square 10. I ask wt 10, 10 feet, inches etc. or 10 points. if the later; I deny there is any such square, tis impossible 10 points should compose a square. if the former, resolve yr 10 square inches, feet etc. into points and the number of points must necessarily be a square number whose side is easily assignable.

475. × You ask me whether there can be an infinite Idea? I answer in one sense there may. thus the visual sphere tho ever so small is infinite, *i.e.* has no end. But if by infinite you mean an extension consisting of innumerable points. then I ask yr pardon. points tho never so many may be number'd the multitude of points or feet, inches etc. hinders not their numbrableness in the least. Many or more are numerable as well as few or least. also if by an infinite idea you mean an idea too great to be comprehended or perceiv'd all at once. You must excuse me. I think such an infinite is no less than a contradiction.

480. × Qu: whether minima or meer minima may not be compar'd by their sooner and later evanescency as well as by more or less points. So that one sensible may be greater than another tho it exceeds it not by one point.

488. (+ The " " and " " ' and " " " etc. of time are to be cast away and neglected as so many noughts or nothings.)

489. + Mem. to make experiments concerning Minimums and their colours. whether they have any or no. and whether they can be of that green wch seems to be compounded of yellow and blue.

516. × If wth me you call those lines equal wch contain an equal number of points. then there will be no difficulty. that curve is equal to a right line wch contains as (many) points as the right one doth.

710. 1 × 3 You cannot say the M.T. is like or one with the M.V. because they be both Minima, just perceiv'd and next door to nothing. You may as well say the M.T. is the same with or like unto a sound so small that it is scarce perceiv'd.

749. 1 × 2 It seems not improbable that the most comprehensive and sublime Intellects see more M.V.s at once *i.e.* that their Visual spheres are the largest.

835. × Tis a perfection we may imagine in superior spirits that they can see a great deal at once with the Utmost Clearness and distinction whereas we can only see a point.

869. × 132 Tho it might have been otherwise yet it is convenient the same thing wch is M.V. should be also M.T. or very near it.

The *Minima*-Theory and the Corpuscularian Theories of *Siris*

SOME comparisons of Berkeley's *minima*-theory with his corpuscularian hypotheses in *Siris* have already been drawn above. However, I would like here to sum up briefly, in a very concise manner, the differences and similarities, and also the logical links, between those two theories which both deal with the composition of manifolds.

1. The *minima*-theory argues from the least and last units of extension. The corpuscularian theories of *Siris* do not refer to those building-blocks of extension. (Even the 'exceeding small' particles of light—which, in Berkeley's view, may be regarded as 'as small as we please'—are not treated as indivisible; cf. *S.* 207–9.) The *minima*-theory is atomistic, whereas Berkeley's corpuscularian hypotheses are not necessarily so.

2. The *minima* are assumed by Berkeley to be of two types only (*m.t.* and *m.v.*), although each type may well include various subdivisions; whereas there is no limitation concerning the varieties of particles mentioned in *Siris* (and even the particles of aether, or 'the substance of light', are considered there as 'heterogeneous').

3. The theoretical status of *minima* as the last and least units of division is seriously impaired by the assumption that they bear the same features as the perceived manifolds. Thus, *ex hypothesi*, the *minima* of a red manifold must themselves be red, although the epistemic 'points' discerned, or discernible, by us (at the very 'threshold' of our abilities of perception) may not be identical with the ultimate *minima*. Particles, on the other hand, are assumed in *Siris* to bear many variegated features which do not have to characterize their compounds.

4. The *minima*-theory is firmly geared to Berkeley's general epistemological contentions. But, as a theory of physical explanation, it only accounted for some correlations between kinematics and optics. In all other realms of physics (geometrical optics included) Berkeley had to have recourse to various corpuscularian theories.

5. Accordingly, the *minima*-theory could not function as a departure-point of various hypothetico-deductive proceedings (subjected to mathematical treatment). It is not, therefore, surprising that it was very seldom referred to by Berkeley after the *TV* period. On the other hand, he did not immediately switch over to the corpuscularian theories which had been identified by him with the metaphysical creeds of his opponents (e.g. Locke's hypothesis of the 'real essence', and Descartes's theory of infinite

divisibility of the extended *material plenum*). In fact, his standpoint remained completely inductivist from *PHK* up to the beginning of the 1730s. Thus, he does not refer in *M*. to *minima*, nor to minute corpuscles. But, ultimately, he had to adopt the corpuscularian theories, and adapt them to his general epistemological (and metaphysical) premisses. This process of adaptation had begun in *TVV*, is quite conspicuous in *An*., and reached its peak in *S*.

6. However, even in that late period of his thought, Berkeley did not discard the thesis of finite divisibility (cf., *inter alia*, all the relevant sections of *An*., *S*. 208, and his own footnote to *S*. 271). His corpuscularian theories are accompanied by an assumption that no extension may be infinitely subdivided. In addition, he never says that the smallest particles are indivisible. His particles are most certainly not atoms. Therefore, they might have been regarded by him as concatenations of indivisible units, be they the *minima* of perceived extensions, or otherwise. There is no lack of fit between the *minima*-theory and the corpuscularian hypotheses of *Siris*, although the former is very seldom referred to within the framework of the latter.

NOTES

Notes to Chapter 1

1. Cf. for instance Locke's *Essay*, III. iii. 17–18, and also II. xxiii. 10–17.

2. Cf. for instance G. Buchdahl, *Metaphysics and the Philosophy of Science* (Oxford, 1969), pp. 204–15 (esp. p. 207) and p. 276. See also G. J. Warnock, *Berkeley* (2nd edn.; Harmondsworth, 1969), pp. 198–9, and also 94–5. For Berkeley's discussion of scepticism (involved, on his view, in the theory of the 'real essence' and the internal 'constitution' of bodies), see, *inter alia*, the very beginning of the *Third Dialogue* (vol. ii, pp. 227–30). Berkeley's rejection of the theory of the 'real essence' is also prominent in the Introduction to *PHK* (sect. 2), and in *PHK* 18, 49, 84, and 95. Particles are always mentioned in *PHK* as involved in the 'real essence' theory. The same may be said of *TD* with one interesting exception (vol. ii, p. 185): Berkeley there assumes that 'inconceivably small animals perceived by glasses . . . must see particles less than their own bodies'.

3. Cf. for instance the *Essay*, II. xvii. 12 and 18, and Descartes, *Principles*, II, pr. XX. Berkeley's view that infinite divisibility is connected with the very concept of matter (and that 'as the later is false, ergo ye former also') is already mentioned in the first entries of his *Phil. Com.* (26).

4. Cf. *inter alia* the very beginning of the *Second Dialogue* (vol. ii, pp. 208–10), and also the *First Dialogue* (ibid., p. 180 and esp. ll. 20–6).

5. For an attack on Cartesian corpuscularianism (especially as connected with thesis 2, i.e. with the distinction into primary and secondary qualities), see *Phil. Com.* 453 and 424a. *Phil. Com.* 424a is accompanied by the marginal signs *P* and *M* which refer respectively to *primary and secondary qualities*, and *matter*, and *Phil. Com.* 453 is accompanied by *P*. The Lockean 'Corpuscularian Essences of Bodies' are mentioned in *Phil. Com.* 533 (which, like *Phil. Com.* 234, is accompanied by the marginal sign *N*). Berkeley's train of thought in *Phil. Com.* 234 and 533 is presumably explained by his remark in *Phil. Com.* 536: 'ffruitless the Distinction twixt real and nominal Essences'. (This last entry is also accompanied by the marginal sign *N* which refers to philosophy of nature.) See also ibid., 601.

6. Cf. also R. Jackson, 'Locke's Distinction Between Primary and Secondary Qualities', *Mind*, 38 (1929), 56–76; and P. Alexander, 'Boyle and Locke on Primary and Secondary Qualities', in I. C. Tipton, ed., *Locke on Human Understanding: Selected Essays*

(Oxford, 1977), pp. 62–76. In any case, there is nothing in Berkeley's concepts, neither in his main writings or in *S.*, which necessitates ascription of various particular qualities, be they 'primary' or 'secondary', to all particles (except for their being constituents of physical—i.e. tangible—or of visual extension). For an interesting exposition of relations between Locke's corpuscularianism and 'secondary' qualities see, *inter alia*, I. C. Tipton, *Berkeley: The Philosophy of Immaterialism* (London, 1974), pp. 28 ff. See also G. Pitcher, *Berkeley* (London, 1977), pp. 115 ff.; and J. O. Urmson, *Berkeley* (Oxford, 1982), chs. 1, 2, and 3. For the place of scepticism in 17th-c. science (e.g. as connected with the division into primary and secondary qualities and the inner constitution of matter) see, especially, R. J. Popkin, *The History of Scepticism from Erasmus to Descartes* (rev. edn.; New York, 1968), ch. 7.

7. In regard to 4, it should be noticed that in *PHK* 10 he does not mention the assumption that particles have powers (for which see again Locke's *Essay*, II. viii. 15), but only refers to the contention that the so-called 'secondary qualities' '*depend* on and are *occasioned* by [*my italics*] the different size, texture and motion' of particles. This careful usage of terminology may be regarded as reflecting a tendency to attack not only Locke, but Malebranche, and other materialist occasionalists, as well.

8. Where Berkeley says, among other things, that ideas cannot be 'copies or resemblances' of entities which 'exist without the mind, in an unthinking substance'. He also says there: 'I appeal to anyone whether it be sense, to assert a colour is like something which is invisible; hard or soft like something which is intangible; and so of the rest.'

9. This argument appears again in the *Third Dialogue* (vol. ii, p. 244) and *Phil. Com.* 67. The relativity of co-ordinations between particular visible and tangible figures and magnitudes, and also an implied distinction between real and apparent magnitude, are upheld by Philonous himself in the *First Dialogue* (pp. 188–9).

10. The terms 'explanatory theory' and 'reticular theory' are defined by H. R. Harré (*Matter and Method* (London, 1964), pp. 13 ff., and p. 18) in the following way: 'A reticular theory can be defined as a set of relationships between refined observational concepts, mediated by one or more theoretical concepts which are to be understood wholly in terms of a complex of the refined observational concepts of the theory.' 'Explanatory theories', on the other hand, 'are such that every relation among observables is mirrored by a corresponding relation among theoretical concepts. Theoretical concepts in explanatory theories are not used to form relations, as are the theoretical

concepts of reticular theories, but explain those relations which are already known . . .'

11. *Berkeley*, p. 200. The emphasis put by Berkeley on reticular theories ('the laws of nature') as distinct from (e.g. corpuscularian) hypotheses is also very prominent in the first *Letter to Johnson* (of 25 Nov. 1729). And in *Alc.* he does not at all uphold, let alone invent, explanatory hypotheses, be they corpuscularian or otherwise. It seems to me, therefore, that one may only consider *TVV* 43 and *An.* 50, Qu. 56 as first indications of Berkeley's change of mind in regard to corpuscularian theories (see also Appendix B, sect. V, and n. 22 below).

12. My italics. This issue is also mentioned, in a very illuminating way, by Buchdahl in *Metaphysics and the Philosophy of Science*, pp. 311 ff. However, Buchdahl speaks of references to 'similitudes', or analogies, in *PHK* as an indication of Berkeley's willingness to accept some 'deductive theories' (as distinct from the purely inductivist ones). This interpretation is rather dubious, since Berkeley's acceptance of limited inductivist procedures, subject to the uniformity of nature, has no bearing on the assumption of hypothetical premisses or of nomothetic necessity. But, in any case, Buchdahl's reference to Berkeley is important as it shows, among other things, that rejections of some metaphysical tenets in *PHK* do not always necessarily involve apparently corresponding moves in the realm of physics.

13. In *PHK* 102 Berkeley expounds the principle of economy, and apparently uses it against all hypotheses, be they metaphysical or explanatory.

14. Those powers may, in their turn, be regarded as either identical with, or different from, the 'represented' instances of the primary qualities. For the attack on causal powers of the corpuscularian 'real essence' and its 'primary qualities' cf. also the *Second Dialogue* (vol. ii, pp. 216–19) where Berkeley even rejects the very notion of 'instrumentality' of certain items in the *rerum natura* (the notion which is the foundation of his philosophy of nature in *S.*). In addition, Philonous (Berkeley) denies (pp. 174–5) the assumption that we perceive the assumed causes of our perception. On his premises, 'sensible things are those only which are immediately perceived by sense' (ibid.). Philonous does not explicitly deny the possibility that entities assumed as causes (e.g. particles) may be 'sensible' themselves. But, in fact, he declines to take into account Hylas' remark in favour of 'deducing of causes or occasions'. It may also be maintained that Berkeley's reliance in *TD* on 'common sense' (cf., for instance, p. 172) is in favour of induction rather than of hypothetico-deductive methods. The very notion of 'immediate perception' (cf. for instance, p. 174, and *PHK* 38) tends also to be more easily connected with

induction (e.g. in regard to 'signs' and 'things signified') than with inference from assumed causes to effects.

15. E.g. of the type mentioned in *S*. 162. The employment of 'secondary causes' in explanatory hypotheses, as expounded in that section of *S*. (and, among others, also in *S*. 165, 181 and 227), is in sharp contrast to, or at least a major modification of, Berkeley's standpoint in *PHK* 102.

16. Berkeley's references to 'the exquisite contrivance' of 'the smaller parts of the creation' are to be found also in *PHK* 146, in the *Second Dialogue* (vol. ii, p. 210), and in the *Third Dialogue* (p. 257), where he denies that the formation of minute parts may be explained by laws of mechanism. For Hylas' accusation that Philonous relies only what he (Hylas) calls 'empty forms and outside of things', and not on their inner structures, see p. 244. For the place of microscopes in (*a*) Berkeley's theory of vision, (*b*) his theory of perception, and (*c*) his immaterialism in general, see G. Brykman, 'Microscopes and Philosophical Method in Berkeley', in C. M. Turbayne, ed., *George Berkeley: Critical and Interpretive Essays* (Minneapolis, 1982), pp. 69–82. Cf. also Tipton, *Berkeley*, pp. 248 ff.

17. These last terms are also, in Berkeley's view, detached from any observation or meaningful use of words. For his criticism of Malebranche's term 'seeing all things in God', cf. the *Second Dialogue*, pp. 213–14. And see also A. A. Luce, *Berkeley and Malebranche* (Oxford, 1934), and Tipton, *Berkeley* pp. 50 ff.

18. Cf., for instance, the discussion of the 'eleventh objection' in *PHK* 60–6, and the *Second Dialogue*, p. 210.

19. Cf. C. M. Turbayne's commentary in *Berkeley: Works on Vision* (New York, 1963).

20. On Berkeley's treatment of the 'proper objects of vision', see also Warnock, *Berkeley*, pp. 25–46.

21. For Berkeley's endorsement of *philosophia prima seu metaphysica*, see e.g. *M*. 72.

22. *TVV* 43 is mentioned by Warnock as a possible indication of Berkeley's change of mind with regard to the value of corpuscularian optics (*Berkeley*, p. 202). Other commentators did not notice Berkeley's change of mind in *TVV* 43, and I relied rather heavily on Warnock's reference to it at the very beginning of my reassessment of Berkeley's approach to 'the corpuscularian philosophy' (in 'Particles and *Minima* in George Berkeley's Immaterialism' (Univ. of Oxford D.Phil. thesis, 1971) and in 'A Note on Berkeley's Corpuscularian Theories in *Siris*', *Studies in History and Philosophy of Science*, 2/3 (Cambridge, 1971), 257–71). But Warnock did not really deal with *S*. In any case, it should also be noticed that the gradual acceptance of the

concept of particle from *TVV* onwards is completely different from a purely tactical reference to *matter* and to its particles in *TV* (during the period of Berkeley's half-way immaterialism).

23. Fraser dates *Of Infinites* 1705 or 1706, and Luce 1707 or 1708. One interpretation of this early reference to particles may be that at some stage of Berkeley's development in *Phil. Com.* (see entries 60, 64, and 242), he referred to particles along with *minima*, before having abandoned their concept in the 'heroic age' of his epistemology. Yet another explanation of that reference may be that he speaks of particles either (1) within the framework of a tactical acceptance of Locke's approach to the idea of 'growing' infinity (which was in any case closer to him than the idea of the immediately perceived or conceived one), of (2) within the framework of the half-way immaterialism of the period of *TV*. (1) and (2) are not incompatible.

24. See also my 'Note on Berkeley's Corpuscularian Theories in *Siris*', mentioned in n. 22 above.

25. And, according to Berkeley's hypothetico-deductive approach in *S.*, particles may be accepted as 'theoretical' in a weak, but not in a strong, sense of the term. I follow R. J. Brook's distinction between the two senses of 'theoretical': 'An entity is said . . . to be "theoretical" in a strong sense if (*a*) it functions in a theory . . . and (*b*) it is in principle unobservable . . . A weak condition for (x) to be a "theoretical entity" would be merely that (x) functions in a "theory" without claiming that (x) is in principle unobservable' (*Berkeley's Philosophy of Science* (The Hague, 1973), pp. 94–5.) As Brook's book was published after the completion of my D.Phil. thesis and after the publication of my 'Note on Berkeley's Corpuscularian Theories in *Siris*', I could not then refer to his distinction between the two senses of 'theoretical', a distinction most helpful for the present purpose of proving that Berkeley did not have to reject the very existence of particles, provided that 'unobservable' is not to be understood in the 'strong sense'.

26. For a very interesting argument that Berkeley not only did not *have* to identify (1) corpuscularian structures of things with (2) their metaphysical essence, but also, in fact, did *not* identify (1) and (2), and even made a distinction between them, see D. Garber, 'Locke, Berkeley, and Corpuscular Scepticism', Turbayne, ed., *George Berkeley: Critical and Interpretive Essays* (Minnesota, 1982) pp. 174–93. Accordingly, Garber's claim concerning this issue is stronger than the relevant assertions made in ch. 2 of my 'Particles and Minima in George Berkeley's Immaterialism' and in my article 'Berkeley: Corpuscularianism and Inductivism', *Manuscrito*, 2/2 (São Paulo, Brasil, 1979), 21–42, and summed up in Ch. 1 above. I

only claim that Berkeley's references to corpuscles in *PHK* and *TD* neither include nor necessitate the rejection of micro-entities *per se*. However, Garber wrongly ascribes to me the view that Berkeley rejected the existence of particles in the *PHK*-period, although he refers to my analyses of Berkeley's corpuscularianism as in *S*. For a valuable comment on Garber's article in general, and on Berkeley's possible approach to perceivability and causality within the realm of micro-entities in particular (but without any reference to *S*.), see M. D. Wilson, 'Berkeley and the Essences of the Corpuscularians', J. Foster and M. Robinson, eds., *Essays on Berkeley : A Tercentennial Celebration*, (Oxford, 1985), pp. 131–47.

Notes to Chapter 2

1. 'Particles' (and also 'corpuscles' and 'minute parts') are mentioned in 54 (out of 368) sections of *S*.; and at least 44 other sections also deal with the corpuscularian subject-matter (e.g. with various problems involved in the incorporation of the concept of particle into the main body of Berkeley's immaterialistic ideism). See the 'corpuscularian index' of *S*. in my Appendix C.
2. Or, rather, we would see in this case, according to Berkeley, their visual counterparts.
3. Cf. G. Maxwell, 'The Ontological Status of Theoretical Entities', in H. Feigl and G. Maxwell, eds., *Minnesota Studies in the Philosophy of Science*, (Minneapolis, 1962), vol. iii, pp. 9–11.
4. According to the Berkeleian view, the ontological status of corpuscles which are mentioned in hypotheses depends, of course, only on God. The Infinite Spirit has no need of two indices, the hypothetical and the real, because his knowledge is absolute. Finite spirits, however, must draw a distinction between epistemic proceedings, such as construction of theories, and ontic states of affairs. The part of the *rerum natura* which is known to finite spirits is completely real (and also, one may say, non-hypothetical); it is not a 'false imaginary glare' (cf. *TD*, vol. ii, p. 211). And our true references to the perceived data do not include any 'uncertain conjectures' (to use Berkeley's own term; cf. *PHK* 59). But our real index of ideas of sense includes only a small part of the *rerum natura*. Hypotheses are, therefore, necessary from any finite point of view. However, it seems that Berkeley's approach to explanatory hypotheses (as exemplified in various corpuscularian theories) is mainly expounded in *S*.; whereas in *M*. (and in *PHK* as well) he puts a stress on 'laws of nature' and on mathematical 'fictions' (cf. *M*. 39).
   Mathematical 'fictions' or 'phantoms' (e.g. 'corporeal forces,

absolute motions, and real spaces') are also mentioned by Berkeley in *S*. 271 and 293. But these 'mathematical hypotheses' seem to be considered by him as quite different from particles which, in his view, may or may not refer to real entities. (Cf., for instance, *S*. 159.) And in fact, the very words 'mathematical fictions', or 'geometrical phantoms', etc., which characterize Berkeley's reference to 'corporeal forces', 'parallelogram of forces', and 'absolute motions and spaces', are not to be found in his treatment of theoretical particles of gases in *S*. 228, nor in his numerous references to the corpuscles of aether.

5. The tendency of some Greek and Arab astronomers to materialize celestial paths of motion is mentioned, *inter alia*, by A. Pannekoek, *The History of Astronomy* (London, 1961), p. 159, and G. Abetti, *The History of Astronomy* (London, 1954), p. 36. Cf. also H. Butterfield, *The Origins of Modern Science 1300–1800* (London, 1950), pp. 15–22.

6. It is for this reason that 16th- and 17th-c. astronomers and commentators frequently refer to them as 'mathematical hypotheses', when they wish to emphasize their 'fictional' character and abstain from any physicalist or realist interpretation.

7. I use here a term coined by H. R. Harré (cf. 'Metaphor, Model and Mechanism', *Proceedings of the Aristotelian Society*, ns 60 (1959–60), 101–22, esp. 105–8).

8. This point is completely clarified with regard to *PHK* and *M*. in G. Buchdahl's *Metaphysics and the Philosophy of Science* (Oxford, 1969), pp. 309–11. For instance, Buchdahl says that Berkeley had 'to formulate a notion of "explanation" that will eliminate reference, not so much to unobservable entities, as to metaphysical level with which the former have become confused'. Therefore, 'it does not follow that ... Berkeley (and other phenomenalists like him) could not make room for concepts (and "entities") like atoms ... Too many philosophers (even nowadays) think that a philosophical analysis which "reduced" certain concepts by moving them to some other level must thereby be involved in corresponding empirical denials also. All that such misunderstandings show is the difficulty of a demarcation of the realm of "metaphysics"' (p. 311). I have independently reached the same conclusions concerning *PHK* and *M*. (the part of my D.Phil. thesis on which my present Ch. 1 is based had been completed in essentials before the publication of Buchdahl's book, as had my exposition of Berkeley's 'corpuscularian' views in *S*., a subject of which Buchdahl makes no mention). Buchdahl's remarks on Berkeley's philosophy of science in *PHK* and *M*. are most illuminating, and influenced and encouraged me considerably both during the final stages of the composition of my thesis and after its completion.

9. 'Possible' means here, of course, 'possible for (what Berkeley calls) finite spirits'.

10. Or the minutest corpuscles of aether, i.e. particles of 'a strong but invisible fire that rules all things without noise' (cf. *S.* 174, where Berkeley speaks of the *De Diaeta* of Hippocrates).

11. Popper wrongly claims that Berkeley's warning (against the assumption that a 'working hypothesis' has to employ terms referring to existents) implies, or is to be identified with, a sort of Machian standpoint which unconditionally rejects the very possibility of existence of corpuscles and corpuscularian structures. See his reference to *S.* 228 in 'A Note on Berkeley as Precursor of Mach and Einstein', in C. B. Martin and D. M. Armstrong, eds., *Locke and Berkeley: A Collection of Critical Essays* (London, 1968), pp. 448–9. And see my Appendix B. For the distinction between (1) 'saving the appearances' by means of epicycles and (2) the claim that epicycles exist, see, e.g., Aquinas, *Summa theologica*, I a, 32, 1. ad. 2.

12. T. E. Jessop draws attention to Plato's distinction between causes and concauses (*aitia* and *synaitia*) in *Timaeus* 46C and 68E, and *Phaedo* 99A (see the *Works of George Berkeley*, vol. v, p. 83 n. 1).

13. 'Instrumental' here means 'functioning as a "secondary" cause', and does not imply 'instrumentalism' in the modern sense, even if all Berkeleian hypotheses in which the 'instrumental' causality is employed may be defined as 'instrumentalist' in a carefully determined and rather restricted way (at least until the possible transposition of their terms from the theoretical level to the real one; cf. also n. 11 above). In any case, against the background of the 'corpuscularian' evidence so abundantly supplied in many sections of *S.*, it is extremely difficult, if not impossible, to accept Popper's view that Berkeley was a Machian or Bellarmino- or Osiander-like instrumentalist. For Popper's view, see e.g. 'Three Views Concerning Human Knowledge', in H. D. Lewis, ed., *Contemporary British Philosophy* (London, 1956), pp. 375–88; and 'A Note on Berkeley as Precursor of Mach and Einstein', in *Conjectures and Refutations* (London, 1963), pp. 166–77 (also in Martin and Armstrong, eds., *Locke and Berkeley*, pp. 436–49). It seems to me that, especially against the background of *S.*, one has rather to endorse a diametrically opposite view, and put an emphasis on Berkeley's 'realism'. In any case, I tend to accept Buchdahl's evaluation of the logical applicability of the *esse = percipi* principle to hypotheses. (See, for instance, Buchdahl, *Metaphysics and the Philosophy of Science*, p. 291 n. 1: 'we should beware of the conclusion . . . that Berkeley must be an "inductivist Newtonian" who is vocal in his opposition to "hypotheses" . . . this is by no means the case. Contrary to what is usually supposed, the "*esse = percipi*"

doctrine in the end liberates the logical situation, and indeed drives Berkeley to a more sustained employment of a hypothetico-deductive approach.') Cf. also my Appendix B. In any event, it should be understood, *pace* Popper, that although Berkeley rejected Newton's materialism, his ascription of causal powers to bodies, and also his semi-Cartesian endorsements of *plenum*-hypotheses, he did *not* reject in *S*. the hypothetico-deductive attempts included in *Opticks* (see my Ch. 2, Sect. 7) and in the *Scholium*, although the inductivist 'hypotheses *non fingo*' maxim of the *Principia* is very close indeed to the outlook of *PHK* and *M*.

14. And it should also be immediately noted that the range of activity of the assumed Cartesian 'animal spirits' is regarded by him as much more limited than that of the heterogeneous particles of aether (cf. *S*. 159).

15. i.e., to the extent that it is considered as a metaphysical or pseudo-physical entity, or activity, detached from spirits and ideas alike. I use here the terms 'spirit' and 'idea' in the Berkeleian sense.

16. 'Some other agent, wherein the force exists and not in them' means here presumably an 'Infinite Spirit'; but it could also mean another (and theoretical) 'instrumental agent' on a different corpuscularian level. Newton speaks in *Opticks* iii, Qu. 31, about 'Agents *(in the plural]* in Nature able to make the Particles of Bodies stick together by very strong attractions' (repr. edn.; New York, 1952; p. 394). Newton seems here to mean by 'Agents' physical causes besides particles, which express God's design. Berkeley's 'agent', on the other hand, is not spelled with a capital letter, and is singular.

17. Assuming that the question of their reality has been settled favourably.

18. This was Homberg's hypothesis, according to which 'acids are shaped like daggers, and alkalies like sheaths, and that, moving in the same liquor, the daggers run into the sheaths' (cf. *S*. 132). Berkeley, too, ascribes to particles various figures and magnitudes and 'angles'; but rejects the hypothesis that impact, and fits between geometrical properties, may explain all, or most, micro-events. Wilhelm Homberg (1652–1715) was a Dutch physician, physicist, and chemist. In *S*. 194 reference is made to Homberg's 'Suite de l'article trois des Essais de Chimie', *Histoire de l'Académie Royale des Sciences* (Paris, 1706).

19. The second part of the sentence is 'still swifter as it goes farther from the sun'. In n. 99 below I try to interpret this rather cryptic dictum.

20. Homology and analogy are defined by J. Agassiz (*An Essay on Classification* (London, 1895), p. 272) in the following way: 'Homology is that kind of relationship which is founded upon identity of

structure in . . . natural divisions of the same kind; while analogy is a
. . . more remote and less definite resemblance arising from the
combination of features characteristic of one natural group with those
of another group.' Agassiz also mentions a supplementary definition,
according to which homology is 'the relationship arising from identity
of structure without reference to function, while analogy is based
upon similarity of function, without reference to structure'.

21. And cf. also *S.* 157, 169, and 201. In *S.* 169 Berkeley speaks very
    cautiously of references to the weight of aether ('the moderns pretend
    further to have perceived it by weight'); but in *S.* 201 he says that
    'aether . . . is sometimes found by experience [*sic*!] to be attracted,
    imprisoned, and detained in gross bodies'.

22. And cf. also *S.* 221 where Berkeley maintains that fire in the
    'philosophic sense' is 'such as is collected in the focus of a burning
    glass'.

23. But even unperceivability from the human point of view could not
    indicate in this context unperceivability demanded by the logical
    structure of the theory, but rather unsurmountable difficulties
    inherent in the epistemic limitations of humans. Cf. G. J. Warnock's
    remark that Berkeley 'could no doubt have maintained that these so-
    called "insensible particles" were in fact perceived by God and thus
    no exception to his principles . . .'. And Warnock continues: 'but he
    was not satisfied with this rather arbitrary-looking solution. Instead,
    with the greatest insight and originality, he relied on a distinction
    between the *observed facts* of science and the *theories* constructed to
    comprehend them.' (*Berkeley* (2nd edn.; Harmondsworth, 1969),
    p. 202.) Even particles regarded as being forever outside the region of
    accessibility to human observers might yet be, on Berkeleian
    principles, either parts of theory only, or real parts of the *rerum
    natura*, i.e. 'fleeting' and 'passive' 'ideas of sense' observed by 'other
    spirits' or God.

24. Berkeley does not ascribe incorruptibility to non-aethereal particles.
    In regard to corruption and generation, he relies heavily on
    Boerhaave's *Elementa Chemiae* (presumably the 1732 edn.).

25. And see n. 62 below. On Berkeley's view in *S.*, even elements have to
    be regarded as compounds whenever they are supposed to be
    penetrated by the corpuscles of aether.

26. And see, *inter alia.*, D. Davie, *The Language of Science and the
    Language of Literature 1700–1740* (London, 1963). Davie explicitly
    refers to Berkeley (pp. 49–59). However, he certainly overempha-
    sized the role of the linguistic ambiguities in *S.* in saying: 'The writer
    is not using the language to think with; he is permitting the language
    to do his thinking for him' (p. 58).

27. The last 'link' of the 'chain' being our own 'incorporeal' sensations, or 'secondary qualities' (ibid.).

28. For the spagyrists and their theory of principles or elements, see Ch. 2, Sect. 11 and Ch. 4, Sect. 4.

29. For instance, he also tried to prove the existence of *homoiomeriae*, i.e. miniature germ-like replicas of plants and animals (cf. *S.* 267 and 281–3, and my Ch. 4, Sect. 3), by reference to the then newly observed spermatozoa, in which some microscopists claimed to have discerned very minute homunculi, etc.

30. Stephen Hales (1677–1761). His *Vegetable Statics* (1727) and *Statical Essays* (1733) are counted as the chief works on physiology in the century. He introduced new methods of measurement of physiological processes.

31. Bernard Nieuwentijdt (1654–1718), a Dutch mathematician, is also mentioned in Berkeley's early essay *Of Infinites*.

32. Cf. *S.* 280, 320, 326, 328, 329, and 344; and also remarks on creation *ex nihilo* in *Phil. Com.* 830–1.

33. 'It may be fixed and imprisoned in a compound, and yet retain its nature, though lost to sense, and though it return into the invisible elementary mass, upon the analysis of the compounded body' (*S.* 198).

34. Berkeley seems, in this particular respect, to be influenced by Newton's hints concerning aether in the famous *Scholium Generale* to the third book of the *Principia*. In the same vein, many sections of *S.* may be considered as comments on, and modifications of, Newton's *Opticks*; see Ch. 2, Sects. 8 and 10. One may even maintain that the influences of the *Scholium Generale* and *Opticks* on the author of *S.* are similar to the influence of Boyle's *Sceptical Chymist* and *Origin of Forms and Qualities* on Locke. In general, he did not accept the famous maxim 'hypotheses *non fingo*', but rather tried to elucidate the status of hypotheses, and, in particular, rejected the Cartesian *plenum*-trends in Newton's approach. For the distinction between Newton's very cautious approach to hypotheses in the *Principia* and his *de facto* endorsement of hypotheses in *Opticks* see I. Bernard Cohen's Preface to it (*Optics* (New York, 1952), pp. xxiv–xxv). See also n. 13 above.

35. Berkeley even says there that he himself 'knew an ingenious man who had experienced it [*i.e. 'fits of seeing in the dark'*] several times . . .'.

36. Berkeley presumably refers to an inner experience of 'acts of will' analogical, in his view, to the Divine ones, and providing us with insights into aesthetic and supposedly teleological features of nature.

37. In *S.* 252–4 Berkeley says that 'there is a certain analogy, constancy and uniformity in the phenomena or appearances of nature, which are

a foundation for general rules: and these are a grammar for the understanding of nature . . . Plotinus observes, in his third *Ennead*, that the art of presaging is in some sort the reading of natural letters denoting order, and that so far forth as analogy obtains in the universe, there may be vaticination. And in reality, he that foretells the motions of the planets, or the effects of medicines, or the result of chemical or mechanical experiments, may be said to do it by natural vaticination. We know a thing when we understand it; and we understand it when we can interpret it or tell what it signifies . . . As the natural connexion of signs with the things signified is regular and constant, it forms a sort of rational discourse, and is therefore the immediate effect of an intelligent cause . . . Therefore, the phenomena of nature, which strike on the senses and are understood by the mind, form not only a magnificent spectacle, but also a most coherent, entertaining and instructive Discourse.'

38. And vice versa, although in one place (*S.* 225) he refers to gravity as a supposedly 'original property'.

39. For this distinction see also *PHK* 110 ff., and *A Defence of Free-Thinking in Mathematics*, 13.

40. But he rather carefully avoids there any mention of Newton's name, and only says that the doctrine was wrongly 'induced' by 'some modern philosophers'.

41. Berkeley also mentioned the theory of fluxions in a footnote to *S.* 271.

42. Or in any 'body of a given size' on the level of macroscopic measurement. Cf. *S.* 227 and 235 where Berkeley mentions particles before other bodies. However, his argument may be conceived (in contrast to the actual order of the terms in the text) as proceeding by analogy from observed bodies to unobserved particles (and aether).

43. It may perhaps be noticed here that even in *M.*, in which Berkeley says that one should not multiply beyond necessity terms referring to motion, nor invent a separate term for every 'part of motion' (see, for instance, *M.* 44), he nevertheless draws a distinction between *gravity* and the *presssure of percussion* (*M.* 13).

44. Berkeley does not accept Newton's suggestions (cf. *Opticks* iii, Qu. 21) that the density of the corpuscles of aether which 'is supposed greater in free and open spaces', and, especially, at 'great distances from the celestial bodies' 'than within the pores' of the 'compact' ones, 'causes' 'those great bodies to gravitate towards one another, and their respective parts towards their centres, every body endeavouring to pass from the denser parts of the medium towards the rarer' (*S.* 223). Berkeley's rejection of this hypothesis (i.e. of an explanation of gravity by means of the corpuscularian structure and density of aether) is most conspicuous in *S.* 225 where he says: 'And gravity seems . . . to be produced by some other cause'. In general, he

relies on Qq. 28 ff. of *Opticks*, and not on Qq. 18–24, with regard to the *plenum*-hypothesis and the assumption of aether which exerts pressure on light, and his rejection of aether as different from light (be it *plenum*-like or otherwise) is more consistent than Newton's 'second thoughts' on all the issue of aether in his Queries at the end of *Opticks*. Newton, in fact, suggests a vague compromise between the vacuum-theory and the theory of ('rare' or 'thin') aether even at the end of his critical examination of *plenum*-hypotheses in Qq. 29, where he says that his references to vacuum are to be understood as indicating the existence of 'exceedingly rare' aether mentioned in Qq. 18, 19, and 20, although he is wary of some blatant difficulties involved in the hypothesis of 'two aethers', or 'two vibrating mediums' (ibid.). Cf. also *Opticks* ii. 3, Prop. iii.

45. Partly only, since another relevant factor is, according to *S*. 225, 'the number of particles contained in a given space'.

46. And see also, *inter alia*, *Phil. Com.* 361, 618, and *M*. 6.

47. And cf. *TV* 143, 144, and 148; *TVV* 13, 39, and, especially, 40; *PHK* 108–10; *Alc.* iv. 7–12, and vii. 11–13; and *An.* 36–7 and 50, Qq. 17–19.

48. Berkeley cites Newton's reference to common salt and vapours (cf. *Opticks* iii, Qu. 31, pp. 376–7) as an instance of 'want of Attraction'. A more representative relevant example would be, no doubt, the reference to 'Salt or Vitriol' on pp. 387–8, where a 'repulsive Force' is explicitly mentioned. However, it should be noticed that even in the case of 'Salt or Vitriol' Newton wavers between two assumptions; namely, (*a*) that some particles simply 'have a repulsive force' in regard to each other, and (*b*) that such 'a repulsive force' only means that particles which 'fly asunder from each other' are attracted by other kinds of particles more strongly than by each other. (But see also ibid., pp. 395–7.) In addition, Newton seems to gear 'attractions and repulsions' of particles very closely to the concept of gravity, or, at least, relates them more closely to it than Berkeley.

49. For the contention that the smallest particles are the fastest, see again *S*. 152, 162–3, and 223–5, among many others.

50. Besides the obvious difficulties involved in postulating two different velocities for the visible light and the corpuscles of its 'substance'. However, it should be noticed that (*a*) on the premises of at least those 'matterists' who assumed the existence of empty space there is no good reason for a distinction between movements of a visible (ray of) light and of its assumed corpuscles, and (*b*) on Berkeley's premises even visible movements are basically located by having recourse to kinaesthetic frames of reference, although, strictly speaking, they are bi-dimensional only.

51. As expounded, for instance, in Qq. 18–23.

52. Thus, for instance, he assumes that the colours of thin plates (explained by Newton by 'fits of easy reflexion and transmission', produced by vibrating aether, cf. *Opticks* ii. 3, Prop. xii–xiii; cf. also Ch. 2, Sect. 10) may be interpreted as an outcome of various vibrations 'excited' by the rays of light and, presumably, also by *attractions* in empty 'pores' of bodies.

53. And, indeed, has to be followed. But I have not found in *S.* any reference to the *necessary* connection between the assumptions of a *plenum* and, say, 'a circular motion' condemned by him in *S.* 232. However, it may well be that he simply accepted the Cartesian arguments concerning the vortical hypothesis and the necessity of the above-mentioned connection.

54. Cf. also *S.* 194 where Berkeley tries to explain, according to his own corpuscularian theory, Homberg's claims that gold is made of mercury by 'introducing light into its pores'. Berkeley says there that such a process can be explained by the assumption of *attractions* between particles of light and mercury which 'fix each other'.

55. Or, as he puts it, 'proper subjects' (i.e. various corpuscularian bodies) 'part and attract' the blended 'luminous substance' of light. But this attraction has to be regarded, at least to a certain extent, as mutual. The same division of roles between the minutest particles of aether, or 'the substance of light', and their grosser counterparts is to be found in many other sections of *S.* (cf., for instance, *S.* 162).

56. Marsiglio Ficino (1433–99), the Neoplatonist of Florence. Berkeley refers several times to Ficinus's commentary on the *Enneads* of Plotinus. For Ficinus's views on the spiritual status of celestial fire, or aether, see, for example, the following description: 'the highest celestial body, the soul's ultimate chariot, is modelled from the fire constituting the heavenly spheres . . . something on the verge of itself becoming immaterial, becoming soul' (M. J. B. Allen, *The Platonism of Marsiglio Ficino* (Berkeley, 1984), p. 100). But Allen is more cautious than both Berkeley and Jessop in that he does not ascribe to Ficinus's light a purely spiritual status, and describes it as 'something on the verge of becoming immaterial'.

57. In Berkeley's view, no appearance is a real cause; but we can regard some real appearances, i.e. some real 'ideas of sense' (whose regularities, of course, are assumed by him to depend on the Divine will), and, especially, appearances assumed by our theories, as 'secondary causes'. I have mentioned above that the theory of concomitant 'causality' is one of the basic tenets in Berkeley's immaterialism. However, in *S.*, where he emphasizes the 'instrumental' role of aether, that theory is expounded as a hypothesis of *privileged* 'secondary causes', whereas in his earlier works he put a

stress on ordinarily concomitant *visible* or (*tangible*, etc.) 'marks' or 'signs'. The theoretical 'secondary causes', assumed in *S.*, function as special and very convenient 'marks' and 'signs', which may be regarded as nearly universal. It is perhaps also noteworthy that the function of those 'secondary causes' is partly modelled on 'analogies' with perceived states of affairs. (See, *inter alia*, *S.* 252–4.)

In addition, a new and special problem arises in *S.*: is the term 'appearances' endowed with exactly the same meaning as the term 'ideas of sense' which appears in Berkeley's earlier writings? (The term 'appearances' now comes in place of the former *terminus technicus*, 'ideas of sense'; and indeed 'idea' as a human sense-datum—and *not* as one of the divine Ideas, for which see e.g. *S.* 337—occurs in *S.* only once, in sect. 308.) 'Appearances' in *S.* are, of course, ideas of sense, but are they ideas of sense 'with nothing behind them' besides spirits, and the only real contents in that universe of discourse which constitutes the *rerum natura*, as in *PHK*; or are they characterized now as mere sensory reflections of the Divine archetypes? In any case, it is very conspicuous that the term 'appearance', which had seldom appeared in Berkeley's earlier writings, and, in at least one case, had been introduced into the discussion by an opponent of immaterialism (Hylas in the *Third Dialogue*, vol. ii, p. 242), superseded in *S.* the term 'idea'.

58. In a similar vein, Euphranor (Berkeley) says in *Alc.* vi. 8 that the 'light of the sun' is 'the most glorious production of Providence in this natural world', but, nevertheless, is far from being perfect ('This light, nevertheless . . . shines only on the surface of things, shines not at all in the night, shines imperfectly in the twilight, is often interrupted, refracted, and obscured, represents distant things and small things dubiously, imperfectly, or not at all . . .'). See I. C. Tipton, 'The "Philosopher by Fire" in Berkeley's *Alciphron*', in C. M. Turbayne, ed., *George Berkeley: Critical and Interpretive Essays* (Minneapolis, 1982), pp. 159–73. Tipton's reference to 'ethereal aura', solar light or fire, and 'volatile essences' or 'souls' of plants as in *Alc.* is most illuminating, especially with regard to Berkeley's discussion of theories of Boerhaave. In fact, he shows that Berkeley's discussion of Boerhaave's views foreshadows some of his corpuscularian views in *S.*, as he does not, in fact, reject Boerhaave's corpuscularian remarks (although in *Alc.* some other views of Boerhaave, or at least some views ascribed to him, are apparently dismissed, whereas in *S.* he has become a respected authority). I completely agree with everything that Tipton says in this context on *S.*, and, especially, with his rejection of over-instrumentalist approaches to Berkeley's philosophy of science on the one hand, and

of the interpretation of Berkeley's aether as *matter* (as put forward by
J. Wild) on the other. Tipton's discussion of *Alc.* contributes yet
another 'missing link' between *M.* (1721) and *S.* (1744) with regard to
Berkeley's philosophy of science (in addition to *TVV* and *An.*), and
fits, so at least it seems to me, my views on *S.* as expounded from 1971
onwards. (And cf. also D. Garber's references to my 1971 Cambridge
article on *S.*, in his 'Locke, Berkeley, and Corpuscular Scepticism', in
Turbayne, ed., *George Berkeley: Critical and Interpretative Essays*,
p. 193, nn. 8 and 15.)

59. Ficinus speaks of the lack of fixity of 'the solar light'; but Berkeley
regards this last argument as applied to all light whatever.

60. Where he maintains, among other things, that the burning bodies
receive some 'substance of light'. This contention certainly amounts
to the rejection of the *phlogiston* theory. But it had been propounded
before the discovery of oxygen.

I have mentioned above that Berkeley certainly did not know
enough about the nature of combustion, or about oxygen and the
precise composition of air. A real insight into the nature of
combustion was first made possible by Priestley's study of gases, and
Scheele's discovery of the two constituents of atmospheric air. But
Scheele, for instance, made his experiments only in the 1760s and
1770s. (Cf., *inter alia*, A. Wolf, *A History of Science, Technology and
Philosophy in the Eighteenth Century* (London, 1952), pp. 345–6.)
Wolf also says: 'As the study of combustion has led to many
difficulties and contradictions, he [Scheele] determined to carry out
many experiments independently in order to fathom the mysteries of
the phenomena of combustion. He soon realised the impossibility of
solving the problems of combustion without a close study of the air.
These problems, accordingly, occupied his attention during the years
1768–1773; and he gave an account of his experiments and results in
his *Chemical Treatise on Air and Fire* (1777). Scheele first determined
the properties which distinguish air from other gases, and then
carried out a series of experiments to show that air is composed of two
different gases.' (Ibid., p. 358.) And T. E. Jessop says in his
introduction to *Siris*: 'air, held from Paracelsus onwards to be a
mixture, was found in the latter half of the seventeenth century to
include among its gases one that is necessary both to combustion and
life. Berkeley, writing a generation before Priestley, was easily able to
identify it with his Aether.' (Vol. v, p. 9.)

61. Purely visual space is not assumed by Berkeley himself; but might, or
even had to, be assumed on his premises (and, besides, can be
suggested as a possible epistemic model independently of his
theories). See also Appendix A above.

62. Thus, for instance, one might assume, on Berkeley's theory, that the 'radiating' points, or *minima*, are interspersed with single, or multiple, 'blank' points (i.e. completely dark from any point of view).

63. However, the following caveat should be taken into account when dealing with Berkeley's entire argument in *S*. 206–10: the thesis of the finite divisibility of extension (in conjunction with the rejection of *plenum*-theories and the assumption of relativity of space) necessitates the conclusion that (*a*) space is not infinitely divisible, and (*b*) mathematically conceived 'points of space' are not to be identified with atoms of (say, tangible) extension, but does not imply anything in regard to the radiation of atoms and parts of space. On the other hand, if Berkeley was inclined to argue that 'points of space' are not radiating, since radiation is only geared to parts of corporeal extension, he did not really need to rely on finite divisibility. In any event, to the extent that his use of 'radiating' implies a visible radiation, he seems to assume that every particle of the 'corporeal' light can, in principle, be seen. But this last contention has nothing to do with the thesis of finite divisibility, or its converse.

64. See also *TV* 83–5.

65. Mind-dependence of even the primary qualities is, *inter alia*, emphasized in *S*. 251.

66. But Berkeley does not reject here, or anywhere else in *S*., the very assumption, or a possible theoretical use, of those different shapes and figures of particles. In addition, he also refers to angles of measurement in the corpuscularian realm (*S*. 132 ff.). He seems also to assume that it is possible to argue by analogy from the observed configurations of 'fixed salts' to motions and figures of the relevant particles (*S*. 131–2, and 162). See also my reference in Appendix B to Popper's confusion in regard to this issue.

67. Cf. *Essay*, II. viii. 9–10, and 23 for the logical grounds of this distinction; and also R. Jackson 'Locke's Primary and Secondary Qualities', *Mind*, 38 (1929), especially pp. 65–9.

68. See, for instance, *Essay*, II. viii. 12 and 17.

69. Cf. *The Second Dialogue between Hylas and Philonous*, vol. ii, p. 211.

70. In a broad sense of 'mechanical' (see Ch. 2, Sect. 6).

71. But God, of course, perceives, on Berkeley's view, infinitely more 'ideas' than any 'finite spirit'.

72. See, for instance, *PHK* 77 and 81.

73. Cf. *Phil. Com.* 830–1.

74. It is true that in the *Third Dialogue* Berkeley admits that God does not 'perceive by sense' any ideas whatever 'as we do'; but in his view 'God knows or hath ideas' although His ideas are not 'conveyed to Him' by organs of sense. In addition, he assumes that pain is only an outcome

of processes which are 'produced against our wills'. Now the dependence (or independence) of any processes on our wills may be regarded as distinct from the very fact of perception (especially on Berkeley's anti-Malebranchian assumption that 'we' ourselves move our bodies; cf., *inter alia., Phil. Com.* 548).

75. See also n. 57 above.

76. Here he says that 'the aromatic flavours of vegetables seem to depend upon the sun's light as much as colours'. What is assumed in *S.* 40 in regard to light is ascribed in *S.* 165 to the corpuscularian structure of aether (identified with 'the substance of light').

77. As I have already mentioned above, 'attraction' is here used as an umbrella-term for the description of various 'idiosyncrasies' of particles among which those of the corpuscles of aether are the most important. But neither the non-aethereal particles nor even the corpuscles of aether have, or are, on Berkeley's view, real forces, nor are they influenced by other corporeal forces. Cf. *S.* 293, and especially *S.* 248 where Berkeley says: 'Nor are they natural agents or corporeal forces which make the particles of bodies to cohere'.

78. See, for instance, what Sir Edmund Whittaker has to say on this subject in the Introduction to *Opticks* (New York, 1952), pp. lxxiii–lxxiv: 'That Newton was more committed to the corpuscular theory than he realised is evident from the proof of the law of refraction which he gives in the sixth Proposition of the first book of the *Opticks*. He tells us that the proof is "general, without determining what Light is, or by what kind of Force it is refracted, or assuming anything farther than that the refracting Body acts upon the Rays in lines perpendicular to its surface"; nevertheless on examining his proof we find that it involves the proposition (afterwards repeated in Proposition ten of Book II) that the velocity of light is greater in a transparent medium than in a vacuum: which is a distinguishing mark of the corpuscular theory. The inclination to the corpuscular theory in his later period is shown also by his treatment of two of the great problems of the subject: the colours of thin plates, and double refraction.' Berkeley himself speaks at the beginning of *S.* of 'rays of light' only (e.g. in *S.* 40); but his reference to rays and particles gradually becomes blended as he introduces the corpuscularian theory of aether, or 'the substance of light', at the middle stages, or links, of his description of the great 'chain of being'. In addition, he insists that what Newton calls 'fits of easy reflexion and transmission' may be explained by movement of particles of light and *vibrations* of grosser bodies, without any compromise with the undulatory theory (*S.* 225). On this issue he is an even more convinced corpuscularian than the author of *Opticks*.

79. Incidentally, he seems to have considered this issue in an early entry of *Phil. Com.* (152). However, that section is marked by the plus sign, which is supposedly used by him in order to refer to somewhat dubious assumptions and to at least temporarily discarded subject-matter.

80. He seems to follow and develop, in this particular respect (i.e. concerning the 'secondary' and 'tertiary' qualities; but *not* in regard to gravity, attractions and repulsions, and 'coherence'), Newton's suggestions in the *Scholium Generale* to the third book of the *Principia*, where an aethereal 'spirit' is a candidate for a universal agent.

81. I say 'most', because on Berkeley's general premises it is quite impossible to assume an uncoloured visible extension. Therefore, *to the extent* that he wanted to argue from the visible items, he could not admit uncoloured particles, or uncoloured concatenations of parti-cles, e.g. 'grosser' than those of aether; and, accordingly, was only allowed, on his own premises, to explain *changes* of colour(s), but not the existence of coloured extension in the first place, by reference to 'generation' by aether. (See also Garber's corrections to his article 'Locke, Berkeley, and Corpuscular Scepticism', in Turbayne, ed., *Berkeley: Critical and Interpretive Essays*.) See also n. 85 below. However, there is nothing in Berkeley's hypotheses which necessi-tates the permanent concomitance of *all* the primary qualities enumerated together by Locke in the *Essay*. It would not be illogical from his point of view to admit the possibility of existence of a completely invisible extension, i.e. of a manifold which, *ex hypothesi*, may not be seen (or, to use Berkeley's own terms, may not be visually signified). The same contention might have been even more easily applied by him to particles, the minutest corpuscles of aether, *minima tangibilia*, etc. (and see, *inter alia*, *TV* 62 where he hints that one has to take into account such possibilities). I admit that the assumption of completely invisible items may sound somewhat strange; but modern physicists assume much stranger entities than Berkeley.

   Now it might be argued that such a 'disengagement' of various data, or loosening of the traditional connection between certain 'primary' and 'secondary' qualities (i.e. between the solid extension and its visible scope considered as necessarily coloured), has no bearing on the permanent concomitance of, at least, the 'primary' qualities. Still, on Berkeley's view, one might well assume *minima* of impact without any velocity, shape, weight, or extension; and such a view might be applied to some particles as well. It may be that the validity of both theses expounded above is impaired by conceptual muddles which I did not notice. Still it seems to me that the very assumption that some 'primary' qualities may, as it were, appear on their own, without being accompanied by various other qualities, be they 'secondary' or even 'primary', might be an asset rather than a handicap in some brands of corpuscularian physics, regardless of Berkeley's, and indeed of any, metaphysical creed.

82. Cf. the reference above to 'medicinal virtues'. However, it might be held that the tertiary qualities have to be discussed under the heading of the primary, and not under that of the secondary, ones, to the extent that one would refer to cases similar to those in which fire makes lead fluid (*Essay* ii. viii. 23), and not to those in which the sun makes wax white (ibid.).

83. Similarly, it may be maintained that Berkeley's reference in *S.* 220 to the 'incorporeal links' in the 'great chain of beings' amounts to an attempt to draw a distinction between perceptions and sensations. It seems that, according to this section, one may regard some tangible qualities, or presumably even visible extensions, as perceptions (or, more accurately, as percepts) of 'things corporeal', whereas 'the sense of heat', and even 'the sense of light', would have to be relegated to the realm of 'incorporeal' sensations (together with pain). The trouble is that such an interpretation would be Cartesian, or Lockean, rather than Berkeleian. Therefore it is, I believe, more plausible to assume that Berkeley deliberately employs the ambiguity of the very term 'incorporeal' which may mean either 'spiritual' or 'intangible' and 'non-extended'.

84. Such an assumption (that the corpuscularian, or any corporeal, realm is 'independent of the soul') necessitates, on his view, the acceptance of (1) non-spiritual forces, and (2) abstract general ideas (e.g. of extension, or *matter*).

85. Berkeley completely rejects in all his writings the infinite divisibility of extension admitted and endorsed by the Cartesians. For more specific criticisms of various tenets of Descartes see, for instance, *Phil. Com.* 780–6, 790, 795, 798, 801, 805, 818, and 819. However, there is only one remark in *Phil. Com.* on Descartes's particular brand of the '*corpuscularian* [*my italics*] philosophy' (453). In that entry Berkeley interprets Newton's optical research as an argument against the existence of uncoloured parts of extension. He says that the 'globules', which in the view of the Cartesians (and of Locke as well) lacked any colour, must in fact be, at least, 'pellucid', and maintains that 'pellucidness is a colour', just like 'the colour of ordinary [*white*] light of the Sun'. And he adds: 'Newton is right in assigning colours to the rays of light.' However, even this single criticism of the Cartesian 'corpuscularian philosophy' is not accompanied in *Phil. Com.* by an endorsement of a non-Cartesian corpuscularianism. (In *Phil. Com.* Berkeley expounds a brand of *atomism* i.e. the finitist theory of *minima*

which refers, instead of to particles, to the last and least indivisible parts of the *rerum natura*; cf. Appendix A. However, the *minima*-theory is scarcely mentioned in *S.*).

86. He certainly owes a debt in this respect not only to Newton, but also to other British famous adherents of 'the corpuscularian philosophy', especially to Boyle and Locke. However, the name of Newton looms large in *S.*, whereas his predecessors (such as Boyle) are mentioned in a few sections only (e.g. 8).

87. I have already mentioned above that Berkeley mainly relies in *S.* (e.g. in sects. 221, 222, 223, and 238) on Newton's *Opticks*, and scarcely refers to the *Principia*.

88. A. G. van Melsen, *From Atomos to Atom* (Pittsburgh, 1952), p. 94.

89. I say 'scarcely' mainly because of *S.* 208–9. See my Ch. 2, Sect. 8, and Appendix A.

90. In fact, Berkeley was closer to Newton than to Descartes in assuming the existence of *empty space*, and closer to Descartes than to Newton in rejecting *absolute space* (i.e. space non-relative to extended objects).

91. Cf. also *M.* 52–5. In sect. 55 Berkeley explains that *empty space* is 'the absence of other bodies'. See also my Appendix A.

92. In any case, *change of place* may, on these premises, occur in empty space and in various media (e.g. in a Cartesian *plenum*) alike.

93. Berkeley is apparently more consistent on this issue than Newton himself, who, even in his almost anti-Cartesian Qu. 28 of *Opticks* iii, speaks only of 'places *almost* empty of matter' (my italics).

94. I have already mentioned above (e.g. when dealing with Berkeley's treatment of aether) many references to gravity in *S.* (e.g. *S.* 225, 241, 243, and 245). Berkeley's references to 'attractions and repulsions', of which gravity is assumed to be only a species, are even more numerous.

95. I am not saying that Berkeley's finitism, and all the corpuscularian theories of *S.*, necessitate the assumption of empty space; but only that Berkeley incorporated the theory of empty space within the framework of his immaterialistic ideism. However, it might be plausibly maintained that (1) any incorporation of a *plenum*-hypothesis within the conceptual framework of immaterialism-cum-finitism would demand many complicated theoretical moves. (Thus, for instance, finite divisibility would have to be defended without having recourse to space relative to tangible *minima*.) In addition, (2) computations of motions in the assumed *plenum* would have involved Berkeley in all the embarrassments of theories of impact in a seemingly empty space (e.g. of the vortical ones). A more empirical reason not to adhere to the Cartesian hypothesis of *plenum* had been, of course, (3) the striking success of Newtonian science.

96. Berkeley meant by *gravity* certain *motions* in the *rerum natura*, and did

not regard it as a force distinct from its effects. 'Action', on the other hand, was used by him in *S*. either as a synonym for a real ('spiritual') force (assumed to exist distinctly from the observed phenomena), or, in a secondary sense, as a technical term for 'causal' concomitance of phenomena. (See, *inter alia*, *S*. 154–5.)

97. Berkeley also seems to assume at least the possibility of combustion *in vacuo* (cf., for instance, *S*. 196), although ordinary combustion depends, in his view, on a fiery element hidden *in the air*. In the same vein, in *S*. 201 he says that life, or 'vital flame', survives *in vacuo* longer than 'culinary fire', because 'less of that thing' (i.e. of aether), is needed 'to sustain it'; and, on this view, it would follow that, when the element necessary for breathing is completely inhaled, what remains is not a field of aether, but an empty space. In brief, on his view, aether indeed 'remains *in vacuo* when the air is exhausted' (cf. *S*. 223); but it is not identical with, and does not fill, space. Similarly, aether penetrates, in his view, even the most solid bodies (cf. *S*. 222); but does not fill their 'pores' (cf. *S*. 244).

98. Those 'attractions and repulsions' are also supposed to explain refraction. M. Hesse is certainly right in claiming that in *S*. Berkeley preferred action from distance to impact in *plenum* (cf. *Forces and Fields* (London, 1961), p. 181), but she is wrong in regarding Berkeley as a 'mathematical positivist' only (ibid., p. 187).

99. Berkeley seems to apply to the movement of light in general Newton's suggestion in *Opticks* iii, Qu. 1: 'Do not Bodies act upon Light at a distance, and by their action bend its Rays; and is not this action (*caeteris paribus*) strongest at the least distance?' (A very similar passage is to be found in Qu. 3.) Newton explicitly mentioned applications of this suggestion (via various 'powers' of corpuscles) to problems of reflection and refraction only (ibid., Qq. 3–5, and 29), or at most with regard to 'inflexion' 'at a very small distance'; and, in addition, tried to connect it with the hypothesis of semi-Cartesian (*plenum*-like) aether (Qq. 19–21), whereas Berkeley seems in *S*. 227 to assume that the transition of rays of light takes more time near the sun than far away from it, and adds that this hypothesis may be better explained by attraction (e.g. of the sun) *in vacuo* than by 'the density and elasticity of aether'. (I refer here to *transition*, and not to *velocity*, since Berkeley refers to light as having fixed velocity—'about ten millions of miles in a minute'—in the preceding section (226). By 'transition' I mean here 'a movement from one point to another along any observed, or assumed, line' and if such a line, or path, is made longer, e.g. curved instead of straight, the time of transition will be longer even in cases when the velocity is fixed.)

In any event, it seems to me that this interpretation takes account of

Berkeley's reference to aether, light-rays, and the sun in the relevant passage of *S.* 227: 'We are not therefore obliged to admit a new medium distinct from light, and of a finer and more exquisite substance, for the explication of phenomena which appear as well to be explained without it. How can the density or elasticity of aether account for the rapid flight of a ray of light from the sun, still swifter as it goes farther from the sun? Or how can it account for the various motions and attractions of different bodies?' However, it should be noticed that Berkeley's rather surprising remark on the motion of light and the sun refers most certainly to a conjecture, and not to observational data. Newton himself referred to this lack of observational data concerning the 'bending' of light-rays (in contexts different from 'thin plates' interference), and regarded it as a good reason for the rejection of certain hypotheses of aether (cf. *Opticks* iii, Qu. 28: 'But light is never known to follow crooked Passages . . . For the fix'd Stars by the Interposition of any of the Planets cease to be seen. And so do the Parts of the Sun by the Interposition of the Moon, Mercury or Venus').

100. He says that 'Sir Isaac Newton in his later thoughts seems (as was before observed) to have adopted somewhat not altogether foreign from this notion [*i.e. Descartes's*], ascribing that to his elastic medium which Descartes did to his second element'. And Berkeley, as usual, attacks the Cartesian leanings and weaknesses of Newton. Truly, *S.* is thoroughly anti-Cartesian. And, at least with regard to the philosophy of nature and all the corpuscularian subject-matter, H. M. Bracken's view that Berkeley was really an 'Irish Cartesian' (cf. his *Berkeley* (London, 1974)) is completely unacceptable. See for example a thoroughly anti-Cartesian entry in *Phil. Com.* 424a: 'I agree in nothing with the Cartesians as to Ye existence of Bodies and qualities.'

101. One might, of course, just equate suitable angles of non-aethereal particles with those of the aethereal ones in order to preserve both the *plenum* and a relatively free movement of the individual particles of aether. But such a Cartesian theory is admittedly a very cumbersome one.

102. See also Jessop's remark on that issue (*Siris*, vol. v, p. 80 n. 2). Incidentally, those references to 'the microcosms' as indicating human, or any living, bodies have, of course, to be distinguished from many references above to the microcosmic level of particles. The technical term 'microcosm' is used in *S.* to designate the organic realm only.

103. The issue of animals' perception and motion is left by Berkeley very much in the dark. They seem to be considered by him as independent

centres of motion and perception (in sharp contrast to Descartes's view). He rejects in *S*. 266 the identification of sensation with a species of thinking, but he certainly could not ascribe to animals intellect and immortality which, in his view, are connected with the spiritual substances only. In his view, there is also no need to assume that animals lack the capacity to form abstract general ideas—the concept of such ideas is rejected by him in any case—in order to draw a distinction between them and humans. He says that it is sufficient to maintain that they lack imagination, and certain other human features. (Cf. *Phil. Com.* 746 and 753.)

104. For aesthetic and teleological reasons (ibid.; see also *PHK* 60–5).
105. See also the second *Dialogue between Hylas and Philonous* (vol. ii, pp. 208–9) where an explanation of sensations by 'animal spirits' is suggested by Hylas.
106. See also *Opticks* iii, Qu. 24, where Newton endorses the Cartesian hypothesis of 'voluntary motions'.
107. Berkeley might assume, on his premises, that muscles are swelled, and 'the fleshy fibres' contracted, not by impact, but only by 'attractions and repulsions' of the aethereal particles of the 'animal spirits'; but he declined to do so.
108. The merits and demerits of the analogy between plants and animals are explored by him in *S*. 29–35.
109. See also *Phil. Com.* 548: 'We move our legs ourselves. 'tis we that will their movement. Herein I differ from Malbranch.' Accordingly, it is impossible to accept Bracken's interpretation of Berkeley as a Malebranchian concerning this issue (cf. H. M. Bracken, *Berkeley*, p. 117); see also n. 100 above. It is quite obvious that Berkeley is not an occasionalist with regard to correlations between human will and voluntary motions of human body.
110. Tar-water is mostly mentioned in those sections of *S*. (1–119) which are considered by Berkeley as the introductory links in his description of the 'great chain of beings'. But, occasionally, it is referred to even in the later parts of the book.
111. See also the reference to the 'animal spirits' and tar-water in *S*. 87.

Notes to Chapter 3

1. 'Therefore' in *S*. 151 may perhaps be considered as the only remnant of theoretical considerations embedded in the sentence quoted above. But see also *S*. 197 where Berkeley says that 'air is *in reality* [*my italics*] nothing more than particles', etc.
2. Berkeley does not refer here to most undulatory theories (e.g. Huygens's) but only to Newton's corpuscularian-cum-undulatory

hypothesis of aether, and to his own corpuscularian theory which is even more anti-Cartesian than Newton's.

3. For the relationships between 'the corpuscularian philosophy' of *S.*, atomism, and Berkeley's own *minima*-theory, see Appendix A and Appendix E.

4. Such purely 'mathematical hypotheses', and their terms, are also mentioned in *M.* 39 (where Berkeley compares geometrical fictions with those of 'the mechanicians'), and in *S.* 293 where he deprecatorily refers to 'corporeal forces, absolute motions, and real spaces'.

5. The same may be said of *S.* 255 and 267. In *S.* 255 reference is made to 'the least particles' in the *rerum natura*, 'formed' by a wise Creator, which even 'the most improved human reason cannot thoroughly comprehend'. Incidentally, that last passage seems to be the very opposite of Berkeley's anti-corpuscularian utterances in *PHK* where the assumed impossibility of comprehending the 'real essence' is regarded by him as one of the best reasons to reject the Lockean model of physical explanation, and *not* to endorse the concept of particles. However, it should also be noticed that the difficulties of 'comprehension' of 'the least particles', as mentioned in *S.* 255, need not be understood as referring to either unperceivability or a hidden 'real essence'. Berkeley refers rather to empirical limitations (see also *S.* 283, where he speaks of the apparently 'inexhaustible' series of *minutiae*, gradually discovered in the corpuscularian realm).

   In *S.* 267 he speaks approvingly of theories referring to 'various regular, and useful . . . attractions and repulsions . . . a concord and discord, union and disunion' of all particles, and does not call in question their existence (especially as he regards even the 'animalcules' discovered by the microscopists as a kind of particles proper).

6. Berkeley mentions, for instance, the research of Grew (*S.* 30 and 37) and Malpighi (*Farther Thoughts on Tar-Water*, vol. v, p. 214), and refers in *S.* 29 to 'those who have examined the structure of trees and plants by microscopes', 'discovered an admirable variety of fine capillary tubes and vessels', and provided thereby a basis for maintaining 'that there are innumerable fine and curious parts in a vegetable body' (*S.* 31). See also the discussion of the 'eleventh objection' in *PHK* 60–6.

7. 'Fine' means, among other things, 'small in comparison to bigger parts', but not necessarily 'extremely small'. Even the 'finest balsamic particles' are described by Berkeley as much bigger than the corpuscles of light which are regarded as 'drawn off' in them (*S.* 110).

8. Cf. *S.* 208–10.

9. See also the following passage in *S.* 128: 'And where fallows are well broken and lie long to receive the acid of the air into all their parts, this

alone will be sufficient to change many terrene particles into salts and consequently render them soluble in water, and therefore fit aliment for vegetables.' It is also noteworthy that the 'molecular' 'terrene particles' are here regarded as 'soluble'.

10. However, the 'molecular' status of particles of mercury is rather dubious in *S.* and they seem to be regarded as existing on a less-than-molecular level (cf. Ch. 3, Sect. 1, above). It is true that they are referred to as entering and causing *damage* to various 'capillaries' (which may imply that they are not much smaller than, say, the blood-vessels). But, on the other hand, the 'capillaries' themselves are called by Berkeley 'most minute', and might well be regarded by him as hypothetical and exceedingly small. In addition, the damage which is supposedly inflicted on the 'capillaries' by particles of mercury is, in Berkeley's view, an outcome of a 'force'; and that 'force' may, in its turn, be an abbreviating term for 'attractions and repulsions' of the most active particles of aether regarded as smaller than even 'the most minute capillaries'.

11. But Berkeley characteristically declines to derive greater attraction from greater size of particles, and assumes that it depends on various corpuscularian 'idiosyncrasies' (ibid.). Some 'idiosyncrasies' may, for instance, depend on *momentum*, which is defined by a species of 'attraction' (i.e. gravity *qua* weight) multiplied by velocity, and *not* by size and shape.

12. The 'grosser particles' are almost always mentioned in *S.* within the context of compounds. But even in those few cases where the relevant reference seems to indicate elements (either in the medieval and spagyrist or in the modern sense of the term), it seems to imply that the particles involved are just beyond the verge of the actual observations.

13. Berkeley refers in *S.* 201 to a far-fetched interpretation of Homberg's experiments, and he also speaks of observations and experiments according to which 'the substance of light' had been assumed to fulfil the decisive role in combustion (instead of the then unknown oxygen).

14. 'Loose' seems, as in *S.* 201, to refer not only to air in general but also to its particles.

15. 'Grosser' than the corpuscles of light.

16. Berkeley refers in *S.* 255 to 'the least particles' of various bodies; but it is not clear if he speaks also of 'the least particles' on each relevant level (say, of animal bodies), or only of the smallest particles of the *rerum natura* in general.

17. I scarcely referred above to *Berkeley's Letters to Prior* in which he mentions some undoubtedly 'grosser' particles. (Cf., especially, the first *Letter to Prior*, 14–15, where 'gross particles' are mentioned;

vol. v, p. 176.) And see also the corpuscularian index of *S.*, Appendix C below.

Notes to Chapter 4

1. Cf. D. Davie, *The Language of Science and The Language of Literature* (London, 1963), pp. 49–59 (see also Ch. 2, n. 26 above). And cf. the following passage of Hobhouse (S. Hobhouse, 'Isaac Newton and Jacob Boehme: An Enquiry', repr. as Appendix 4 in *Selected Mystical Writings of William Law* (London, 1948), pp. 416–17: 'The conceptions of aether and of aethereal spirit or spirits as used by Gilbert, Descartes, Boyle, and other physicists, have a long and varying history. Though the terms have at times theological and mystical, or perhaps we should say animistic, associations, it seems to me clear that in Newton's mind there was nothing properly metaphysical or "spiritual" (as God and thought are spiritual) about "aethereal spirit", which was merely an extremely thin, elastic, penetrating wavelike medium, allied not to thought but to matter, even if apparently different from it in some of its properties.' The same may be said of the 'aethereal spirit' in *S.*, although Berkeley rejects the matterist interpretation of aether and its wave-like structure.
2. Mixed with Aristotelian references to 'forms', and with Stoic tenets (e.g. the endorsement of *pneuma*).
3. Cf. also various references to 'spirits' 'virtues', and 'most medicinal and active particles', in Berkeley's first *Letter to Prior* (vol. v), sects. 15, 18, and 19.
4. See also *S.* 140.
5. See *S.* 140 and 142, and also 138 and 281–2.
6. 'Small particular seeds' are also mentioned by Euphranor (Berkeley) in *Alc.* iii, 1, but *without any reference* to corpuscularian contexts. In *Alc.* iii. 1, Berkeley also says that 'organised bodies' are 'produced of seeds' by either 'growth' or 'gradual unfolding', and the latter of these two possibilities fits the *homoiomeriae*-theory.
7. The approach of *S.* is also similar to a theory of generation mentioned by Plato in *Timaeus* 91D. Plato's animalcules are described as gradually 'matured', but also as initially 'without form' and gradually subdivided.
8. As applied, for instance, to the composition of air and acids, and to the physiology of plants and animals. Berkeley's remarks on the physiological observations of the microscopists seem to refer primarily to Leeuwenhoek (1632–1723), Swammerdam (1637–80), and Malpighi (1628–94); cf. also *Works of George Berkeley*, vol. v, p. 132 n. 1.
9. And see also Berkeley's reference in *S.* 47 to 'the native spark or form

... which differenceth a plant, or makes it what it is'. It is noteworthy that to the extent that he was inclined to speak in *S.* of 'essences', the perceived qualities seem to have been regarded by him as a sort of Lockean 'nominal' essence, and the corpuscularian composition as a possible, non-metaphysical and non-material, equivalent of the 'real' one. He seems to fall back upon some tenets of Locke's 'corpuscularian philosophy' without subscribing to their metaphysical and epistemic implications (although leaning heavily, and rather clumsily, on some Neoplatonic terms).

10. J. Myhill says that Berkeley was inclined to interpret as formal causes what others tended to interpret as efficient ones. Myhill does not speak of Berkeley's approach to particles; but his dictum may be applied to it (cf. 'Berkeley's "De Motu"—An Anticipation of Mach', in *George Berkeley: Lectures Delivered before the Philosophical Union of the University of California* (Los Angeles, 1957), pp. 142–57).

11. The 'modern' and anti-scholastic trend in Berkeley's writings (cf., *inter alia, M.* 40) had always been strongly expressed in his assertions that various laws of motion (e.g. of Newton) apply, or may apply, to the earth and 'the heavens' alike (cf., *inter alia, PHK* 103–5). This trend is very prominent in *S.* as well. See, for instance, references to Heraclitus' monistic theory of fire in *S.* 166, and to the application of laws of motion, and the theory of aether, to various bodies of this 'mundane system' (*S.* 161). The applicability of the theory of aether to 'the whole universe', or 'the whole system', which is emphasized in *S.* 161 and 166, is also endorsed in *S.* 157–8 in which he refers to that 'latent and unobserved' medium as 'present in all parts of the earth and firmament', and as 'shaking' 'the earth and heavens' alike. In addition, he speaks approvingly in *S.* 211 of a Neoplatonic doctrine, according to which the 'celestial fire' 'is not defined ... by its local situation'. ('The purest and most excellent fire, that is heaven, saith Ficinus. And again, the hidden fire that everywhere exerts itself, he calls celestial.') It is true that Berkeley was not inclined to accept gravity as the unique law of the universe; but this reluctance to rely unconditionally on gravity, e.g. in the realm of the 'fixed stars', had nothing to do with anachronistic references to peculiarities of the 'sublunary' region. It seems, therefore, that the above-mentioned anachronism (i.e. the reference to 'sublunary forms') in *S.* 137 may be explained as an outcome of Berkeley's tendency in *S.* to deal with biological phenomena, and to provide quotations and paraphrases from all possible sources, in order to reinforce the plausibility of his theory of aether. In any event, the reliance on Aristotelian terms, which is conspicuous in *S.*, had been condemned by Berkeley himself in his reference to Borelli in *M.* 20.

12. It is true that not all the paraphrases and quotations in *S.* express Berkeley's own views. But very many of them include some crucial tenets endorsed by him, perhaps because he wanted to rely on as many sources as possible in his last, and partly eclectic, book. Only assertions which completely contradict the foundations of immaterialism are rejected, or referred to for polemical purposes.

13. *De Mundo* is no longer attributed to Aristotle; it is regarded now rather as an eclectic work with Stoic tendencies. For the Stoic view of fire as the main agent of physical changes, see e.g. Cicero, *De natura deorum*, ii. 9.

14. 'Spirits' in an unequivocal sense.

15. It is amazing that Lovejoy does not refer to Berkeley in his *The Great Chain of Being* (Cambridge, Mass., 1936). For Berkeley's reliance in *S.* on the 'Great Chain of Being' theory and some alchemical tenets traditionally connected with it, see also A. D. Ritchie, 'George Berkeley's *Siris*, The Philosophy of the Great Chain of Being and the Alchemical Theory', *Proceedings of the British Academy*, 40 (1954), 41–55. However, Ritchie does not refer to Berkeley's corpuscularian theories. He only indicates briefly that alchemical tenets as in *S.* are sometimes integrated with some views propounded in the early 18th-c. chemistry (e.g. of Boerhaave).

16. i.e. operating as if by rules of art (and see T. E. Jessop's remark, and references to Zeno and Cicero; *Siris*, in *Works of Geoerge Berkeley*, vol. v, p. 110 n. 1).

17. A historian of science, C. Singer, says that the discovery of 'animalcules' of sperm, or *spermatozoa*, in 1679 aroused speculations and, indeed, led to misleading interpretations according to which the newly discovered entities were assumed to include minute 'homunculi' (*Short History of Scientific Ideas to 1900* (Oxford, 1959), p. 283).

18. (Univ. of Oxford D.Phil. thesis, 1971), pp. 171–83.

19. And cf. also *S.* 197, 198, 200–2, 227, 229, 277, and the reference to (Plotinus' remark on) fire in *S.* 316.

20. J. B. van Helmont (1577–1644), Flemish chemist and physician. Cf. also Jessop's remark in his Introduction to *Siris* (*Works of George Berkeley*, vol. v, p. 9): 'Paracelsus's pupil, Van Helmont, whom Berkeley mentions, retained the alchemists' theory of three "elements", called sulphur, mercury, and salt, but meaning respectively the combustible, liquid and solid factors in all substances. This theory, although challenged by Boyle, who defined "element" in the modern way, persisted into and after Berkeley's time.' And Jessop adds that the rejection of the homogeneity of the air, which is very conspicuous in *S.*, had also been an important feature of Van Helmont's theory. And see also Berkeley's reference to Van Helmont

in *S.* 49 (he speaks there of tenets expounded in Van Helmont's *Arcana Paracelsi*).

21. In the same vein, *sulphur* had been supposed to be the universal 'principle' of combustion, and *mercury* of metallic properties (including liquidity).

22. However, Berkeley apologizes for the rather eclectic conjectures concerning the 'elements'-theory in this group of sections and says (in *S.* 125): 'I am very sensible that on such subjects arguments fall short of evidence, and that mine fall short even of what they might have been if I enjoyed better health, or those opportunities of a learned commerce from which I am cut off in this remote corner [*Cloyne*]. I shall, nevertheless, go on as I have begun, and proceed, by reason, by conjecture, *and by authority* [*my italics*] to cast the best light I can on the obscure paths that lie in my way.'

23. Conceived either as an observed body, or as a 'principle'. Mercury is put on the footing of observed bodies, such as iron, oil, and water, in *S.* 227.

Notes to Appendix A

1. I am indebted for this remark to G. J. Warnock. Incidentally, a uniform (i.e. evenly distributed) change in number of *minima* would seem to modify neither real (atomic) proportions nor 'greatness' (or 'smallness') of any compared bits of extension.

In any case, a *m.s.* can, in certain circumstances (e.g. when moved from *a* to *b*), be regarded as 'greater' than another *m.s.*, or, for that matter, than itself in the past, simply because of different numerical relations between its fixed value and varying frames of reference. Such changes in regard to apparent magnitudes are, accordingly, taken into account by Berkeley even without reference to 'the confusion or distinctness', and 'the vigorousness or faintness', of 'the visible appearances' (which are mentioned by him—e.g. in *TV* 56—as two other indications of 'greatness' and 'smallness' of visible parts of the universe). Therefore, Berkeley might well agree that what looks small to a giant may not look small to a mite. In the first place, a giant is composed of more 'sensible atoms' than a mite. Secondly, if some *m.s.* (e.g. *m.v.*) 'signify' other *m.s.* (e.g. *m.t.*), then various numerical proportions may obtain between the 'signifying' and the 'signified' extensions. In the third place, some observers may be endowed with more encompassing epistemic fields than others, i.e. with epistemic fields which include more basic units of measurement. Thus, according to *Phil. Com.* 749 (accompanied by the marginal signs 1 × 2, which refer to estimates of distance and magnitude), 'It seems not improbable that the most comprehensive and sublime Intellects [*i.e.*

intellectual and perceptual giants rather than physical ones] see more
M.V.s at once *i.e.* that their visual spheres are the largest'. Cf. also
Alc., IV, 23, and Berkeley's references to 'a system of spirits' (*ibid.*,
III, 11), and to 'several kinds of beings which are, or may be . . . in the
universe' (*ibid.*, VI, 30). A rather tricky argument of Philonous
(Berkeley) which, prima facie, gears relative sizes to mind-dependence, but may be interpreted as referring to discrepancies between
haptic and optic measurements, is to be found in *First Dialogue
between Hylas and Philonous*, vol. ii, pp. 188–9.

2. I use here A. A. Luce's suggestion that Berkeley's *minimum* is, in
   effect, a 'sensible atom'; cf. *The Dialectic of Immaterialism* (London,
   1963), p. 76.

3. This contention is also summed up in *TV* 86 ('the *minimum visibile* is
   never greater or lesser, but in all cases constantly the same').

4. See, for instance, *TV* 80–1.

5. e.g. ibid.

6. However, it is not always clear whether the thesis of the fixed atomic
   composition is regarded by Berkeley as a theoretical assumption, or as
   a summary of the known empirical facts.

   Sometimes, he refers to 'points' 'perceived by us' as *minima*. But in
   many cases he does not base his main (and theoretical) arguments with
   regard to *minima* on identification of these 'sensible atoms' with
   human epistemic points, and speaks in most cases of *minima* as of
   hypothetical limits of division whose postulation ensures the possibility of common measurement and objective enumeration without
   relying on mere 'greatness', or 'smallness' of frames of reference.
   Thus he indicates, first, that *minima* are not singly perceived by 'us',
   and, secondly, says that 'we' hardly can even imagine them. (*Phil.
   Com.* 321). The reason for our lack of ability to observe, or imagine, a
   single *minimum* is, on his view, that 'we are not us'd to take notice of
   ''em singly' (ibid.). It is true that this last argument ('because we are
   not us'd', etc.) seems, on the face of it, to be ambiguous. Possibly, 'we'
   can, after all, 'take notice' of a *minimum*, without any aid of
   instruments and have only to try hard enough. But the ending of the
   entry indicates very clearly that such an approach (i.e. a simple
   reliance on attention) would be over-optimistic. We do not 'take
   notice' of the individual *minima* because they are not 'able singly to
   pleasure or hurt us', and 'thereby to deserve our regard' (ibid.). This
   utilitarian argument (namely, that we ordinarily perceive without the
   aid of instruments whatever is useful for our bodily preservation)
   refers to both kinds of *m.s.*, and resembles Berkeley's argument in
   TV 86 and 147 (and Locke's remarks in the *Essay* II. x. 3, and II. xxiii,
   11–13, in regard to the microscopic vision). The utilitarian argument

is usually accompanied in Berkeley's writings by teleological and aesthetic considerations. (See, for instance, the *Second Dialogue*, vol. ii, pp. 210 ff.) Its exposition above is also certainly modelled on similar arguments of Malebranche which constantly refer to God's design. (Cf., *inter alia*, *De la recherche de la vérité* (Paris, 1965), I. i. 6, pp. 29–34.) After saying that all the works of God—even the smallest creatures—are 'worthy of our respect' because of the wonderful craftsmanship revealed in their structures, Malebranche adds, relying on utilitarian arguments, that every species of seeing creatures has eyes and kind of vision (e.g. microscopic) which conform to its respective size. Thus, 'si nous avions les yeux fait comme les microscopes, ou plutôt si nous étions aussi petits que les cirons et les mites, nous jugérions tout autrement de la grandeur de corps'. ('. . . if we had Eyes after the manner of Microscope, or rather, if we were as little as Hand-worms and Mites, we should judge of the Magnitude of bodies in a far different manner'.) However, he adds, extension is only seen by us as it is in proportion to our bodies, and since very small bits of extension can neither hurt nor be useful for us, our sight does not at all take notice of them. And all this line of reasoning does not take into account small malignant microbodies, or those having healing powers. But Malebranche also assumes, mainly for theological reasons, the existence of material objects apart from ideas. (Criteria of objective measurement and the objective status of geometry are, therefore, ensured, on his view, not by *m.s.*, but by the 'absolute size' of bodies, which is independent of any perception, and determined by the 'intelligible Idea' of extension 'seen in God'.) And this view of Malebranche is also adopted by his British disciple John Norris (the author of *The Theory of the Ideal World* (1704)).

7. Strictly speaking, the 'Continuity' of *m.v.* is regarded by Berkeley as different in certain respects from the extension which is seen 'at once and in confuso' (*Phil. Com.* 460). Thus a line (or a square, etc.) whose parts are distinctly (e.g. successively) observed, enumerated, etc., would not precisely resemble one immediately 'perceiv'd by a confus'd view' (ibid., 400). But the two lines, or figures, may be regarded as practically the same, following operative criteria of identity, if (1) no discontinuity is discerned between various parts in each of them and (2) the spatial relations between the above-mentioned lines, or figures, and their identical frames of reference do not change, e.g. when 'the plain is suppos'd to keep the same distance' (ibid., 283).

The *locus classicus* with regard to the distinction between these two aspects of visible extension is to be found in an entry which has been referred to in this Appendix above, *Phil. Com.* 400: '1 × 3 Qu: if there be not two kinds of visible extension, one perceiv'd by a confus'd view, the other by a distinct successive direction of the optique axis to each point'. This rather rhetorical query (see also ibid., 283–4, and *TV* 145) is certainly regarded as answered in the affirmative in *Phil. Com.* 443: '1 × 3 if visible extension be the object of Geometry 'tis that which is survey'd by the optique axis'. Here Berkeley already assumes the distinction between 'two kinds of visible extension'. ('If' indicates here that, on Berkeley's view, the tangible extension is, strictly speaking, the only primary and proper object of geometry.) The distinction is also assumed ibid., 460, where he says: '. . . extension qua Mathemat: cannot be conceiv'd but as consisting of parts wch may be distinctly and successively perceiv'd. Extension perceiv'd at once and in confuso does not belong to Math.' The most interesting feature of this entry is, to my mind, that it seems to refer not only to the visible, but also to the tangible extension. Cf. also *Phil. Com.* 353.

8. Whenever geometry is taken into account. Cf., for instance, Berkeley's remark on the tangible basis of geometry in *Phil. Com.* 101, and, especially, 297: '1 × 3 Stated measures, inches, feet, etc. are tangible not visible extensions'. He also says that, strictly speaking, movements of bodies, or, indeed, any spatial movements whatever, cannot be perceived by purely visual means. Even what seems to us to be movement of light and colours in space is, strictly speaking, either a rearrangement of bi-dimensional patterns, or 'a successive change' (e.g. a continuous decrease of size, or of intensity) which is only interpreted as a three-dimensional motion because of reference to bodies in space. Cf. *Phil. Com.* 262: '1 × 3 A Body moving in the Optique axis not perceiv'd to move by sight merely and wthout experience, there is (tis true) a successive change of ideas it seems less and less, but besides this there is no visible change of place'. It seems that Berkeley detached the origin of the concept of visible motion from that of solidity (cf. *Phil. Com.* 533), but not from that of movements of one's own body. However, this last contention concerning the impossibility of purely visual reference to space and to movement in space is not necessitated by any other of Berkeley's premises and conclusions. Heterogeneity of objects of sight and touch does not have to indicate (1) non-existence of the visible (bi-dimensional) extension and motion, independent of the tangible ones; and (2) non-existence of the purely visual perception of (*a*) space, or depth; and of (*b*) movements in space, or in three dimensions. Moreover, the very contention that the visual depth is not to be included among, or construed from, the 'proper ideas of sight' does not seem to be consistent with the main premises of Berkeley's epistemology. One may, of course, maintain, on Berkeley's premises,

that certain sets, or arrangements, of 'ideas' (e.g. visual depth) customarily follow other ones (e.g. 'faintness', or 'the turn of the eye'). In the same vein, there is nothing anti-Berkeleian in the contention that one's perception of visual depth gradually develops. The only thing that Berkeley may not consistently say on this issue is that certain 'ideas' revealed by one sense-modality are not, in fact, its proper objects, and have, accordingly, to be ascribed to another sense-modality, or to be regarded as 'blended' with 'proper objects' of another sense-modality. At any rate, Berkeley's inconsistent attitude is very conspicuous in *TV*, *TVV*, and *Alc*. He is completely inconsistent when claiming that some ideas which seem to be 'proper ideas' of sight are, in fact, 'blended' with ideas of other senses, or that *m.v.* (which are, in his view, completely independent of *m.t.*) are not allowed to constitute their own extension or space.

9. e.g. not merely as arithmetical operations and algebraic equations.

10. Berkeley there compares *m.s.* with a mathematical point, and says: 'The *M.S.* is not nearly so inconceivable as this Signum in magnitudine individuum.'

11. Bonaventura Cavalieri (1598–1647), Professor of Mathematics at Bologna, was the author of *Geometria indivisibilibus continuorum nova quadam ratione promota* (1635), and *Exercitationes geometricae sex* (1647). He was regarded by Berkeley as a well meaning but rather clumsy ally against the majority of 'the Mathematicians'. Most of the 'Mathematicians' relied on the concept of mathematical point, and, accordingly, assumed that lines 'are divisible *ad infinitum*' (cf. *Phil. Com.* 393–4), i.e. do not consist of indivisible units. Cavalieri, on the other hand, endorsed a partly finitist view.

12. It seems doubtful, however, whether the finitist approach has to be based on immaterialistic premisses. The finite divisibility of any given bit of extension may be maintained even by 'matterists' (to use a term coined by Prof. Luce), and, in general, it certainly may be upheld, either as a necessary condition of a universally accepted measurement, or as a hypothesis (which may be confirmed), by various schools of ontology, epistemology, and the philosophy of science. However, it is also plausible to argue that the finite divisibility of *material* things can or has to be considered as an empirical feature of nature, rather than being regarded as made likely by epistemic analogies with limits, or 'thresholds', of perception, or as necessitated by a priori rationalist assumptions in regard to possibilities of objective measurement.

13. See also *Phil. Com.* 469, where Berkeley indicates that the ascription of numerical values to geometrical (and physical) units is useless whenever one does not know what units are referred to ('Say you assign unto me the side of the square 10. I ask wt 10, 10 feet, inches, etc., or 10 points.').

14. Incidentally, I would argue that there is nothing within the framework of Berkeley's atomistic theory which necessitates limitation of number of *minima* (or, indeed, of any other 'ideas') in an *infinite rerum natura*. Thus, for instance, nothing is said in *Phil. Com.* 475, an entry which deals with infinity, against the possibility of existence of infinite number of finite and measurable stretches of extension in an infinite *rerum natura*. Berkeley only rejects the concept of infinity of any given extension, i.e. of '*an* extension consisting of innumerable points' (*ibid.*). (The emphasis on 'an' is mine.)

15. Berkeley is not, of course, against metaphysics, which is regarded by him as *philosophia prima* of 'incorporeal things . . . causes, truth and . . . existence' (*M*. 71). He is only against a tendency of many metaphysicians to regard 'abstract and general terms' of certain 'mathematical hypotheses' as real explanations of nature (cf. ibid., 39, 71, and 72).

16. Ideas perceived by God may, of course, be called 'Divine'; but, on the Berkeleian view, they are *not* to be regarded as Neoplatonic archetypes just because they are perceived by God.

17. Objects, and not only causal powers. Berkeley rejected in the later entries of *Phil. Com.* his early metaphysics of 'pan-psychism', according to which objects have an intermittent existence only, and are always being created at any given moment of perception by permanent powers inherent in God. According to the extreme version of pan-psychism, our perceptions are merely 'modifications of the soul', and as the concept of matter is rejected as well, one is left with no objects at all. Cf. *Phil. Com.* 52 and 802, and Luce's notes (pp. 109 and 136, vol. i). *Phil. Com.* 52 is one of the entries accompanied by the plus sign, which in many (but not all) instances may be interpreted as representing discarded views, and *Phil. Com.* 802 represents Berkeley's final view concerning the existence of objects of sense.

18. Without any loss of 'clearness and distinctness' of perception. Reference to this last condition is made in *TV* 83–5. Incidentally, it seems to me that Berkeley's heavy reliance in *TV* 79–87 on the clearness and distinctness of some particular ideas, or sets of ideas, is one of the few relics of Cartesian epistemology in his writings. Cf. also *Phil. Com.* 720.

19. For example, he uses expressions like '*thinking* of points' and '*perceived* squares' (the italics are mine).

20. He emphasizes repeatedly in *Phil. Com.*, and from *PHK* onwards—after the interim period of *TV*—that there is no insensible extension.

21. The italics are mine. The perceivability of *minima* (e.g. in geometrical figures), and various degreees of the actual differentiation of points, are also asserted in *Phil. Com.* 250. A distinction is drawn there

between (1) *m.v.* (which are 'fixt' for all 'beings' whatever), and (2) the least differentiated visual points whose 'smallness' may be evaluated by an angular measurement. Spatio-temporal specifications may provide us, on the Berkeleian view, with criteria for identifying a figure in which 'perceived points' are distinguished with a similar one in which no such 'points' are distinguished.

22. i.e. of concrete lines, surfaces, and volumes of bodies to the extent that they are not considered as perceived by sight.

23. e.g. in *PHK* 47, 50, and 101–2.

24. One may here mention that the doctrine of Lucretius draws a sharp line of distinction between materialism on the one hand and the thesis of the infinite divisibility on the other. Lucretius endorses the first, but rejects the second. Cf. *De rerum natura*, i. 418–48, and 551–98.

Another useful instance would be Boyle's reference to *minima naturalia*. Boyle, of course, was a convinced 'matterist'. Nevertheless, he assumed the existence of *minima naturalia*, of which all physical bodies are composed. These *minima*, on his view, are not actually subdivided in the ordinary course, or the 'experimental history', of nature. (But they can be mentally subdivided, and God can surely dismantle them by means of His infinite powers.) In addition, Boyle maintained that *minima naturalia* are too small to be individually detectable by human observers. He also assumes that such smallest parts are 'very solid', and have shape. (Cf. *Origin of Forms and Qualities, The Works of the Honourable Robert Boyle* (Birch edn., London, 1744), vol. iii, pp. 470–1; and also Marie Boas Hall, *Robert Boyle on Natural Philosophy* (Bloomington, Ind., 1965), e.g. p. 69.) However, Boyle's references to the smallest parts of (material) extensions are not always consistent with each other.

Boyle's intermediate position between atomism and theories of *minima* on the one hand and the hypothesis of infinite divisibility on the other, is mentioned, *inter alia*, by A. G. van Melsen in *From Atomos to Atom* (Pittsburgh, 1952), pp. 99 ff.). On van Melsen's view, Boyle ascribes to the 'concretions' of *prima naturalia* the role of the smallest and practically indivisible particles of elements (ibid., p. 103).

25. On Berkeley's *finitism, atomism*, or *particularism*, in epistemology and mathematics alike, see also G. A. Johnston, *The Development of Berkeley's Philosophy* (London, 1923), pp. 92–3 and 280.

26. i.e. the absurd conclusion is seen by Berkeley to prove his view that the *conjunction* of the two premisses must be false. However, he seems to assume that the two premisses *must* be conjoined and uncritically accepts their conjunction in the corpuscularian hypotheses of his opponents; see also Ch. 1 above. It seems to me that his hesitations in

regard to the necessity of the conjunction of (1) the thesis of infinite divisibility ('Nihilarianism') and (2) 'matterism', or 'materialism', are indicated in one place only: a very brief entry (399) at the very end of Notebook B of *Phil. Com.*: '+ The Materialists and Nihilarians need not be of a party'. But it seems that he did not pay heed to his own suggestion; and entry 399 may be regarded as completely discarded.

27. I use here again a term coined (so far as I know) by A. A. Luce, the chief merit of which is to indicate that Berkeley was not an opponent of the reality of physical *bodies*, but rather of 'matter'. However, the assertion that 'matter' is a metaphysical term does not have to lead one to the obviously metaphysical conclusion that there is no matter.

28. Mathematics, purified from the conceptual muddles of the 'nihilarians' (as exemplified by reference to *matter* and *infinite* divisibility), would, on Berkeley's view, be either an essentially practical science, or a notational game. In both capacities it cannot be regarded as having an equal status with *philosophia prima* which, according to him, includes not only metaphysics, natural theology, and ethics, but also the primary science, or 'theory', of the proper objects of sense, i.e. epistemology. This classification is, for instance, referred to in *TVV* 43, and in *M.* 71–2. See also Johnston, *The Development of Berkeley's Philosophy*, pp. 261–3.

Concerning geometry and physics alike, Berkeley rejected Descartes' and Locke's theses of infinite divisibility of extension (or space). But his theory of finite divisibility of time-sequences, which may be connected with intuitionist foundations of arithmetic, resembles some aspects of the Cartesian concept of time as consisting of discrete moments, in spite of many obvious differences between the two theories. For the best analysis of Berkeley's approach to time, see I. C. Tipton, *Berkeley: The Philosophy of Immaterialism* (London, 1974), pp. 271–80.

29. Cf. again *Phil. Com.* 347: 'Unperceivable perception a contradiction'. This entry is accompanied by the marginal sign *M.P.*, which indicates reference to matter and 'matterist' concepts (and to the division between primary and secondary qualities).

30. 'Blending' of 'immediate and mediate objects of sight' is mentioned, for example, in *TV* 51.

31. Berkeley often says that the visible extension (i.e. every two-dimensional visual manifold as distinct from concave, convex, or even flat, surfaces of bodies; cf. D. M. Armstrong, *Berkeley's Theory of Vision* (Melbourne, 1960), pp. 5–6) is an immediate object of sight. Cf., *inter alia*, the reference to various *figures* as immediate objects of sight in the *Three Dialogues*, vol. ii. p. 175; *TV* 43, where colour is regarded as inseparable from extension (in contrast to distance);

TVV 44 and 46 (where he speaks of 'bounds' or limits between colours); and *TV* 56 (which is most important in this context; Berkeley speaks there of 'the magnitude of extension or the visible object . . . immediately perceived by sight'); etc. However, Armstrong is certainly right in saying that Berkeley sometimes speaks as if the only immediate objects of visual perception were 'light and colours' (op. cit., p. 6). The author of *TV* and *TVV* seems to waver between (1) the contention that light and colours are the only immediate objects of sight, just as sounds are the only *audibilia*; and (2) a quite different view, referred to above, according to which extension may also be regarded as such an immediate visual datum. *TV* 130 exemplifies this confusion very clearly. Berkeley says there that 'as for figure and extension, I leave it to any one that shall calmly attend to his own clear and distinct ideas [*this reference to 'clear and distinct ideas' is one of the few remaining Cartesian undertones in* TV *and in Berkeley's writings in general*] to decide whether he has any idea intromitted immediately and properly by sight save only light and colours . . . It must be owned that by mediation of light and colours other far different ideas are suggested to my mind; but so they are by hearing, which beside sounds which are peculiar to that sense, doth by their mediation suggest not only space, figure, and motion, but also other ideas whatsoever that can be signified by words.' However, in the same section he rather confusedly identifies the query whether the only immediate objects of sight are light and colours with a quite different problem, namely whether the visible extension can be seen or imagined, or conceived of, as uncoloured. In addition, he raises yet another query which seems to undermine, and not to support, his initial assumption that light and colours are the only immediate objects of sight. This rather rhetorical query, which seems to run against the general drift of his argument, is whether one 'can conceive colour without visible extension'. But if one cannot conceive colour without visible extension, it would follow that 'visible extension' has to be included among the 'proper and immediate objects of sight'.

The same tensions between these two basic, but opposite, contentions (i.e. (*a*) that the visible extension is 'immediately perceived'; and (*b*) that it is not 'immediately perceived') can be revealed by comparing *Phil. Com.* 28, 54, 70, 108, 121, 240, 287, etc., to 32, 59, 174, 196, 328; and presumably (I say 'presumably' because of the marginal plus sign, which in *Phil. Com.* usually seems to indicate doubt) 216 may also be regarded as supporting (*b*).

32. Berkeley also sometimes seems to indicate that the visible magnitude is, as it were, less stable than the tangible one, because it depends heavily on ever-shifting kinaesthetic frames of reference (e.g. the

place of our bodies in space), and on certain other (e.g. optical) conditions, whereas measurement by touch is much simpler. See, for instance, *TV* 61.

This 'argument from difficulty of measurement' is not only quite different from the rejection of the immediate perception of visible extension (see also *TV* 153–5); it also does not contradict Berkeley's thesis that *m.v.* are completely independent of *m.t.* But this last thesis ensures, in fact, the independence of visual from tangible extension. All that the 'argument from difficulty of measurement' boils down to is that the co-ordinations between the seen magnitude and physical objects in space may, and sometimes do, vary. (In the same vein, one may maintain that the co-ordinations between *m.v.* and *m.t.* differ as well.) In addition, one may well agree with Berkeley that estimations of purely visual proportions (or purely visual computations of angles), or sometimes even an enumeration of purely visual units, are more difficult than tactual measurement. But it does not follow from all this that there is no 'settled and stated' visual length which may be enumerated by various observers. Berkeley seems to forget that, according to his own premises, an enumeration of quanta of 'light and colours' cannot be less objective (or, for that matter, less 'stable') than an atomic measurement by means of *m.t.*, since those quanta's objective status is not different from that of *m.t.* He emphasizes some empirical features of visual measurement (which might vary under other epistemic conditions) at the expense of his own theory of measurement based on *minima*.

33. Cf. *TV* 132. Berkeley's anticipation of an empirical answer to the 'Molyneux problem' (whether the congenitally blind made to see would identify at the first sight geometrical figures previously perceived by touch and studied by them; cf. also *An Appendix* to 2nd edn. of *TV*, and *TVV* 71) is identical, to all practical purposes, with Locke's standpoint (cf. the *Essay* II. ix, 8). He differs from Locke only in regard to certain epistemic and linguistic implications of the answer.

34. Berkeley says in *Phil. Com.* 321 that single *minima* are not able 'to pleasure or hurt us'. This remark refers to *m.t.* and *m.v.* alike; and, accordingly, seems to have a bearing on the intensity of *m.v.* In addition, the general argument that 'visibles cannot be made up of invisibles' (cf. *Phil. Com.* 464, and also 438) has to be applied not only to extension, but to intensity as well. The crucial entry, in this respect, is without doubt *Phil. Com.* 480, in which he inquires whether *minima* 'may not be compar'd by their sooner or later evanescency as well as by more or less points'. Luce calls it 'an obscure question'. But the meaning seems to be quite clear here; and, in fact, Berkeley provides

more than a clue to it in the last sentence of the entry: 'So that one sensibile may be greater than another tho it exceeds it not by one point'. Thus, quanta of light and colours may be perfectly equal as units of enumeration of visual extension, and yet differ from each other in their colour and intensity. The greater intensity would be accompanied on Berkeley's view, by 'later evanescency'; and, conversely, 'later evanescency' would indicate greater intensity.

It should also be mentioned again in this context that *minima* of light and colours are compared by Berkeley to *sounds* 'so small' that they are 'scarce perceiv'd' (*Phil. Com.* 710). He says that *m.v.*, being 'just perceiv'd and next door to nothing', resemble not only *tangibilia*, but also *audibilia*. Sounds are perceived not via extension, but, among other things, *qua* intensity (or changes of intensity); and, on Berkeley's view, may not be infinitely diminished, being sometimes 'next door to nothing'. (See *Phil. Com.* 394: 'now we Irish men are apt to think something and nothing are next neighbours'.) However, one of the reasons why Berkeley does not postulate *minima* different from *m.v.* and *m.t.* (e.g. *minima audibilia*) in spite of his relevant queries (see e.g. *Phil. Com.* 137) might be his reluctance to completely detach the concept of *minima* from the context of *extension*. In any case, the least degrees of visual intensity (and, of course, the least units of what he considers as the relevant extension) verge, on his view, on complete *absence* of light and colours. (The same contention might also be applied to heat. But heat, according to Berkeley, is not connected with quanta of light and colours which are regarded by him as purely visual, and not as endowed with any thermal qualities.)

Be that as it may, in *TV* he does not refer any more to the 'later or earlier evanescency' of *m.v.*, but only speaks of their 'clearness or darkness' (83–4). This whole problem of various degrees of intensity and 'clearness' of *m.v.* is not really elucidated by him; and *minima* are mainly considered by him as constituents of extension. However, constituents of extension may themselves be unextended. This last possibility is referred to in *Phil. Com.* 442 ('Qu: whether a M.V. be of any colour? a M.T. of any tangible quality?'). This entry, and similar queries (such as in *Phil. Com.* 273, 321), may be interpreted as speaking, among other things, of two quite different possibilities: (1) a state of affairs in which *m.t.* would lack any 'tangible qualities' whatever, or (2) a state of affairs in which it would be extensionless, but, nevertheless, characterized by some other 'tangible qualities' (e.g. heat and coldness, hardness and softness, smoothness and roughness, and, especially, impact). The first assumption (namely, a postulation of non-tangible *minimum tangibile*) is clearly a contradiction in terms, and is also completely repulsive from the Berkeleian point of view. A. A. Luce is, therefore, quite right in maintaining that Berkeley would have had to answer his own query in the affirmative in so far as tangible qualities are concerned (cf. the note on this entry, and on 273 in the *editio diplomatica* of *Phil. Com.*). On the other hand, Luce seems to assume too hastily that *m.t.* has, on Berkeley's premisses, to be extended. Non-tangible *m.t.* would be patently absurd, just like uncoloured *m.v.*, transparent opaque screens, etc. But it seems to me that there is a certain difference between the query in *Phil. Com.* 442 ('whether a *M.T.* be of any tangible quality?') and the query in *Phil. Com.* 273 where Berkeley asks 'whether a m.v. or T be extended?' The more general query (in *Phil. Com.* 442) has to be answered in the affirmative. But the more specified query (in *Phil. Com.* 273) remains problematic, and may, even on Berkeley's premisses, be answered in more than one way. For instance, the very position (i.e. spatial co-ordinates) of a 'point' (e.g. as indicated by lines or rays in an angular measurement) may be considered as its extension. But this is not the only legitimate answer. Another one, for instance, is discussed by Armstrong: 'The minima, it may be said, should be conceived of as extensionless (which does not imply that they do not exist), comprising an extension only by being linked in spatial *relation* with other minima. The extension is, as it were, something that is brought into existence between one minimum and the adjoining one: and so a finite number of extensionless minima can make up an extension.' (*Berkeley's Theory of Vision*, p. 43). In any case, H. M. Bracken seems to me to be wrong when he claims that Berkeleian *minima* are unequivocally conceived of as extended (*Berkeley* (London, 1974), p. 23). But, on the other hand, he is right in claiming that Berkeley's *minima* are designed to evade 'Zenoist strictures' as exposed by Boyle.

It may well be that Berkeley's particular brand of atomism is not free of antinomies inherent in any atomism whatsoever (or, at least, inherent in non-Kantian approaches to atomism); see Kant's references to Berkeley and space in *Critique of Pure Reason*, ed. N. Kemp Smith (London, 1968), pp. 89, 244) and also the Second Antinomy, and Kant's *observations* on its thesis and antithesis where he refers to his own principles of 'transcendental atomism', or 'dialectical monadology'. However, it seems that Strawson is right in maintaining that Kant's argument for the antithesis of the Second Antinomy is not completely convincing (*The Bounds of Sense* (London, 1968), pp. 182–4, and 203–4). Strawson suggests two possible ways out of the antinomy, and other solutions may be suggested as well. But even on the assumption that Berkeley's finitism suffers from certain antinomies, it is difficult to understand Armstrong's a priori contention that objects of sense *have* to be indeterminate, and, therefore, are, or have to be, regarded as neither divisible nor indivisible *ad infinitum* (op. cit., p. 44).

35. The thesis that heterogeneous (visible and tangible) *minima* have to be co-ordinated in order to establish a visual extension (and space; the above-mentioned thesis concerning space can here be held either on its own, or as an *a fortiori* version of the rejection of the immediate perception of visual bi-dimensional figures) is clearly theoretical, as it deals with theoretical terms (*m.v.* and *m.t.* are entities which are not singly observed, and their assumed relations are also postulated within an hypothetical framework). On the other hand, the thesis that 'ideas' of sight and touch have to be co-ordinated in order to establish a visual extension (and space) seems to be empirical to the extent that it depends on case-histories of the congenitally blind made to see (and, presumably, also to the extent that the relevant empirical findings do not leave room for alternative theoretical models). It seems that modern research (e.g. of M. von Senden and R. L. Gregory) has established Berkeley's contention (as exemplified, for example, in *An Appendix* to 2nd edn. of *TV*, and in *TVV* 71) that (1) the visually achieved concepts of space and extension are not immediately identified with the kinaesthetically achieved ones (the case in point would be examined by the behaviour of the congenitally blind made to see), and (2) they can be neither identified nor co-ordinated by a purely geometrical reasoning. ('Kinaesthetically achieved' as above means 'not found to exist without kinaesthetic experience', and 'visually achieved' means 'not found to exist without visual experience'. Berkeley's attempt to provide a general model for such cases is very conspicuous in his hypothesis of 'a nation of men blind from their infancy' (*Alc.* iv, p. 161).) And even if the relevant case-histories (from Jones's and Chesselden's cases onwards) do not *completely* establish the heterogeneity of all concepts of visual extension, or space, on the one hand, and of their assumed kinaesthetic counterparts, on the other, the evidence clearly contradicts some extreme features of a geometrical approach suggested by Leibniz, although not necessarily Locke's more modest and empirical arguments concerning the point at issue.

However, it is not clear whether the relevant case-histories have established that the visually achieved concepts of space *depend* on the kinaesthetically achieved ones. It even seems that Berkeley was wrong concerning this last issue. It is true that most of the empirical findings may be much more plausibly interpreted and correlated by Berkeley's theory than by a lot of others; but this plausibility does not mean that the very general queries raised by the 'Molyneux problem' are unambiguously answered by the clinical research, or that Berkeley is right on *all* the relevant issues.

Most of the relevant case-histories are mentioned in M. von Senden's *Space and Sight: The Perception of Space and Shape in the Congenitally Blind Before and After Operation,* tr. P. Heath (London, 1960). It is noteworthy that, in one very crucial respect, von Senden reveals a conviction directly opposite to Berkeley's; namely, he maintains that concepts of space and spatial relations are purely visual. A similar 'anti-kinaesthetic' and 'ultra-visual' thesis had also been endorsed by T. K. Abbott (cf. *Sight and Touch: An Attempt to Disprove the Received (or Berkeleian) Theory of Vision* (London, 1864), e.g. pp. 10 and 28, and ch. 5, pp. 60 ff.). However, G. J. Warnock seems to be right in saying that this approach of von Senden is sometimes rather dogmatic, especially when it leads him to reject kinaesthetically achieved concepts of space and spatial relations, because 'it does not appear . . . to be required by the evidence, and indeed at key-points it is manifestly reinforced by extraneous considerations of great philosophical interest, but most uncertain authority'. (Cf. the third appendix to *Space and Sight,* p. 322). And Warnock adds that von Senden's 'ultra-visual' approach to space is 'hardly less dogmatic' than Berkeley's 'directly opposite' 'ultra-kinaesthetic' approach (ibid.). Be that as it may, there is nothing in Berkeley's *basic* theses which compels him to reject visual space.

36. In any case, Berkeley seems to maintain that visual proportions are immediately perceived. He clearly indicates in *Phil. Com.* 204 that *proportion* and 'greatness per se' of 'visible appearances' do *not* depend on their unified geometrical organization *qua* extension (neither 'the visual orb' nor any other geometrical forms of the visual manifold, e.g. 'a plain', are regarded by him as immediately perceived). The thesis that there are immediate proportions between various 'visual appearances' is logically completed by the assumption of perceivable *units* of comparison. Berkeley's assumptions (1) that *m.v.* is totally different from *m.t.*, and (2) that proportion and 'greatness per se' of 'visual appearances' do not depend (at least in some cases) on 'blended extension', which is perceived 'by reasoning', support each other.

37. I say 'simultaneously', and 'static', because measurement of successive parts of a bi-dimensional tangible extension would seem, on Berkeley's view, to imply motion (in third dimension). But I would like, for the sake of simplicity and clarity, momentarily to detach kinaesthetic factors from tactual ones.

38. Even on Berkeley's 'weaker thesis', which refers to the visible extension as an immediate object of sight, space is not immediately

seen. Berkeley's contention was that, as we learn 'from infancy' to co-
ordinate sight and touch, we wrongly assume that visual depth is
immediately seen. (However, Berkeley seems to indicate in one place
(*First Dialogue between Hylas and Philonous*, vol. ii, p. 202, ll. 36–40)
that immediate perception of distance could be allowed on his own
premisses.) But this contention might not have been considered as
empirical in absence of any study of congenitally blind adults made to
see. However, due to the gradual accumulation of the relevant
evidence from Jones's and Chesselden's cases onwards (Berkeley
himself mentions the first empirical cases relevant to his theory in *An
Appendix* to 2nd edn. of *TV*, and in *TVV* 71), one can now try to
confirm, or reject, (1) the heterogeneity of (*a*) the original concepts of
movement in space and of (*b*) the newly acquired concepts of visual
co-ordination, and (2) the thesis that visual depth is (*a*) not
immediately seen, and (*b*) lacking 'real' three-dimensionality in
comparison with purely kinaesthetic co-ordination. In this context it
is particularly noteworthy that, according to the case-histories
assembled by von Senden (cf. n. 35 above), the empirical evidence
does not seem to confirm theses 2*a* and 2*b* above. 2*b* in particular
remains without any substantial empirical support (see also n. 35
above). The relevant case-histories clearly indicate that the spatial
concepts of the sighted people are more comprehensive than those of
the congenitally blind, and, moreover, that this comprehensiveness is
not merely an outcome of an acquaintance with new series of data,
different from any formerly perceived, but also a result of a
simultaneous co-ordination, or, as one may perhaps label it,
'togetherness-cum-simultaneity', which is not acquired by touch.
See, for instance, von Senden, *Space and Sight*, pp. 37, 41, and 67.
(See also Armstrong's remarks in *Berkeley's Theory of Vision*, pp. 66;
and H. H. Price, *Perception* (2nd edn., London, 1930), p. 245.
Armstrong's remarks on Berkeley's treatment of visual surfaces
(pp. 66 and 57) are especially useful. According to Price, Berkeley's
rejection of the visually achieved concept of space is not immune from
phenomenological criticism.) I would also remark in passing that
Berkeley was evidently afraid that any assumption of the 'visual space'
would indicate the existence of the 'pure' and 'absolute' one. Thus,
for instance, he says in *PHK* 116: 'Some perhaps may think the sense
of seeing doth furnish them with the idea of pure space; but it is plain
from what we have elsewhere shewn, that the ideas of space and
distance are not obtained by that sense. See the *Essay concerning
Vision*.' However, the idea of the visual space, i.e. of three visual
dimensions, does not seem, on Berkeley's own premises, to
necessitate the existence of quite another idea, namely that of the

kinaesthetic space independent of any frame of reference. In addition, the assumption that the visually achieved concept of three-dimensional expanse has to refer to the 'absolute' space, i.e. to space independent of any standpoint or frame of reference (or, indeed, of any arrangement of units, data, etc.) is not justified by any relevant evidence. (For an analysis of Berkeley's rejection of visual depth see also M. Merleau-Ponty, *Phenomenology of Perception* (London, 1961) pp. 254–6. On Merleau-Ponty's view, bi-dimensionality ('breadth') is, plausibly enough, regarded by Berkeley as more properly belonging to the pure visual data than depth. But he does not deal with various other aspects of Berkeley's theory of visual three-dimensionality.)

In any event, it seems that all the relevant evidence does not really confirm von Senden's thesis, according to which there are no kinaesthetically achieved concepts of space and spatial relations. It seems to indicate rather that the visually achieved spatial concepts are, at least, on the same footing as their kinaesthetic counterparts. See also G. N. A. Vesey, *Berkeley, Reason and Experience* (Cosham, Portsmouth, 1982) pp. 42–3.

39. Motion, or change of place, is possible on Berkeley's view, only when two bodies are concerned. See *PHK* 112: 'To conceive motion, there must be at least conceived two bodies, whereof the distance or position in regard to each other is varied. This seems evident, in that the idea I have of motion doth necessarily include relation.' (But what would have been Berkeley's evaluation of cases in which the (assumed) second body is merely signified by a source of light?) 'Pure space', on the other hand, seems to be regarded by him as conceivable even on the assumption of one body only. 'When I excite a motion in some part of my body, if it be free or without resistance, I say there is *space*: but if I find a resistance, then I say there is *body*' (*PHK* 116). And I have already mentioned those two definitions in Ch. 2, Sect. 10 above. But the logical distinction between (1) space as a relational frame of reference, and (2) space as an absence of resistance (and, *eo ipso*, of bodies), is not consistently held by him. However, in due course, he clarified the distinction between those two concepts of relative space (in *M.* 55). But in *PHK* 112 and 116 his use of the relevant terms is seemingly somewhat confused. In the first place, the term 'motion' stands for *change of place* (i.e. varied 'distance or position', 112), and kinaesthetic *'ideas'* (116) alike (although he tries to clarify this issue by drawing a distinction between *impressed force* and potential motion, on the one hand, and actual motion, on the other). Secondly, the concept of 'one body' is not sufficiently defined. Thirdly, it is not clear whether the *lack of resistance* (i.e. 'free

motion'), and, consequently, *pure space*, are introduced as theoretical terms, or as empirical data.

In any case, there is an obvious difference between space as a relational frame of reference of 'at least two bodies' (cf. *PHK* 112) and 'pure space', i.e. a kinaesthetic datum whose existence may be assumed to the extent that it is not conceived of as 'exclusive of all body'. It should also be mentioned that both Berkeley's conceptions of space refer to tangible objects and kinaesthetic data, and not to *visibilia*. (See the reference to *TV* at the end of *PHK* 116.)

40. But it is noteworthy that the lack of recognition of visual figures by the congenitally blind immediately after the operation (say, after the removal of cataract) does not necessarily mean that light and colours are only arranged into extension after co-ordination with touch, but rather that classification of visual figures has to be gradually learnt, and also that they cannot immediately be seen because of the eye's intolerance of light on the first days of testing. (See, for instance, Franz's case, referred to in von Senden's *Space and Sight* pp. 130–1.) In brief, the need to learn the use of visual co-ordinations and of visually achieved spatial concepts, does not necessarily mean that they depend on touch. Thus, for example, Piaget refers to 'the respective (spatial) fields of various sensory organs', visual, kinaesthetic, etc., put, as it were, on an equal footing during the first stage of the very young children's perception of space. According to Piaget, neither of those primary 'respective fields' depends on three- or two-dimensionality as perceived by other sense-modalities. Only at relatively late stages of the child's development 'coordination of sight and prehension' is achieved and 'a single system' of the different sensory spaces is constituted. (J. Piaget, *The Constitution of Reality in a Child* (New York, 1954), p. 211.)

However, within the framework of the above-mentioned reference to various perceptual fields, Piaget also thinks that the sensory-topological spaces, and, especially, the projective and geometrical spaces, constituted on the basis of the sensory-topological ones, are (*a*) based on various perceptual and physical *activities*, and (*b*) 'mediated' and developed by means of images and schemata (J. Piaget and B. Inhelder, *The Child's Conception of Space* (London, 1967). In his view, the relevant perceptual activities are mainly tactile-kinaesthetic; but the relevant images are mainly visual, although connected with non-visual data, and the constituted—perceived and conceived—percepts and concepts of spaces are, accordingly, regarded by him as (1) based mainly on tactile-kinaesthetic data, and (2) constituted, none the less, with the help of visual imagery. (See, especially, op. cit., pp. 41 and 445.) But it should be noted that

Piaget's analyses and conclusions in the *Child's Conception of Space* deal with normal children, and not with congenitally blind.

It is true that Berkeley might argue against all those objections and comments that there are certain asymmetries between visual perception of distance and that of other spatial relations. These asymmetries seem to indicate that steroscopical vision is 'mediated', not only in contrast to 'light and colours', but to bi-dimensional manifolds as well. (Cf. Armstrong, *Berkeley's Theory of Vision*, p. 67.) However, even in this last case, one might yet argue that Berkeley had no need to assume that the stereoscopical asymmetries have to be explained by references to the primacy of the kinaesthetic space.

41. Cf. *An Appendix* which was added to the second edition of *TV* (at the beginning of 1710).

42. Berkeley says in *TV* 54, that 'it is certain' that 'sensible extension is not infinitely divisible'; but he also admits that the infinite divisibility may, and, indeed, has to, be assumed when speaking of *matter*, or 'extension in abstract'. However, the crucial words 'whatever may be said of extension in abstract' (ibid.) seem to suggest double, if not triple, meaning. First, Berkeley seems to toy with the notion of distinction between 'sensible' and 'insensible' extension. This *ad interim* use of terms is consonant with the half-way immaterialism of *TV* (and also with a possible interpretation of *Phil. Com.* 11, where he says that extension is 'not infinitely divisible in *one* [*my italics*] sense'). The second meaning of this dictum ('whatever may be said of extension in abstract') would be that both 'extension in abstract' *and* the infinite divisibility are mere fictions. (However, Berkeley did not reject in *TV* material extension, but only the abstract 'sensory' one, 'common both to sight and touch'; cf. 129, *ibid.*) Thirdly, Berkeley assumes in the whole sentence ('For, whatever may be said of extension in abstract, it is certain sensible extension is not infinitely divisible') that 'insensible extension' entails the infinite divisibility and vice versa. What he really does is to accept a 'package deal' suggested by his 'matterist' opponents. He assumes that *matter* has to be infinitely divisible, and adds that 'sensible extension' can be divided into finite parts only. (It is, however, noteworthy that the units of 'insensible extension', referred to in *TV*, are not regarded as *mathematical points*, but as infinitely divisible *particles* of matter (see again *An Appendix* to 2nd edn. of *TV*).) Accordingly, it would seem that in passages like *TV* 54 the theory of *minima* is not expounded as an explanatory hypothesis whose function is to ensure the logical ground of objective measurement. Instead, it is based on metaphysical (and supposedly epistemic) grounds of ideism.

43. Thus a triple hierarchy of minimal units of extension is introduced: (*a*) material particles; (*b*) *m.t.*; (*c*) *m.v.*

44. Berkeley does not reject in *TV* the existence of absolute space and its infinite divisibility either. In any case, his contention that visual distance is not 'without the mind' is ambiguous since his 'without' is a sort of blended *sine-cum-extra*. This aspect of the epistemic situation in *TV* has already been dealt with satisfactorily by A. J. Furlong ('Berkeley and the "Knot about Inverted Images"', *Australasian Journal of Philosophy*, 41 (1963), 308–9), Armstrong (*Berkeley's Theory of Vision*, p. 27), and A. R. White ('The Ambiguity of Berkeley's "Without the Mind"', *Hermathena*, 83 (1954), 55–65). See also Tipton, *Berkeley*, pp. 202–9, where reference is made to Warnock's treatment of this problem. Warnock's and Tipton's remarks completely elucidate the ambiguity of the expression 'without the mind' with regard to visual space, which indicates either outness or independence on perceiving minds. See G. J. Warnock, *Berkeley* (2nd edn.; Harmondsworth, 1969), pp. 57–8, and also George Pitcher, *Berkeley* (London, 1977), pp. 29–30.

45. i.e. are regarded as real parts of the *rerum natura*.

46. Moreover, in some places he even seems to indicate that, strictly speaking, space is not mediately seen in the same sense that extension is. (See the reference to space in n. 35 above.) In the present note I try to sum up the status of visual three-dimensionality, within the framework of Berkeley's immaterialism with particular reference to 'unconscious inferences'. According to Berkeley's 'stronger thesis', the visual perception of *horizontal* and *vertical* relations is 'mediated' by relations of *tangibilia* to which the same adjectives are applied, although the tangible-cum-kinaesthetic horizontal, or vertical, relation is, in his view, quite different from its visual counterpart (cf. *TVV* 46). It follows that not only space but extension too is not immediately seen. And, as I have already mentioned above, his 'weaker thesis' is merely that the visible extension and the tangible one are heterogeneous. The 'weaker thesis' does not imply that the visible extension is mediated by touch. However, according to Berkeley, space is not immediately seen even if visual figures are. We may, therefore, conclude that according to both his theses space is not immediately seen. But the crux of the matter is that according to the weaker thesis visual space is 'mediated' by (1) touch, and (2) *immediately* perceived extended patterns of light and colours, whereas according to the stronger thesis it is 'mediated' by (1) touch and (2) *mediately* perceived extension (which itself is a construct elaborated out of extensionless light and colours by means of '*unconscious*', or '*praenotional*', reliance on kinaesthetic experience). Such 'praenotions', i.e. assumptions concerning shape, distance, etc. of 'tangible objects', 'gained by [previous] experience of touch, or of sight and

touch conjunctly', are assumed by Berkeley to influence directly our visual perception, although we are not ordinarily aware of that influence, and even constitute, on his view, 'the true medium by which we apprehend the various degrees of tangible distance' when seeing objects (*TVV* 62). This 'praenotional' reliance of three-dimensional vision on kinaesthetic experience is firmly endorsed by Berkeley. In fact, it is quite amazing that the unconscious or 'praenotional' inferences loom large in his theory of vision, despite his phenomenological reliance on the 'given' percepts. See, for instance, *TVV* 59–64, where 'praenotional apprehensions' of magnitude and distance, i.e. 'praenotional' perceptual constructions of magnitude, distance, etc., elaborated in due course of epistemic evolution out of mixed visual and kinaesthetic clues on the unconscious level, are suggested as substitutes for (*a*) purely immediate phenomenological data, and also for (*b*) geometrical (conscious or unconscious) deductions. And the 'anti-deductive', or 'anti-geometrical', anti-Cartesianism of *b*-substitution is much more consistent with Berkeley's general phenomenological approach than his equally anti-Cartesian reliance on unconscious perception as in *a*-substitution.

47. i.e. the contention that *m.v.* are basic units of measurement which may be distinctly observed by various 'perceivers'. Accordingly *m.v.* may, in this respect, be regarded as similar both to *m.t.* and to the real magnitude of the fixed particles of matter assumed by the 'corpuscularians'—i.e. to assumed particles of *one and the same kind*, and also to particles conceived of as ultimate atoms. Obviously, material particles of *different* kinds and sizes (e.g. as assumed by Boyle in *The Excellency and Grounds of Corpuscular and Mechanical Philosophy*) may hardly function as units of common measurement. In addition, Berkeley maintains that even identical material particles would lack that magnitude *per se* which depends on an enumeration of fixed atomic constituents, i.e., on his view, of *minima*. Cf. also *PHK* 47, and Luce's n. 65, *Phil. Com.*, vol. i.

48. 'Kinematics' here would not refer unconditionally to changes of position of 'light and colours' in visual fields; it would only refer to their co-ordination with movements of bodies, and, especially, to movements of bodies themselves.

49. In the same vein, the atomic structure of (2) is, of course, regarded by him as independent of the atomic structure of (1).

50. Relations mentioned in (2) indicate not only a purely visual magnitude, but also an absolute visual magnitude which has to be considered as countable by means of enumeration of quanta of 'light and colours'. The same contention seems to be applicable to relations mentioned in (1), in so far as the sphaera visualis is considered as

composed of *m.v.* But Berkeley sometimes tends to refer to the sphaera visualis as primarily based on angular measurement, e.g. as 'less that 180°' and the angular measurement that he suggests may be either consistent or inconsistent with the atomic one. For an emphasis put on angular measurement combined with reliance on 'the field of view size', a proportion of any given visual object to the entire visual field, see H. V. Stainsby, 'Sight and Sense-Data', *Mind*, 79 (1970), 170–87. Stainsby refers to Berkeley's, Moore's, and Price's views on angular-cum-proportional measurement, but not to Berkeley's concept of quanta-based measurement.

51. I have already more than once briefly mentioned above that the concept of *minima* may be considered either as based on epistemic assertions, or on a tautology, or as a theoretical term. I have also indicated that the use of this concept by Berkeley seems to be justified in so far as it is employed as a theoretical term, linked, of course, in its turn, to certain metaphysical assumptions and to some analyses of matters of fact (e.g. of extended physical objects). And it should also be noticed again that Berkeley's hypothesis of *minima* was not incorporated, in spite of its many valuable theoretical insights, within the framework of scientific hypotheses of the 18th c. The fault was not entirely Berkeley's own. After all, he did suggest a completely new and previously unknown linguistic model for explanation of the physical universe, instead of the then prevailing mechanistic one. (Perhaps the best discussion of Berkeley's application of linguistic models to nature, to perception, and to scientific hypotheses, is to be found in C. M. Turbayne's well-known commentary, *Berkeley's Works on Vision* (New York, 1963).)

However, it must be mentioned that, in addition to the novelty of the linguistic model, there were also some other features in Berkeley's theories which impaired their influence. In many cases, his explanatory suggestions were not useful enough, and, in sharp contrast to his analysis of vision, did not enable the relevant theories to function as parts of a scientific machinery of prediction and discovery. Thus, the theory of *minima* failed to provide explanatory links between hypotheses and observations in physics, and was, accordingly, completely detached from any scientific context, although it certainly is very interesting from the respective points of view of epistemology, mathematics (calculus), history of philosophy of science, theory of measurement, and modest metaphysics. (It is, of course, also most pertinent from the point of view of experimental psychology of perception. But this last science was practically non-existent at the beginning of the 18th c.) In any case, Berkeley was not able to introduce it as a substitute for the corpuscularian theory of light in explanatory hypotheses and actual computations of geometrical optics, nor as a substitute for Huygens's explanations. His finitist approach to the theory of light had been couched before *TVV* (mainly in *Phil. Com.* and *TV*) in terms of the *minima*-theory, and not in terms of particles; but he was not able to refer to most problems of physical optics (and to physics—and chemistry—in general) without reference to corpuscularian units bigger than his *minima*.

It is, therefore, not at all surprising that Berkeley virtually abandoned reference to *minima* (and unified his finitism with corpuscularian hypotheses accepted by him from *TVV* onwards). As a young man he expounded the *minima*-theory enthusiastically. Its various aspects were most carefully discussed in *Phil. Com.* and *TV* (54, 62, 79–83), but *minima* are scarcely referred to after *TV* (1709): the theory is mentioned only once in *PHK* (132) and not at all in his later works. (See also Luce's n. 59, *Phil. Com.*, vol. i.) However, it is noteworthy that the finitist doctrine, as applied to mathematics, is once more expounded by Berkeley in the 1730s (in *An.*). In any case, the author of *Siris* remained a convinced finitist (see also *S.* 271), but preferred to rely on divisible particles in physics, chemistry, and optics.

Be that as it may, it seems to me that not only Berkeley's later corpuscularian theories, but even his early arguments concerning *minima*, include some highly original, and, one may say, modern insights. It is certainly noteworthy that both particles (e.g. as mentioned in *Siris*) and *minima* may be regarded as theoretical entities. However, there are many differences between Berkeley's theoretical approach to *minima* in *Phil. Com.* and *TV* and his treatment of particles in *Siris*. I try to sum up these differences in Appendix E below.

52. Berkeley refers here principally to human epistemic conditions, and, by implication, to epistemic states of affairs in general. On the other hand, there is on his premises nothing, in principle, infelicitous in a different, and, one may say, diametrically opposite, assumption, according to which 'visible magnitudes' and physical objects, i.e. 'bodies', might be correlated in unchanging proportions in some, or all, states of affairs.

53. However, one might maintain that $(\sim c)$ (i.e. the lack of a uniform correspondence between *m.v.* and *m.t.*) is logically connected with what may be regarded as an observation-statement (a), and a theoretical statement (b) mentioned in the Appendix above, only if there are no further empirical factors—e.g. various correlations of media—which have to be taken into account. But this last condition seems to be completely hypothetical, being neither an accepted matter

of fact nor something deduced from any premiss. Moreover, one might argue that any given 'lack of constancy' on various macroscopic or macrocosmic levels is a mere empirical feature which does not necessarily hold in all parts of the universe, and which does not characterize all possible visual fields. It is also noteworthy that Berkeley himself says that fluctuations in 'lack of constancy' occur sometimes because of various changes of context. (Cf. his reference to intermediate objects and other 'media' in *TV* 3; and also in 67–8, where he deals with 'the phenomenon of the horizontal moon' and various ways for estimating 'the magnitude of outward objects'.)

54. The size of particles is here regarded as uniform. Berkeley speaks, for instance, of a state of affairs in which 'the same particle of matter' that 'is marked to a man by one *minimum visibile*, exhibits to an insect a great number of *minima visibilia*' (*An Appendix* to 2nd edn. of *TV*, vol. i., p. 239).

55. In 1709, i.e. before the exposition of the full-fledged immaterialism in *PHK*. However, it seems reasonable, as G. J. Warnock pointed out to me, that Berkeley's assumption that particles exist even apart from tangible *minima* may be explained as an instance of his 'as if' semi-materialist tactical approach which is so characteristic of *TV*. See also n. 42 above.

56. e.g. in *TV* 55.

57. An exemplification of the Cartesian (and Malebranchian) approach to the issue of the infinite divisibility may be found in J. Norris's *The Theory of the Ideal World* (London, 1704), Part II, p. 44: '. . . all the matter is divisible as such, it being not to be conceiv'd that a thing should be extended and not divisible, which by the way shews the Doctrine of Democritus concerning Indivisibles to be impossible'. It is also noteworthy that, according to the Neoplatonic and Malebranchian contentions of Norris, the infinite divisibility of matter is here modelled on the infinite divisibility of the Idea of intelligible extension (as found in *Nous* and reflected on by any mind whatever).

58. I do not mean here by 'real' 'non-relative', but merely 'in which one can move'.

59. According to which the very concept of *matter* implies infinite divisibility, and vice versa.

60. Locke refers in the *Essay* II. xv. 9 to 'a *sensible* point, meaning thereby the least particle of matter or space we can discern'. He also says (ibid.), in a footnote added to the fifth edition that 'the least portion of space or extension whereof we have a clear and distinct *idea* may perhaps be the fittest to be considered by us as a *simple idea* of that kind, out of which our complex modes of space and extension are made up. It may fitly be called a *simple idea*, since it is the least *idea* of

space that the mind can form to itself and that cannot be divided by the mind into any less whereof it has in itself any determined perception.'

61. But, in this case, it would follow that indivisible *minima* represent divisible particles of matter.

62. i.e. it would follow, on this view, that matter and tangible extension may be distinct, and yet peacefully co-exist. The same would hold in regard to particles of matter and *m.t.* However, in this case, it would also follow that *m.t.*, being merely epistemic, do not exist in, and do not constitute, common space, or extension.

63. x and y have on Berkeley's premisses, to be integers. But it has already been mentioned above that this contention does not apply to values of y/x (or x/y).

64. See also my 'Particles and *Minima* in George Berkeley's Immaterialism' (Oxford Univ. D.Phil. thesis, 1971), ch. 1, iii–iv. I tried there to sum up various Renaissance *minima*-theories (pp. 184–207), although I was not able to provide any evidence that Berkeley was influenced by them. For an earlier *minima*-theory, that of Wyclif, see N. Kretzmann, 'Continua, Indivisibles, and Change in Wyclif's Logic of Scripture', in A. Kenny, ed., *Wyclif in His Times* (Oxford, 1986), pp. 31–63. It is interesting that one of Wyclif's labels for the minimal units of division is *non-quanta*, apparently since they are regarded as having no enumerable parts. However, Berkeley's *minima* may be regarded as *quanta* because he emphasizes that any given extension consists of a finite and, in principle, countable number of such minimal and indivisible units. (The countability hypothesis stands in sharp contrast to Cavalieri's method of indivisibles; see also n. 11 to this Appendix.) I am grateful to Anthony Kenny for drawing my attention to Kretzmann's article.

Notes to Appendix B

1. First published in *The British Journal for the Philosophy of Science*, 4 (1953). Reprinted as ch. 6 of Popper's *Conjectures and Refutations* (3rd edn. revised, 1969), and in *Locke and Berkeley: A Collection of Critical Essays*, ed. C. B. Martin and D. M. Armstrong (1968), pp. 436–49. The pagination of my quotations refers to the latter.

2. Ibid., p. 447.

3. *Conjectures and Refutations*, p. 266. And see also p. 256 n. 12, where Popper claims that, in Berkeley's view, 'words purporting to denote unobservable entities cannot have any meaning'. And Popper clarifies in his references to Berkeley that 'unobservable' in the above-mentioned passage means 'unobservable by human perceivers under

present conditions', i.e. that not only *forces* or *absolute space* but even *particles* are considered by Berkeley as unobservable.

4. See also Chs. 2–4 above and Appendix C. For Berkeley's inductivist approach to particles in the period of *PHK* and *TD*, see, *inter alia*, Ch. 1 above, and my 'Berkeley: Corpuscularianism and Inductivism', *Manuscrito*, 2/2 (São Paulo, Brasil, 1979), 21–42. For later references to Berkeley's corpuscularianism, and to relations between his inductivism and hypothetico-deductive proceedings, see I. C. Tipton's and D. Garber's articles in C. M. Turbayne, ed., *Berkeley: Critical and Interpretive Essays* (Minneapolis, 1982), and M. D. Wilson, 'Berkeley and the Essences of the Corpuscularians', in J. Foster and H. Robinson, eds., *Essays on Berkeley: A Tercentennial Celebration* (Oxford, 1985), pp. 131–47.

5. See, for instance, sects. 139, 145, 151, 197, 222, 227, 232, 238, 239, 240, 244, 248, 250, 255, 267, 277, and 182. *S.* 250, in particular, refers to particles as undoubtedly real. Berkeley only rejects there the *causal powers* of particles. The relevant passage of *S.* 250 is quoted above, in sect. III of this appendix, and in Ch. 2 Sect. 2 and Ch. 3, Sect. 1 above.

6. In *A*, *B*, *C*, and *D* editions of *Siris* Berkeley employed here 'supposed' and 'explained'; but in the *E*-edition, also published during his life, 'suppose' and 'explain' appear.

7. *A Note*, p. 449.

8. Ibid., pp. 448–9.

9. Cf. Popper's criticism of Berkeley, ibid.

10. Ibid., p. 444. The emphasis is Popper's.

11. And cf. Ch. 2 n. 18 above.

12. And cf. Ch. 2 n. 19 above.

13. Assuming that the question of their reality has been settled favourably by observation and experiments independent of at least these theories in which their names, or designations, had functioned as terms. [See also reference to 'PIC theories' in H. R. Harré's 'Metaphor, Model and Mechanism', *Proceedings of the Aristotelian Society*, NS (1955–60), 101–22, esp. 105–8.) My views on the theoretical impact of Berkeley's treatment of particles in *S.* were influenced by Harré's approach to the possibilities of 'realistic' evaluation involved in existential hypotheses. It is also noteworthy that, in *S.* 222, Berkeley seems to assume that at least some particles, e.g. of water, acids, and earth, may be referred to as undoubtedly real, and so provide a sound basis for corpuscularian analogies in further fields of research.

14. Not considered as terms in mathematical hypotheses only.

15. Not necessarily the same laws as in the macrocosmic realm.

16. The relevant part of the section, omitted by Popper, runs as follows: 'for it would then follow that the constituent particles of air were of

equal densities and diameters; where it is certain that air is a heterogeneous mass, containing in its composition an infinite variety of exhalations, from the different bodies which make up this terraqueous globe.' See also Ch. 2 Sect. 2 above.

17. It should be noted again that Berkeley relied on and referred to the theory of *minima* in his early writings (the *Phil. Com.* and his first Essay on Vision), but it is scarcely mentioned from *PHK* onwards; however, he did not abandon it (see, for example, references to indivisibility in *S.* 207–9, and 271, and *PHK* 132).

18. On useful 'mathematical hypotheses' (or useful terms in such hypotheses), which, however, do *not* refer to real terms or qualities in the *rerum natura*, cf. *M.* 17 and 28. Sect. 17 runs as follows: '*Vis, gravitas, attractio*, et huiusmodi voces utiles sunt ad ratiocinia, et computationes de motu et corporibus motis: sed non ad intelligendam simplicem ipsius motus naturam, vel ad qualitates totidem distinctas designandas. Attractionem certe quod attinet, patet illam ab Newtono adhiberi, non tanquam qualitatem veram et physicam, sed solummodo ut hypothesin mathematicam. Quin et Leibnitius, nisum elementarem seu solicitationem ab impetu distinguens, fatetur illa entia non re ipsa inveniri in rerum natura, sed abstractione facienda esse.' ('*Force, gravity, attraction*, and terms of this sort are useful for reasonings and reckonings about motion and bodies in motion, but not for understanding the simple nature of motion itself or for indicating so many distinct qualities. As for attraction, it was certainly introduced by Newton, not as a true, physical quality, but only as a mathematical hypothesis. Indeed, Leibniz, when distinguishing elementary effort or solicitation from impetus, admits that those entities are not really found in nature, but have to be formed by abstraction.' (Trans. A. A. Luce.)) And see also *PHK* 101–17.

Attraction and gravity (considered as forces), *force* itself, *parallelogram of forces*, and alike are considered by Berkeley as useful mathematical fictions with no possible reference in the physical universe. Now *absolute time, absolute space* and *absolute motion* are considered by him as mere 'phantoms', as *flatus vocis* with neither use nor reference; i.e. in his view, they are not even useful mathematical fictions, being concepts riddled with contradictions, and because one can do mathematical physics without them (see, for instance, *M.* 52–65, and *S.* 271 and 293. But in *S.* 293 he even refers to 'corporeal forces' as 'phantoms'). In any case, *particles*, in sharp contrast to 1) *attraction, gravity, and forces*, and 2) *absolute time*, and *absolute motion* alike, are never referred to in *Siris* as terms in *mathematical* hypotheses. They are considered rather as terms in possibly existential hypotheses. See Chs. 2–4.

19. See, for instance, *S.* 147, 150, 151, 207–9, and 228.

20. *A Note*, pp. 442–3.
21. Cf. sect. III above and n. 13 and references to 'animal spirits' in *S.* 156 and 161.
22. *A Note*, p. 443.
23. Ibid.
24. G. Buchdahl, *Metaphysics and the Philosophy of Science* (Oxford, 1969), pp. 309–11. I myself reached a conclusion in this matter similar to that of Buchdahl, but quite independently of him, in ch. 2 of my D.Phil. thesis prior to the appearance of Buchdahl's book. In any case, Buchdahl refers to *S.* only occasionally whereas my thesis and the present book try to map accurately Berkeley's entire corpuscularian philosophy in *Siris* (cf. also my 'Note on Berkeley's Corpuscularian Theories in *Siris*', *Studies in History and Philosophy of Science*, 2/3 (1971), 257–71), and strengthen Buchdahl's view that one must distinguish Berkeley's rejection of the Lockean 'real essence' from the rejection of the very existence of the corpuscularian realm. Regarding the period of *PHK*, see also nn. 2 and 12 to Ch. 1 above, and my 'Berkeley: Corpuscularianism and Inductivism', pp. 21–42.
25. *TVV* 43. The relevant passage in this section runs as follows: 'To explain how the mind or soul of man simply sees is one thing, and belongs to philosophy. To consider particles as moving in certain lines, rays of light as refracted or reflected, or crossing, or including angles, is quite another thing, and appertaineth to geometry. To account for the sense of vision by the mechanism of the eye is a third thing, which appertaineth to anatomy and experiments. These two latter speculations are of use in practice, to assist the defects and remedy the distempers of sight, agreeably to the natural laws obtaining in this mundane system.' G. J. Warnock refers in a most illuminating way to this section's place in Berkeley's change of mind with regard to corpuscles (from their rejection as unnecessary fictions to the acceptance of their theoretical use) in his *Berkeley* (2nd edn., p. 202).
26. Incidentally, it should be noted here that R. J. Brook, in *Berkeley's Philosophy of Science* (The Hague, 1973), also points out that Popper seriously misinterpreted *S.* 228 in his well-known *Note on Berkeley as Precursor of Mach and Einstein*. Popper wrongly assumes that *S.* 228 rejects explanatory hypotheses. Brook, following Buchdahl, realizes that Popper exaggerates in picturing Berkeley as an arch-Machian; however, he maintains (cf. pp. 96–7) that *S.* 228 is criticizing the 'ad-hoc hypotheses' 'whose sole purpose is to explain certain phenomena', whereas, in fact, the 'sole purpose' of *S.* 228 is to criticize the view that explanatory hypotheses are logically entailed by the phenomena they explain (see my detailed interpretation of *S.* 228 in

Ch. 2 above). But Brook is right in maintaining that Berkeley attacked the Cartesians not so much from the immaterialist as from the ultra-Newtonian point of view (op. cit., p. 98). Both Berkeley's anti-Cartesianism and the rejection of Popper's instrumentalist misinterpretation of *Siris* have an important place in my Oxford D.Phil. thesis and in my article in *Studies in History and Philosophy of Science,* respectively completed and published two years before the publication of Brook's book.

However, Brook's brief and *en passant* mention of particles as in *S.* is clearly wrong on one major issue. He rejects T. E. Jessop's contention that Berkeley's treatment of aether in *S.* is consistent with immaterialism. Aether is regarded by Berkeley as 'insensible'. Brook asks how an insensible entity can be regarded as an 'idea'. He concludes that this is 'an unresolved dilemma' in *S.*, especially since Berkeley did *not* treat particles as completely fictitious mathematical devices (op. cit., pp. 100–2). But, in fact, the Berkeley of *S.* conceives of *aether* as a theoretical term which *may* refer to a 'sensible entity'. And, concerning the non-mathematical status of particles in *S.*, Brook attacks Warnock's remarks on Berkeley's mathematical hypotheses (in *Berkeley*, 2nd edn., pp. 202–3). However, Warnock's relevant remark does not refer to *S.* at all, but to *TVV*, and his remark is most ingenious as it takes notice of Berkeley's acceptance of the use of corpuscularian theories, in contrast to the very existence of micro-entities, in the 1730s.

BIBLIOGRAPHY

A. BOOKS

ABBOTT, T. K., *Sight and Touch: An Attempt to Disprove the Received (or Berkeleian) Theory of Vision* (London, 1864).

ABETTI, G., *The History of Astronomy* (London, 1954).

AGASSIZ, J., *An Essay on Classification* (London, 1895).

ALLEN, M. J. B., *The Platonism of Marsiglio Ficino* (Berkeley, Calif., 1984).

ARDLEY, G., *Berkeley's Renovation of Philosophy* (The Hague, 1968).

ARMSTRONG, D. M., *Berkeley's Theory of Vision* (Melbourne, 1960).

BAILEY, S., *A Review of Berkeley's Theory of Vision* (London, 1842).

BENNETT, J., *Locke, Berkeley, Hume: Central Themes* (Oxford, 1971).

BLACKMORE, J. T., *Ernst Mach: His Work, Life and Influence* (Berkeley, Calif., 1972).

BOAS HALL, M., *Robert Boyle on Natural Philosophy* (Bloomington, Ind., 1965).

BOERHAAVE, H., *Elementa Chemiae* (Leiden, 1732).

BOYLE, R., *Works of Robert Boyle, The Origin of Forms and Qualities* (Birch edn., London, 1744, vol. iii; 2nd edn., London, 1772).

—— *The Sceptical Chymist* (London, 1661, 1911; Birch edn., vol. i).

BRACKEN, H. M. *Berkeley* (London, 1974).

BROOK, R. J., *Berkeley's Philosophy of Science* (The Hague, 1973).

BUCHDAHL, G., *Metaphysics and the Philosophy of Science* (Oxford, 1969).

BUTTERFIELD, H., *The Origins of Modern Science 1300–1800* (London, 1950).

CAVALIERI, B., *Geometria indivisibilibus continuorum nova quadam promota ratione* (Bologna, 1635).

—— *Exercitationes geometricae sex* (Bologna, 1647).

DAWES HICKS, G., *Berkeley* (London, 1932).

DAVIE, D., *The Language of Science and the Language of Literature* (London, 1963).

DESCARTES, R., *Œuvres*, ed. C. Adam and P. Tannery (Paris, 1897–1913).

ENGLE, G. W. and G. TAYLOR, eds., *Berkeley's Principles of Human Knowledge: Critical Studies* (Belmont, Calif., 1968).

FOSTER, J., and H. ROBINSON, eds., *Essays on Berkeley: A Tercentennial Celebration* (Oxford, 1985).

GASSENDI, P., *De apparente magnitudine solis humilis atque sublimis, Epistolae quatuor* (Paris, 1642).

HALES, S., *Vegetable Statics* (London, 1727).

—— *Statical Essays* (London, 1733).

HARRÉ, H. R., *Matter and Method* (London, 1964).

HESSE, M., *Forces and Fields* (London, 1961).

HUXLEY, T. H., *Hume: With Helps to the Study of Berkeley* (London, 1971).

JOHNSTON, G. A., *The Development of Berkeley's Philosophy* (London, 1923).

KANT, I., *Critique of Pure Reason*, ed. N. Kemp Smith (London, 1968).

LENIN, V., *Materialism and Empiriocriticism* (Moscow, 1948).

LOCKE, J., *An Essay Concerning Human Understanding*, ed. J. W. Yolton (London, 1961; revised 1965).

LOVEJOY, A. O., *The Great Chain of Being* (Cambridge, Mass., 1936).

LUCE, A. A., *Berkeley and Malebranche* (Oxford, 1934).

—— *Berkeley's Immaterialism* (Edinburgh, 1946).

—— *The Dialectic of Immaterialism* (London, 1963).

MACH, E., *The Analysis of Sensations* (English tr.; Chicago, 1911).

—— *The Science of Mechanics* (English tr., La Salle, Ill., 1960).

MALEBRANCHE, N., *De la recherche de la vérité* (Amsterdam, 1688; Paris, 1965).

MARTIN, C. B., and D. M. ARMSTRONG, eds., *Locke and Berkeley: A Collection of Critical Essays* (London, 1968).

MELSEN, VAN A. G., *From Atomos to Atom* (Pittsburgh, 1952).

MERLEAU-PONTY, M., *Phenomenology of Perception* (London, 1961).

NEWTON, SIR ISAAC, *Opticks* (Dover edn.; New York, 1952; based on the 4th edn.; London, 1730).

—— *The Mathematical Principles of Natural Philosophy* (New York, 1964).

NORRIS, J., *The Theory of the Ideal World* (London, 1704).

OLSCAMP, P. J., *The Moral Philosophy of George Berkeley* (The Hague, 1970).

PANNEKOEK, A., *The History of Astronomy* (London, 1961).

PARK, D., *Complementary Notions: A Critical Study of Berkeley's Theory of Concepts* (The Hague, 1972).

PEPPER, S. C., K. ASCHENBRENNER, and B. MATES, eds., *George Berkeley: Lectures Delivered before the Philosophical Union of the University of California* (Los Angeles, 1957).

PIAGET, J., *The Constitution of Reality in a Child* (New York, 1954).

—— and B. INHELDER, *The Child's Conception of Space* (London, 1967).

PITCHER, G., *Berkeley* (London, 1977).

POPKIN, R. J., *The History of Scepticism from Erasmus to Descartes* (rev. edn., New York, 1968).

POPPER, SIR KARL, *The Logic of Scientific Discovery* (London, 1959).

—— *Conjectures and Refutations* (3rd edn., revised; London, 1969).

—— *Unended Quest: An Intellectual Autobiography* (London, 1976).

PRICE, H. H., *Perception* (London, 1932; 2nd edn., 1950).

RITCHIE, A. D., *George Berkeley: A Reappraisal* (Manchester, 1967).

SENDEN, VON M., *Space and Sight: The Perception of Space and Shape in the Congenitally Blind Before and After Operation*, tr. P. Heath (London, 1960).

SINGER, C., *Short History of Scientific Ideas to 1900* (Oxford, 1959).

STACK, G. J., *Berkeley's Analysis of Perception* (The Hague and Paris, 1970).

STEINKRAUS, W. E., ed., *New Studies in Berkeley's Philosophy* (New York and Chicago, 1966).

STRAWSON, SIR PETER, *The Bounds of Sense* (London, 1966).

TIPTON, I. C., *Berkeley: The Philosophy of Immaterialism* (London, 1974).

TURBAYNE, C. M., *The Myth of Metaphor* (New Haven, Columbia, SC, 1970).

—— ed., *A Treatise concerning the Principles of Human Knowledge: George Berkeley, with Critical Essays* (Indianapolis and New York, 1970).

—— *Berkeley: Critical and Interpretive Essays* (Minneapolis, 1982).

URMSON, J. O., *Berkeley* (Oxford, 1982).

VESEY, G. N. A., *Berkeley, Reason and Experience* (Cosham, Portsmouth, 1982).

WARNOCK, G. J., *Berkeley* (2nd edn., Harmondsworth, 1969).

WILD, J., *George Berkeley* (1st edn., Harvard, 1936; New York, 1962).

WOLF, A., *A History of Science, Technology and Philosophy in the Eighteenth Century* (London, 1952).

YOLTON, J. W., *Locke and the Compass of Human Understanding* (Cambridge, 1970). (This book on Locke is important for understanding Berkeley as well.)

References to various works of Plato, Aristotle, Plotinus, and Aquinas as above follow the standard and the *Basic Works* editions:

Plato, *The Works*, tr. B. Jowett (3rd edn.; Oxford, 1892).

The *Basic Works of Aristotle*, Oxford tr.; edited and with an introduction by R. McKeon (New York, 1941).

Plotini Opera Omnia, ed. G. H. Moser and F. Creuzer (Oxford, 1835). *Plotinus: The Enneads*, tr. S. MacKenna and B. S. Page (3rd edn.; London, 1962).

St Thomas Aquinas, *Opera Omnia* (Leonine edn.; Rome, 1882).

B. ARTICLES

AARON, R. I., 'Locke and Berkeley's Commonplace Book', *Mind*, 40 (1927), 439–59.

ACTON, H. B., 'George Berkeley' in P. Edwards, ed., *Encyclopaedia of Philosophy*, vol. i (New York, 1967), pp. 295–304.

AGASSI, J., 'The Future of Berkeley's Instrumentalism', *International Studies in Philosophy*, 7 (1975), 167–78.

ALEXANDER, P., 'Boyle and Locke on Primary and Secondary Qualities', in I. C. Tipton, ed., *Locke on Human Understanding: Selected Essays* (Oxford, 1977), pp. 62–76.

BARNES, W. H. F., 'Did Berkeley Misunderstand Locke?', *Mind*, 49 (1940), 152–7.

BAUM, R. J., *Philosophy and Mathematics: From Plato to the Present* (San Francisco, 1973). (Ch. 8 on Berkeley.)

BERMAN, D., 'Francis Hutcheson on Berkeley and the Molyneux Problem', *Proceedings of the Royal Irish Academy*, 74/8 (1974), 259–65.

BRYKMAN, G., 'Microscopes and Philosophical Method in Berkeley', in C. M. Turbayne, ed., *Berkeley: Critical and Interpretive Essays* (Minneapolis, 1982), pp. 69–82.

COHEN, B. I., Preface to Sir Isaac Newton's *Opticks* (New York, 1952), pp. ix–lviii.

DAVIE, G. E., 'Berkeley's Impact on Scottish Philosophers' *Philosophy*, 40 (1965), 222–34.

DAVIS, J. W., 'Berkeley and Newton on Space', in R. E. Butts and J. W. Davis, eds., *The Methodological Heritage of Newton* (Oxford, 1970), pp. 59–71.

FLAMM, D., 'Boltzmann, His Influence on Science', *Studies in History and Philosophy of Science*, 14 4 (1983), 255–78.

FLEW, A., 'Critical Notice of Jonathan Bennett's *Locke, Berkeley, Hume: Central Themes*', *Canadian Journal of Philosophy*, 3 (1974), 691–701.

FURLONG, A. J., 'Berkeley and the "Knot about Inverted Images"', *Australasian Journal of Philosophy*, 41 (1963), 306–16.

GARBER, D., 'Locke, Berkeley, and Corpuscular Scepticism', in C. M. Turbayne, ed., *George Berkeley: Critical and Interpretive Essays* (Minneapolis, 1982), pp. 174–93.

GLOUBERMAN, M., 'Berkeley and Kant: Archetypes Vs. Ectypes', *Rivista Critica Di Storia Della Filosofia*, 2 (1981), 139–55.

GREGORY, R. L., 'The Scientific Past and the Practising Scientist', *Times Literary Supplement* 764/3 (26 Apr. 1974), 429–30. Includes discussion of Molyneux Problem. Followed by replies by: J. L. Mackie (3 May), Gregory (17 May), D. Park (31 May), and D. Berman (21 June).

HARRÉ, H. R., 'Metaphor, Model and Mechanism', *Proceedings of the Aristotelian Society*, ns 60 (1959–60), 101–22.

HINRICHS, G., 'The Logical Positivism of Berkeley's *De Motu*', *The Review of Metaphysics*, 3 (1960), 491–505.

HOBHOUSE, S., 'Isaac Newton and Jacob Boehme: An Enquiry', *Selected Mystical Writings of William Law* (London, 1948), Appendix 4, pp. 416–17.

HOMBERG, W., 'Suite de l'article trois des Essais de Chimie', *Mémoires de l'Académie française des sciences* (Paris, 1706).

JACKSON, R., 'Locke's Distinction Between Primary and Secondary Qualities', *Mind*, 38 (1929), repr. in C. B. Martin and D. M. Armstrong, eds., *Locke and Berkeley*, (London, 1968), pp. 53–77.

JESSOP, T. E., Introduction and Notes to *Siris, The Works of George Berkeley, Bishop of Cloyne*, ed. A. A. Luce and T. E. Jessop (London and Edinburgh, 1948–57), vol. v.

KRETZMANN, N., 'Continua, Indivisibles and Change in Wyclif's Logic of Scripture', in A. Kenny, ed., *Wyclif in His Times* (Oxford, 1986), pp. 31–63.

LUCE, A. A., 'The Alleged Development of Berkeley's Philosophy', *Mind*, 53 (1943), 141–56.

—— Introduction and Notes to *Philosophical Commentaries, The Works of George Berkeley, Bishop of Cloyne*, ed. A. A. Luce and T. E. Jessop (London and Edinburgh, 1948–57), vol. i. (And see also A. A. Luce's 1944 *editio diplomatica* of *Philosophical Commentaries*.)

MABBOT, J. D., 'The Place of God in Berkeley's Philosophy', *Journal of Philosophical Studies*, 6 (1931), 18–29.

MARGOLIS, J., 'Esse est Percipi Once Again', *Dialogue*, 5 (1967), 516–24.

MAXWELL, G., 'The Ontological Status of Theoretical Entities', in H. Feigl and G. Maxwell, eds., *Minnesota Studies in the Philosophy of Science*, (Minneapolis, 1962), vol. iii, pp. 9–11.

MOKED, G., 'A Note on Berkeley's Corpuscularian Theories in *Siris*', *Studies in History and Philosophy of Science*, 2, no. 3 (Cambridge, 1971), 257–71.

—— 'Particles and *Minima* in George Berkeley's Immaterialism' (Univ. of Oxford D.Phil. thesis, 1971).

—— 'On New Aspects in George Berkeley's Philosophy of Nature in *Siris*' *The Rational and Irrational: A Collection of Papers* (Ben Gurion University of the Negev, Beersheba, Israel, 1975), pp. 129–45. (In Hebrew).

—— 'Berkeley: Corpuscularianism and Inductivism', *Manuscrito*, 2/2 (São Paulo, Brasil, Apr. 1979), 21–42.

—— 'Lenin, Mach and Berkeley', *Proceedings of the Israeli Association for Studies of Marx and Socialism* (Haifa, 1983), 165–78. (In Hebrew.)

—— 'Two Central Issues in Bishop Berkeley's "Corpuscularian Philosophy" in the *Siris*', *History of European Ideas*, 7/6 (Oxford, 1986), 633–41.

MYHILL, J., 'Berkeley's "De Motu"—An Anticipation of Mach', in S. C. Pepper, K. Aschenbrenner, and B. Mates, eds., *George Berkeley: Lectures Delivered before the Philosophical Union of the University of California* (Los Angeles, 1957), pp. 142–57.

PARK, D., 'Locke and Berkeley on the Molyneux Problem', *Journal of History of Ideas*, 30 (1969), 253–60.

POPKIN, R. H., 'Berkeley's Pyrrhonism', *The Review of Metaphysics*, 5 (1951), 223–46.

POPPER, SIR KARL, 'A Note on Berkeley as Precursor of Mach and Einstein', in C. B. Martin and D. M. Armstrong, eds., *Locke and Berkeley: A Collection of Critical Essays*, (London, 1968), pp. 436–49.

—— 'Three Views Concerning Human Knowledge', in H. D. Lewis, ed., *Contemporary British Philosophy* (London, 1956), pp. 375–88.

—— 'Replies to my Criticis', in P. A. Schilpp, *The Philosophy of Karl Popper* (La Salle, Ill., 1974), pp. 961–1197.

RITCHIE, A. D., 'George Berkeley's *Siris*, The Philosophy of the Great Chain of Being and the Alchemical Theory', *Proceedings of the British Academy*, 40 (1954), 41–55.

STAINSBY, H. V., 'Sight and Sense-Data', *Mind*, 79 (1970), 170–87.

STRONG, E. W., 'Mathematical Reasoning and its Objects', in S. C. Pepper, K. Aschenbrenner, B. Mates, eds., *George Berkeley: Lectures Delivered before the Philosophical Union of the University of California* (Los Angeles, 1957), pp. 65–88.

THOMAS, G. H., 'The Implications of Berkeley's Earliest Philosophy concerning Things', *Journal of the History of Philosophy*, 10 (1972), 425–30.

THOMSON, J. F., 'Berkeley', in D. J. O'Connor, ed., *A Critical History of Western Philosophy* (New York, 1964), pp. 236–52.

TIPTON, I. C., 'The "Philosopher by Fire" in Berkeley's *Alciphron*', in C. H. Turbayne, ed., *George Berkeley: Critical and Interpretive Essays*, (Minneapolis, 1982), pp. 159–73.

TURBAYNE, C. M., 'Berkeley and Molyneux on Retinal Images', *Journal of the History of Ideas*, 16 (1955), 339–55.

—— Editor's Commentary to *Berkeley, Works on Vision* (The Library of Liberal Arts, New York, 1963), pp. vii–xlv.

VESEY, G. N. A., 'Berkeley and the Man Born Blind', *Proceedings of the Aristotelian Society*, 61 (1960–1), 189–206.

WARNOCK, G. J., Third Appendix to *M. von Senden: Space and Sight*, tr. P. Heath (London, 1960), pp. 319–25.

WHITE, A. R. 'The Ambiguity of Berkeley's "Without the Mind"', *Hermathena*, 83 (1954), 55–65.

WHITTAKER, SIR EDMUND, Introduction to Newton's *Opticks* (New York, 1952), pp. lxi–lxxvii.

WILSON, M. D., 'Berkeley and the Essences of the Corpuscularians', in J. Foster and H. Robinson, eds., *Essays on Berkeley: A Tercentennial Celebration* (Oxford, 1985), pp. 131–47.

C. SELECTED COLLECTIONS OF BERKELEY'S WORKS

ARMSTRONG, D. M., ed., *Berkeley's Philosophical Works*, (New York and London, 1965).

FRASER, A. C., ed., *The Works of George Berkeley* (4 vols.; Oxford, 1901).
LUCE, A. A. and T. E. JESSOP, eds., *The Works of George Berkeley, Bishop of Cloyne* (9 vols.; London and Edinburgh, 1948–57).
TURBAYNE, C. M., ed., *George Berkeley: Principles, Dialogues, and Philosophical Correspondence* (Library of Liberal Arts, Indianapolis, New York, and Kansas City, 1965).
—— *Berkeley: Works on Vision* (New York, 1963).
WARNOCK, G. J., ed., *Berkeley: The Principles of Human Knowledge, Three Dialogues between Hylas and Philonous* (London, 1962).

Index of Subjects

aether, aethereal fire 26, 27, 33,
  40–64, 66, 69, 71–8, 84–94, 97, 100,
  101, 104–6, 109, 110, 114, 116–18,
  122, 123, 129, 131, 163, 168, 169,
  175, 183–4, 186–9, 191, 192, 194,
  195, 198–201, 203, 204, 233
air, composition of 57, 108, 116–19,
  122, 128, 131, 155, 162, 163, 192,
  198, 200, 205, 231
analogy 41–4, 185–7, 191, 193, 200,
  230
animal spirits 18, 22, 46, 61, 101–6,
  121, 126, 131, 165, 185, 200
animalcules 123, 127, 201, 203, 205
archetypes, archetypal Ideas, Forms
  90, 95, 191, 208, 228
arithmetics, arithmetical operations
  210, 213
atomism, atoms 6, 13, 97, 108, 117,
  133, 137, 138, 142–4, 152, 155–8,
  165, 176, 183, 193, 196, 197, 201,
  206, 207, 211, 212, 217
attraction(s) 28, 29, 34, 36, 39, 64, 69,
  70, 75, 89, 91–3, 99, 109, 112, 118,
  189, 190, 197, 198, 200–2, 231

Berkeley's fork 63, 163, 164
Berkeley's razor 63, 163, 164, 166

candidates-for-reality 29, 45, 46, 53,
  108, 110, 159, 162, 163
causality, causal powers 15, 32, 34,
  85, 94–6, 162, 167, 182, 184, 187,
  191, 193, 198, 200, 211, 230
causes, instrumental 32, 33, 60, 61,
  86, 87, 94, 106, 184, 190, 191
chain of beings 121, 126, 187, 200,
  205
colours 20, 21, 77, 92, 144, 145, 153,
  155, 156, 173, 174, 213, 214, 216,
  222, 224
combustion 28, 56–8
corpuscularianism 6, 9, 11, 12, 14,
  18, 19, 21–3, 25, 32, 51, 67, 68, 88,
  95, 96, 102, 110, 113, 116, 118, 142,
  143, 157–9, 161, 163, 165–9, 175–7,
  179, 182, 187, 190–2, 194, 196, 197,
  199, 200, 201, 204, 205, 212, 226,
  227, 230, 232, 233

Creation 128

divisibility, finite and infinite 7, 10,
  11, 18, 62, 83, 96, 134, 136, 137–9,
  142, 148, 154, 162, 170, 172, 175–7,
  193, 196, 210, 212, 213, 223, 224,
  228, 231

electricity 112
electron 157
elements 129, 130, 131, 168, 205,
  206, 212
epicycles 27–9, 31, 184
epistemology, epistemic limitations
  16, 25
extension, blended 149, 219
extension, tangible 18, 69, 87, 98,
  133–5, 141–4, 146, 148, 150, 154,
  170, 172, 178, 193, 209, 215, 224
extension, visible 74, 133–5, 142,
  144–6, 150, 170, 172, 178, 195, 208,
  209, 214–16, 218, 224, 229

finitism 6, 13, 157, 210
force, *vis* 28, 29, 34, 64, 97, 110, 129,
  157, 161, 162, 182, 183, 189, 201,
  202, 221, 230, 231
forms, Aristotelian; formal causes
  122–6, 168, 194, 196, 203, 204

geometry 133, 134, 172, 213, 231
God 18, 60, 67, 89, 90, 103, 105, 120,
  126, 139, 140, 141, 180, 182, 185,
  186, 193, 203, 208, 211, 212
gravity 28, 35–7, 39, 40, 62, 64, 69,
  70, 75, 76, 99, 100, 112, 164, 188,
  189, 197, 208, 209

homoiomeriae 26, 124, 127, 168, 187,
  203
homology 41–4, 185–6
hypotheses, explanatory; hypothetico-
  deductive theories 12, 16, 18, 22,
  23, 25, 27, 29, 30–2, 34, 64, 68, 111,
  113, 129, 132, 140, 160, 162, 163,
  165, 175, 178, 179, 181, 182, 185,
  187, 227, 230, 231
hypotheses, metaphysical 18, 139

ideas 19, 28, 30, 63, 75, 79, 162–4, 168, 172, 173, 182, 185, 190, 191, 193, 196, 200, 211, 228
ideas, relations of 28, 30, 95, 178, 210
idiosyncrasies of particles 34, 35, 38–41, 54, 61, 64, 66, 68–71, 86, 88, 90, 97–100, 106, 117, 161, 162, 167, 189, 194, 197, 198, 200–2
immaterialism, ideism 17, 84, 89, 139, 143, 155, 156, 164, 181, 182, 191, 197, 223, 224, 228, 233
inductivism 13, 18, 24, 25, 181, 184, 185, 230, 232
infinitesimal analysis, differential calculus 24, 134, 135, 142, 143, 172
infinity 181
insensible parts 136
instrumentalism 25, 110, 140, 157–66, 184, 233

kinaesthetic, data and frames of reference 144, 146, 148, 149, 189, 214, 218, 219, 221, 222, 225

laws of nature, laws of motion, reticular theories 12, 13, 16, 17, 19, 27, 29, 30, 37, 40, 62, 64, 66–8, 109, 111, 160, 162, 164, 166, 178, 182, 230
light 20, 21, 26, 37–9, 51, 52, 59, 72–84, 91, 92, 100, 108–10, 114, 115, 129, 144, 145, 153, 155, 156, 169, 189–91, 193, 194, 196, 198, 199, 201, 202, 209, 214, 216, 221, 222, 224, 226
linguistic models 19, 226
logoi spermatikoi 124, 126, 168

macrocosm 46, 68, 72, 101, 103, 105, 106, 132
magnetism 112
manifolds, two- and three-dimensional 144, 148, 153, 175, 189, 199, 209, 213, 219, 221–3
materialism, matterism 140, 143, 212, 212, 213
mathematical fictions 29, 110, 143, 159, 160, 162–5, 182, 183, 201, 211, 230, 231, 233
mathematical notation 213
measurement 210, 215, 226
mechanical philosophy, mechanism 64, 66–8, 71, 99, 166, 193

metaphysics and its rejection 23, 67, 167, 183, 211, 213
microcosm 46, 68, 72, 101–3, 105, 106, 132
microscopic observations 17, 113, 123, 127, 130, 170, 180, 201, 203, 208
mind 154
minima 6, 24, 49, 54, 63, 82, 107, 133–52, 154–6, 163, 170–6, 181, 192, 195–7, 201, 206–8, 211, 212, 215–18, 225–9
Molyneux problem 145, 215, 218
momenta 136, 202
motion, absolute and relative 160, 164, 201, 221, 231
motion, circular 36, 37, 67, 96, 109, 190

Neoplatonism, Neoplatonic 72, 78, 121, 132, 190, 204, 211, 228
nominal essence 177, 204

occasionalism 178
optics 110, 134, 180, 227
oxygen 28, 73, 104, 192, 202

perception 180, 211, 213, 220, 225
perceivability, unperceivability 22, 48, 52, 67, 73, 139, 143, 182, 186, 201, 211, 229
phlogiston 56, 73, 192
physics 133
physiology 113, 187
plenum, Cartesian 35, 39, 40, 55, 64, 67, 69, 71, 76, 87, 96, 98, 99, 101, 176, 190, 192, 197–9
points, mathematical 82, 136, 138, 193, 210, 211, 223
points, sensible 82, 83, 140, 141, 150–2, 154, 170–3, 192, 211, 212, 217, 228
primary and secondary qualities 7, 8, 16, 35, 60, 84–91, 93–5, 167, 177–9, 192, 195, 196, 213
proper objects of vision 180, 210, 213
positivism 157, 164

real essence 6–8, 14, 15, 97, 167, 175, 177, 201, 204
realism 184
rerum natura 28, 30, 31, 33, 68, 74, 89, 107, 120, 135, 139, 150, 162, 197, 201, 202, 224, 231

saving the phenomena 30
scepticism 177, 178, 181
space, absolute 62, 64, 96, 111, 147, 160, 164, 183, 197, 201, 221, 224, 230, 231
space, empty 74, 76, 83, 87, 97–101, 197, 221, 222
space, kinaesthetic 74, 146, 221, 223
space, physical 148
space, relative 147, 193, 221
space, visual 50, 83, 148, 149, 192, 209, 218–21, 223–5
spirit(s) 52, 120–2, 125, 168, 174, 182, 184, 185, 193, 203, 205

tar-water 25, 105, 106, 114, 168, 200, 201
theoretical entities and terms 33, 75
time 213, 231

unconscious inferences, praenotions 224, 225

visual field, visual sphere 145, 150, 151, 171, 174, 207, 219, 225, 226, 228

Index of Names

Abbott, T. K. 219
Abetti, G. 183
Agassiz, J. 185, 186
Alexander, P. 177
Allen, M. J. B. 190
Anaxagoras 128
Aquinas, St Thomas 184
Aristotle 128, 205
Armstrong, D. M. 184, 213, 214, 217, 218, 220, 223, 224, 229

Bacon, F. 159
Bellarmino, F. R. 25, 157
Blackmore, J. T. 158
Boas Hall, M. 212
Boehme, J. 203
Boerhaave, H. 36, 130, 186, 191, 205
Borelli, G. A. 204
Boltzmann, L. 158
Boyle, R. 4, 36, 38, 51, 86, 128, 129, 131, 154, 177, 197, 203
Bracken, H. M. 199, 200, 217
Brook, R. 181, 232, 233
Brykman, G. 180
Buchdahl, G. 166, 177, 179, 183, 184, 232
Butterfield, H. 183

Cavalieri, B. 137, 138, 172, 210
Cicero 205
Cohen, B. I. 187

Dawes Hicks, G. 1, 157
Davie, D. 120, 186, 203
Democritus 13, 97
Descartes, R. 2, 4, 6, 10, 36, 37, 64, 68, 70, 96, 97, 103, 122, 142, 143, 175, 177, 196, 197, 199, 200, 203, 213, 228

Einstein, A. 157
Epicurus 13, 97

Feigl, H. 182
Feyerabend, P. K. 158
Ficinus, M. 78, 80, 81, 83, 132, 190, 204
Flamm, D. 158
Foster, J. 182, 230

Fraser, A. C. 181
Furlong, A. J. 224

Garber, D. 181, 182, 195, 230
Gassendi, P. 97, 154, 155
Gilbert, W. 203
Gregory, R. L. 218
Grew, N. 113, 201

Hales, S. 57, 187
Harré, H. R. 178, 183, 230
Heath, P. 219
Helmont, van, J. B. 205, 206
Heraclitus 127, 204
Hesse, M. 198
Hobbes, T. 13
Hobhouse, S. 184
Hippocrates 127, 184
Homberg, W. 35, 36, 42, 44, 130, 131, 185, 202
Hume, D. 159
Huygens, C. 200, 227

Jackson, R. 177
Jessop, T. E. 51, 67, 84, 85, 88, 184, 190, 192, 205, 233
Johnston, G. A. 212, 213

Kant, E. 217
Kemp Smith, N. 217
Kenny, A. 229
Kretzmann, N. 229

Leibniz, G. 218
Lenin, V. I. 158
Leucippus 13, 97
Leeuwenhoek, A. van 203
Lewis, H. D. 184
Locke, J. 1, 4, 6, 7, 8, 10, 14, 24, 86–9, 93, 96, 97, 142, 143, 175, 177, 178, 181, 196, 197, 213, 215, 218, 228
Lovejoy, A. O. 205
Luce, A. A. 180, 181, 207, 210, 211, 213, 217, 227
Lucretius 212

Mach, E. 157–9, 163

Malebranche, N. 89, 105, 178, 180, 208
Malpighi, M. 200, 201, 203
Martin, C. B. 184, 229
Maxwell, G. 182
Melsen, A. G. van 97, 197, 212
Merleau-Ponty, M. 221
Myhill, J. 204

Newton, I. 2, 15, 34–6, 38, 39, 42, 51, 62, 64, 70, 71, 73, 74, 76, 77–8, 91, 92, 96, 98–100, 109, 110–11, 115, 116, 128, 129, 154, 160, 161, 185, 187–90, 194, 196–200, 203, 204
Nieuwentijdt, B. 57, 187
Norris, J. 208, 228

Osiander, A. 25, 157

Pannekoek, A. 183
Paracelsus 192, 205
Piaget, J. 222
Pitcher, G. 178, 224
Plato 95, 123, 132, 203
Plotinus 205
Popkin, R. H. 178
Popper, K. 1, 5, 23, 25, 63, 157–67, 184, 185, 229, 233
Price, H. H. 220
Priestley, J. 28, 192

Ritchie, A. D. 205
Robinson, H. 182, 230
Roemer, O. 80

Scheele, K. W. 192
Senden, M. von 218–22
Singer, C. 205
Spinosa, B. 13
Stainsby, V. H. 226
Strawson, P. 217
Swammerdam, J. 203

Tipton, I. C. 162, 177, 178, 180, 191, 213, 224, 230
Turbayne, C. M. 180, 181, 191, 195, 226, 230

Urmson, J. O. 178

Vanini, L. 13
Vesey, G. N. A. 221

Warnock, G. J. 12, 177, 180, 186, 206, 219, 224, 228, 232, 233
Whittaker, A. 194
Wilson, M. D. 182, 230
White, A. R. 224
Wolf, A. 192
Wyclif, J. 229

Zeno, the Stoic 205